Houghton
Mifflin
Harcourt

CALIFORNIA

GO MATH!

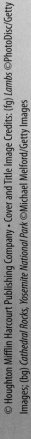

Made in the United States
Text printed on 90%
recycled paper

Houghton Mifflin Harcourt

CALIFORNIA

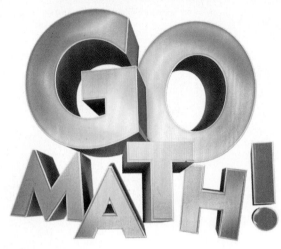

GO MATH!

Curious George by Margret and H.A. Rey. Copyright © 2010 by Houghton Mifflin Harcourt Publishing Company. All rights reserved. The character Curious George®, including without limitation the character's name and the character's likenesses, are registered trademarks of Houghton Mifflin Harcourt Publishing Company.

Copyright © 2015 by Houghton Mifflin Harcourt Publishing Company.

All rights reserved. No part of this work may be reproduced or transmitted in any form or by any means, electronic or mechanical, including photocopying or recording, or by any information storage and retrieval system, without the prior written permission of the copyright owner unless such copying is expressly permitted by federal copyright law. Requests for permission to make copies of any part of the work should be addressed to Houghton Mifflin Harcourt Publishing Company, Attn: Contracts, Copyrights, and Licensing, 9400 Southpark Center Loop, Orlando, Florida 32819-8647.

Common Core State Standards © Copyright 2010. National Governors Association Center for Best Practices and Council of Chief State School Officers. All rights reserved.

This product is not sponsored or endorsed by the Common Core State Standards Initiative of the National Governors Association Center for Best Practices and the Council of Chief State School Officers.

Printed in the U.S.A.

ISBN 978-0-544-20379-2

11 12 13 14 15   0029 23 22 21 20 19 18
4500742713   B C D E F G

If you have received these materials as examination copies free of charge, Houghton Mifflin Harcourt Publishing Company retains title to the materials and they may not be resold. Resale of examination copies is strictly prohibited.

Possession of this publication in print format does not entitle users to convert this publication, or any portion of it, into electronic format.

Dear Students and Families,

Welcome to **California Go Math!**, Kindergarten! In this exciting mathematics program, there are hands-on activities to do and real-world problems to solve. Best of all, you will write your ideas and answers right in your book. In **California Go Math!**, writing and drawing on the pages helps you think deeply about what you are learning, and you will really understand math!

By the way, all of the pages in your **California Go Math!** book are made using recycled paper. We wanted you to know that you can Go Green with **California Go Math!**

Sincerely,

The Authors

Made in the United States
Text printed on 90% recycled paper

CALIFORNIA

GO MATH!

Authors

Juli K. Dixon, Ph.D.
Professor, Mathematics Education
University of Central Florida
Orlando, Florida

Edward B. Burger, Ph.D.
President, Southwestern University
Georgetown, Texas

Steven J. Leinwand
Principal Research Analyst
American Institutes for
    Research (AIR)
Washington, D.C.

Contributor

Rena Petrello
Professor, Mathematics
Moorpark College
Moorpark, CA

Matthew R. Larson, Ph.D.
K-12 Curriculum Specialist for
    Mathematics
Lincoln Public Schools
Lincoln, Nebraska

Martha E. Sandoval-Martinez
Math Instructor
El Camino College
Torrance, California

English Language Learners Consultant

Elizabeth Jiménez
CEO, GEMAS Consulting
Professional Expert on English
    Learner Education
Bilingual Education and
    Dual Language
Pomona, California

Number and Operations

 COMMON CORE **Critical Area** Representing, relating, and operating on whole numbers, initially with sets of objects

1 Represent, Count, and Write Numbers 0 to 5 — 9

Domains Counting and Cardinality
Operations and Algebraic Thinking
CALIFORNIA COMMON CORE STANDARDS
K.CC.3, K.CC.4.a, K.CC.4.b, K.CC.4.c

2 Compare Numbers to 5 — 57

Domain Counting and Cardinality
CALIFORNIA COMMON CORE STANDARDS
K.CC.6

GO DIGITAL

Go online! Your math lessons are interactive. Use *i*Tools, Animated Math Models, the Multimedia *e*Glossary, and more.

Chapter 1 Overview

In this chapter, you will explore and discover answers to the following **Essential Questions**:
• How can you show, count, and write numbers?
• How can you show numbers 0 to 5?
• How can you count numbers 0 to 5?
• How can you write numbers 0 to 5?

Chapter 2 Overview

In this chapter, you will explore and discover answers to the following **Essential Questions**:
• How can building and comparing sets help you compare numbers?
• How does matching help you compare sets?
• How does counting help you compare sets?
• How do you know if the number of counters in one set is the same as, greater than, or less than the number of counters in another set?

Chapter 3 Overview

In this chapter, you will explore and discover answers to the following **Essential Questions:**

• How can you show, count, and write numbers 6 to 9?

• How can you show numbers 6 to 9?

• How can you count numbers 6 to 9?

• How can you write numbers 6 to 9?

3 Represent, Count, and Write Numbers 6 to 9   85

Domain Counting and Cardinality
CALIFORNIA COMMON CORE STANDARDS
K.CC.3, K.CC.5, K.CC.6

Chapter 4 Overview

In this chapter, you will explore and discover answers to the following **Essential Questions**:

• How can you show and compare numbers to 10?
• How can you count forward to 10?
• How can you show numbers from 1 to 10?
• How can using models help you compare two numbers?

Chapter 5 Overview

In this chapter, you will explore and discover answers to the following **Essential Questions**:

• How can you show addition?
• How can using objects or pictures help you show addition?
• How can you use numbers and symbols to show addition?

6 Subtraction 221

Domain Operations and Algebraic Thinking
CALIFORNIA COMMON CORE STANDARDS
K.OA.1, K.OA.2, K.OA.5

Sheep and Ducks

Geometry and Positions

 Critical Area Describing shapes and space

Go online! Your math lessons are interactive. Use *iTools*, Animated Math Models, the Multimedia *e*Glossary, and more.

Chapter 9 Overview

In this chapter, you will explore and discover answers to the following **Essential Questions**:

• How can you identify, name, and describe two-dimensional shapes?

• How can knowing the parts of two-dimensional shapes help you join shapes?

• How can knowing the number of sides and vertices of two-dimensional shapes help you identify shapes?

Chapter 10 Overview

In this chapter, you will explore and discover answers to the following **Essential Questions**:

- How can identifying and describing shapes help you sort them?
- How can you describe three-dimensional shapes?
- How can you sort three-dimensional shapes?

Measurement and Data

 COMMON CORE **Critical Area** Representing, relating, and operating on whole numbers, initially with sets of objects

11 Measurement   465

Domain Measurement and Data

CALIFORNIA COMMON CORE STANDARDS
K.MD.1, K.MD.2

12 Classify and Sort Data   493

Domain Measurement and Data

CALIFORNIA COMMON CORE STANDARDS
K.MD.3

GO DIGITAL

Go online! Your math lessons are interactive. Use *i*Tools, Animated Math Models, the Multimedia *e*Glossary, and more.

Chapter 11 Overview

In this chapter, you will explore and discover answers to the following **Essential Questions**:

• How can comparing objects help you measure them?

• How can you compare the length of objects?

• How can you compare the height of objects?

• How can you compare the weight of objects?

Chapter 12 Overview

In this chapter, you will explore and discover answers to the following **Essential Questions**:

• How does sorting help you display information?

• How can you sort and classify objects by color?

• How can you sort and classify objects by shape?

• How can you sort and classify objects by size?

• How do you display information on a graph?

Fall Festival!

written by Alison Juliano

© Houghton Mifflin Harcourt Publishing Company

CRITICAL AREA Representing, relating, and operating on whole numbers, initially with sets of objects

Fall is here! What do you see?

One big apple tree.

Science

What season is this?

Fall is here! What do you see?

Two pumpkins for you and me.

Science

What do you know about fall?

Fall is here! What do you see?

Bales of hay—1, 2, 3!

Science

What do people wear in fall?

Fall is here! What do you see?

Four leaves falling from a tree.

Science

What changes in fall?

Fall is here! What do you see?

Five stalks of corn. Do you see me?

Science

How is fall different from
the other seasons?

Name _____

Write About the Story

Vocabulary Review

one	four
two	five
three	

DIRECTIONS Look at the picture of the fall scene. Using the numbers you have learned, draw a story about fall. Invite a friend to count the objects in your story.

Count How Many

 1

1 2 3 4 5

 2

1 2 3 4 5

 3

1 2 3 4 5

 4

1 2 3 4 5

 5

1 2 3 4 5

DIRECTIONS 1–5. Look at the picture. Count how many. Circle the number.

8 eight

Represent, Count, and Write Numbers 0 to 5

Curious About Math with Curious George

Navel oranges have no seeds.

- How many seeds do you see?

Show What You Know ✓

Explore Numbers

 1

Match Numbers to Sets

2

| 1 | 2 | 3 | 4 | 5 |

This page checks understanding of important skills needed for success in Chapter 1.

DIRECTIONS 1. Circle all of the sets of three oranges.
2. Draw a line to match the number to the set.

 **Personal Math Trainer**
Online Assessment
and Intervention

Vocabulary Builder

match

set

DIRECTIONS Draw a line to match a set of chicks to a set of flowers.

• **Interactive Student Edition**
• **Multimedia eGlossary**

Game Bus Stop

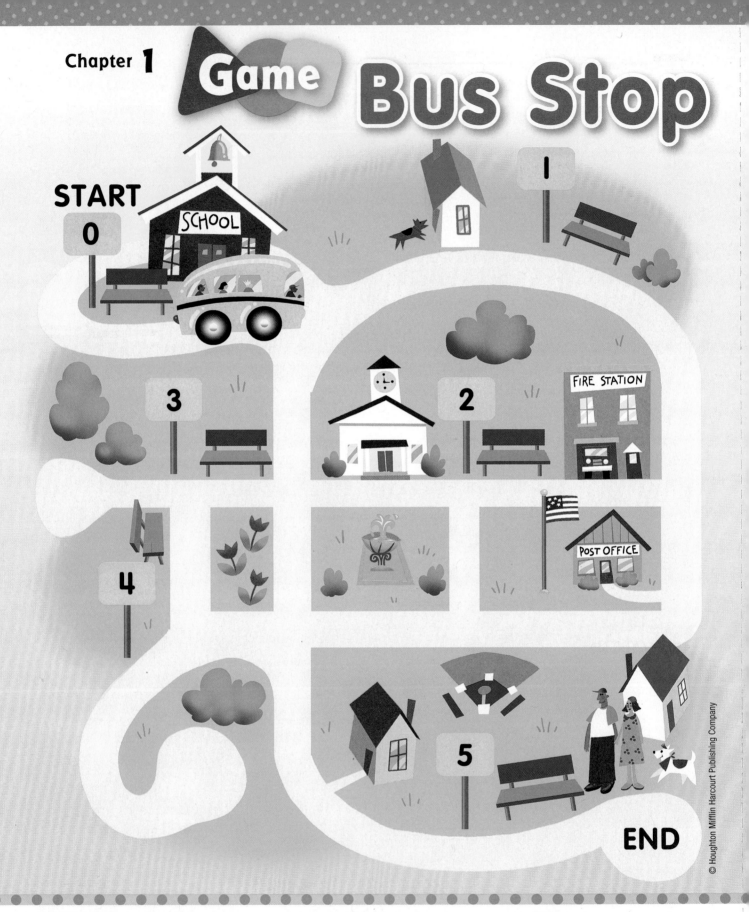

DIRECTIONS Each player rolls the number cube. The first player to roll a 1 moves to the bus stop marked 1. Continue playing until each player has rolled the numbers in sequence and stopped at each bus stop. The first player to reach 5 wins the game.

MATERIALS game marker for each player, number cube (0–5)

Name _____

Model and Count 1 and 2

Essential Question How can you show and count
1 and 2 with objects?

Counting and Cardinality—**K.CC.4a**
Also K.CC.4b, K.CC.4c, K.CC.5
MATHEMATICAL PRACTICES
MP.2

DIRECTIONS Place a counter on each object in the set as you count
them. Move the counters to the five frame. Draw the counters.

1

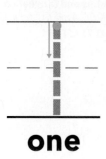

one

2

two

DIRECTIONS 1–2. Place a counter on each object in the set as you count them. Tell how many counters. Trace the number. Move the counters to the five frame. Draw the counters.

Name ______________________________

3

1

one

4

2

two

5

1

one

6

2

two

DIRECTIONS **3–6.** Say the number. Count out that many counters in the five frame. Draw the counters.

Problem Solving • Applications

7

8

9

DIRECTIONS **7.** Jen has 2 matching lunch boxes. Max has 1 lunch box. Circle to show Jen's lunch boxes. **8.** Draw to show what you know about the number 1. **9.** Draw to show what you know about the number 2. Tell a friend about your drawings.

HOME ACTIVITY • Ask your child to show a set that has one or two objects, such as books or buttons. Have him or her point to each object as he or she counts it to tell how many objects are in the set.

16 sixteen

FOR MORE PRACTICE:
Standards Practice Book

Name _____

Count and Write 1 and 2

Essential Question How can you count and write 1 and 2 with words and numbers?

Counting and Cardinality—K.CC.3
Also K.CC.4b, K.CC.5
MATHEMATICAL PRACTICES
MP.2

Listen and Draw Real World

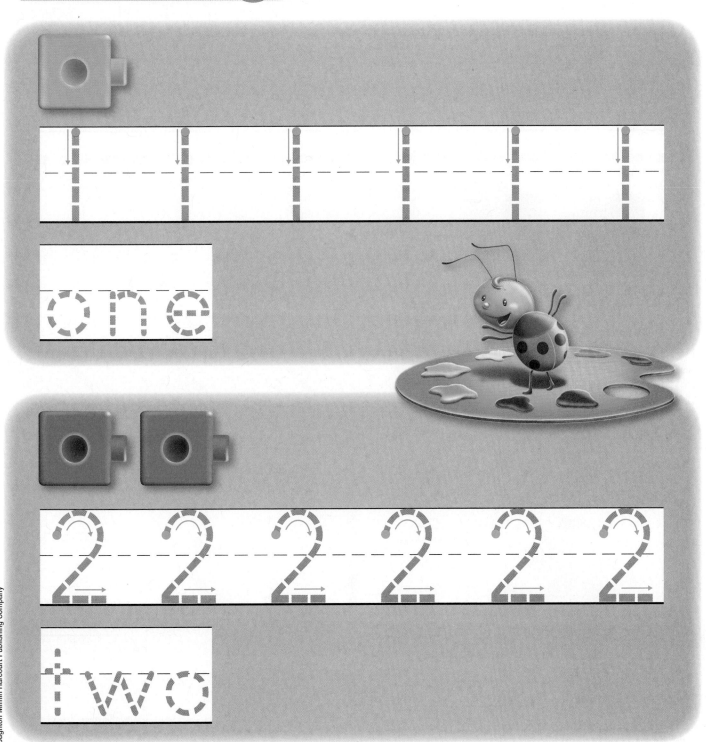

DIRECTIONS Count the cubes. Tell how many. Trace the numbers and words.

Chapter 1 • Lesson 2

seventeen **17**

Share and Show

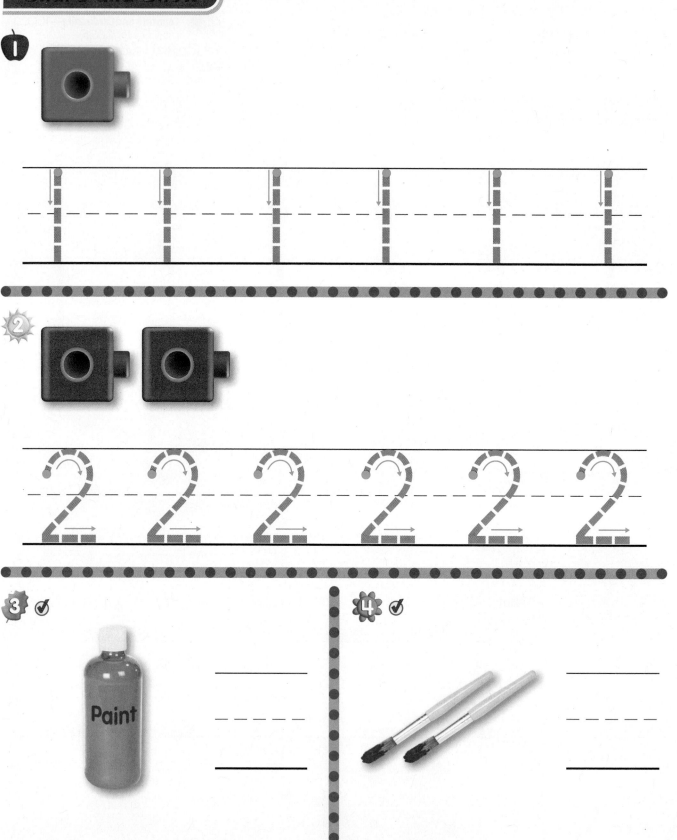

DIRECTIONS 1–2. Count the cubes. Say the number. Trace the numbers. 3–4. Count and tell how many. Write the number.

Name _____

5

_____

_ _ _ _ _ _ _

_____

6

Glue Stick   Glue Stick

_____

_ _ _ _ _ _ _

_____

7

_____

_ _ _ _ _ _ _

_____

8

_____

_ _ _ _ _ _ _

_____

9

Paint

_____

_ _ _ _ _ _ _

_____

10

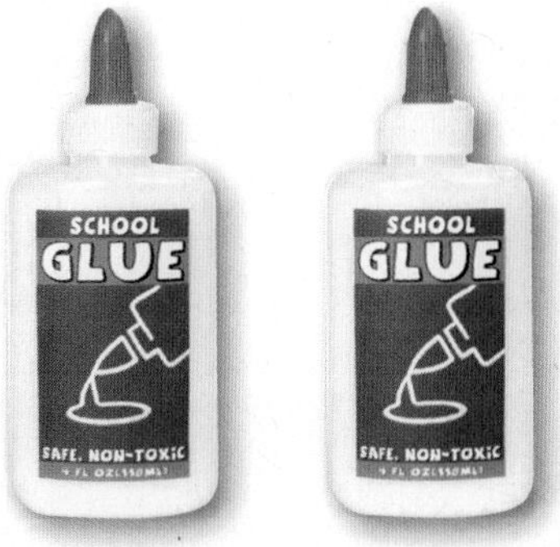

SCHOOL GLUE   SCHOOL GLUE
SAFE. NON-TOXIC   SAFE. NON-TOXIC

_____

_ _ _ _ _ _ _

_____

DIRECTIONS 5–10. Count and tell how many. Write the number.

Problem Solving • Applications

11.

_____

- - - - - - - -

_____

_____

- - - - - - - -

_____

DIRECTIONS 11. Draw to show what you know about the numbers 1 and 2. Write the number beside each drawing. Tell a friend about your drawings.

HOME ACTIVITY • Ask your child to write the number 1 on a sheet of paper. Then have him or her find an object that represents that number. Repeat with objects for the number 2.

20 twenty

FOR MORE PRACTICE:
Standards Practice Book

Name _____

Model and Count 3 and 4

Essential Question How can you show and count 3 and 4 with objects?

Counting and Cardinality—K.CC.4a
Also K.CC.4b, K.CC.4c, K.CC.5
MATHEMATICAL PRACTICES
MP.1, MP.2

 **Listen and Draw**

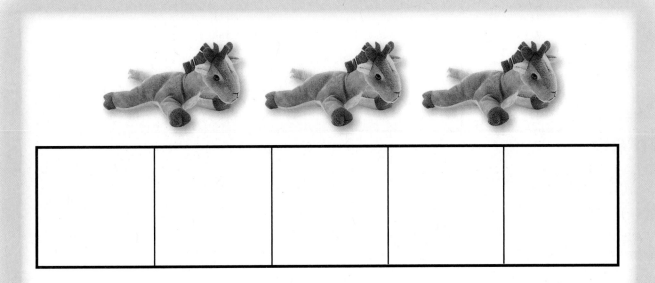

DIRECTIONS Place a counter on each object in the set as you count them. Move the counters to the five frame. Draw the counters.

Chapter 1 • Lesson 3

three

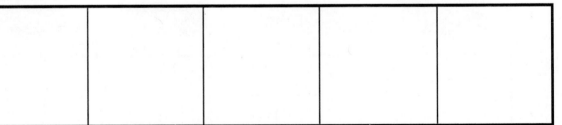

four

DIRECTIONS   1–2. Place a counter on each object in the set as you count them. Tell how many counters. Trace the number. Move the counters to the five frame. Draw the counters.

3 ✓

3

three

4 ✓

4

four

5

4

four

6

3

three

DIRECTIONS 3–6. Say the number as you trace it. Count out that many counters in the five frame. Draw the counters.

Problem Solving • Applications

7

8

9

© Houghton Mifflin Harcourt Publishing Company

DIRECTIONS **7.** Lukas has 3 matching toys. Jon has a number of matching toys greater than Lukas. Circle to show Jon's toys. **8.** Draw to show what you know about the number 3. **9.** Draw to show what you know about the number 4. Tell a friend about your drawings.

HOME ACTIVITY • Draw a five frame or cut an egg carton to have just five sections. Have your child show a set of up to four objects and place the objects in the five frame.

FOR MORE PRACTICE:
Standards Practice Book

Name _____

Count and Write 3 and 4

Essential Question How can you count and write 3 and 4 with words and numbers?

Counting and Cardinality—K.CC.3
Also K.CC.4b, K.CC.4c, K.CC.5
MATHEMATICAL PRACTICES
MP.2

Listen and Draw *Real World*

DIRECTIONS Count the cubes. Tell how many. Trace the numbers and the words.

Chapter 1 • Lesson 4

twenty-five **25**

1

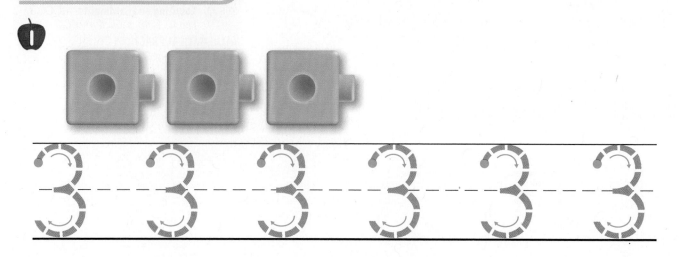

$3 \quad 3 \quad 3 \quad 3 \quad 3 \quad 3$

2

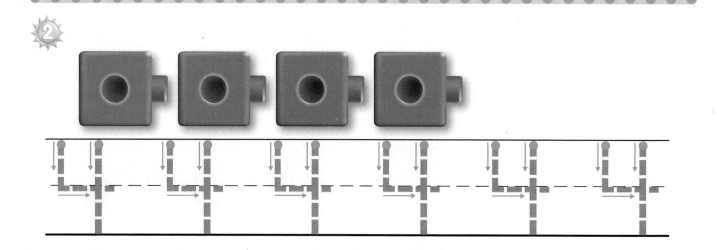

3 ✓

4 ✓

DIRECTIONS 1–2. Count the cubes. Say the number. Trace the numbers. 3–4. Count and tell how many. Write the number.

Name _____

 5

_____

- - - - - - - - - - -

_____

 6

_____

- - - - - - - - - - -

_____

 7

_____

- - - - - - - - - - -

_____

 8

_____

- - - - - - - - - - -

_____

 9

_____

- - - - - - - - - - -

_____

  10

_____

- - - - - - - - - - -

_____

DIRECTIONS 5–10. Count and tell how many. Write the number.

HOME ACTIVITY • Ask your child to show a set of three or four objects. Have him or her write the number on paper to show how many objects.

FOR MORE PRACTICE:
Standards Practice Book

Chapter 1 • Lesson 4

Concepts and Skills

 1

 2  **3**

4 THINK SMARTER

DIRECTIONS 1. Place counters in the five frame to show the number 3. Draw the counters. Write the number. (K.CC.4a)   2–3. Count and tell how many. Write the number. (K.CC.3)
4. Count each set of bags. Circle all the sets that show 3 bags. (K.CC.4b)

28 twenty-eight

Name _____

Model and Count 5

Essential Question How can you show and count 5 objects?

Listen and Draw

Counting and Cardinality—K.CC.4a
Also K.CC.4b, K.CC.5
MATHEMATICAL PRACTICES
MP.1, MP.2

DIRECTIONS Place a counter on each orange as you count them. Move the counters to the five frame. Draw the counters.

Chapter 1 • Lesson 5

twenty-nine **29**

five

five

DIRECTIONS 1–2. Place a counter on each object in the set as you count them. Tell how many counters. Trace the number. Move the counters to the five frame. Draw the counters.

3 ☑

4

5

6

DIRECTIONS 3. Place counters to show five. Draw the counters. Write the number. 4. Place counters to show four. Draw the counters. Write the number. 5. Place counters to show five. Draw the counters. Write the number. 6. Place counters to show three. Draw the counters. Write the number.

Problem Solving • Applications Real World

7

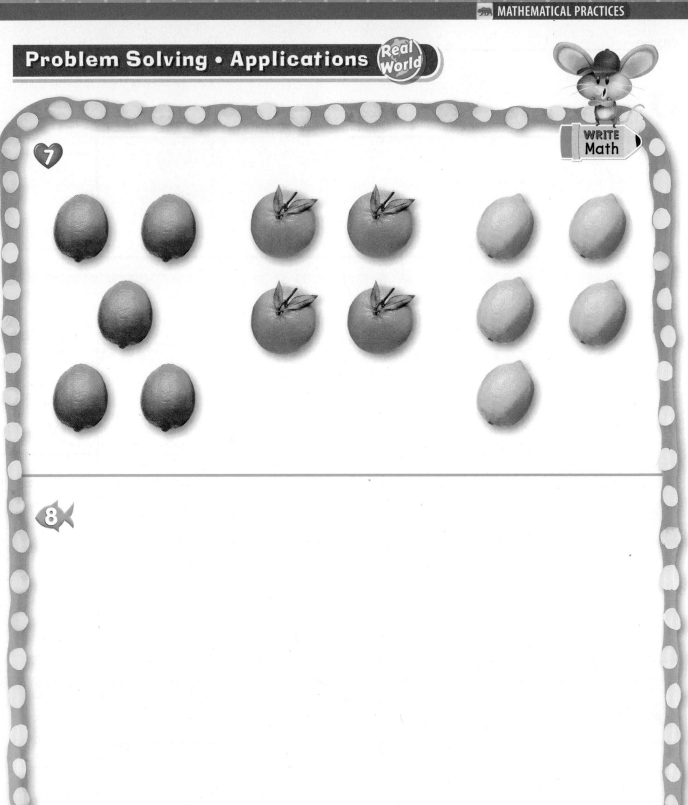

8

DIRECTIONS **7.** Carl needs 5 pieces of each kind of fruit. Circle to show all the sets Carl could use. **8.** Draw to show what you know about the number 5. Tell a friend about your drawing.

HOME ACTIVITY • Draw a five frame or use an egg carton with just five sections. Have your child show a set of five objects and place the objects in the five frame.

32 thirty-two

FOR MORE PRACTICE:
Standards Practice Book

Name _____

Count and Write to 5

Essential Question How can you count and write up to 5 with words and numbers?

Counting and Cardinality—K.CC.3
Also K.CC.4b, K.CC.5
MATHEMATICAL PRACTICES
MP.2

Listen and Draw *Real World*

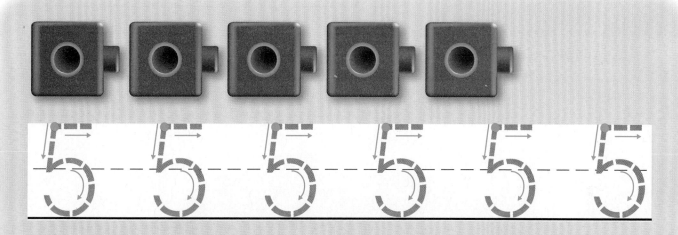

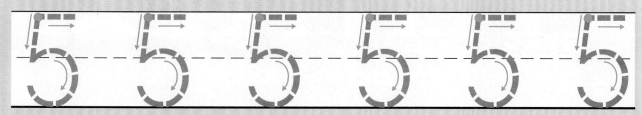

DIRECTIONS Count the cubes. Tell how many. Trace the numbers and the word. Count the apples. Tell how many. Trace the numbers.

Chapter 1 • Lesson 6

1

5 5 5 5

five

2

DIRECTIONS I. Count and tell how many apples. Trace the numbers.
2. Circle all the sets of five apples.

34 thirty-four

Name _____

 3

_____

‒ ‒ ‒ ‒

_____

 4

_____

‒ ‒ ‒ ‒

_____

5

_____

‒ ‒ ‒ ‒

_____

6

_____

‒ ‒ ‒ ‒

_____

DIRECTIONS 3–6. Count and tell how many apples.
Write the number.

© Houghton Mifflin Harcourt Publishing Company

Chapter 1 • Lesson 6

Problem Solving • Applications

WRITE
Math

7

_____

_ _ _ _ _

_____

DIRECTIONS 7. Draw to show what you know about the number 5. Write the number. Tell a friend about your drawing.

HOME ACTIVITY • Ask your child to write the number 5 on a sheet of paper. Then have him or her find objects to show that number.

FOR MORE PRACTICE:
Standards Practice Book

Name _____

Algebra • Ways to Make 5

Essential Question How can you use two sets of objects to show 5 in more than one way?

Counting and Cardinality—K.CC.4b
Also K.OA.3
MATHEMATICAL PRACTICES
MP.4, MP.7

DIRECTIONS Jessica has 5 marbles in the bag. The marbles can be red or yellow. Describe the marbles that might be in Jessica's bag. Use counters to show one pair of marbles. Trace and color the counters.

Chapter 1 • Lesson 7

1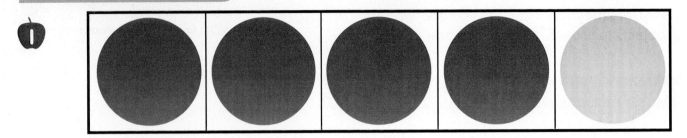

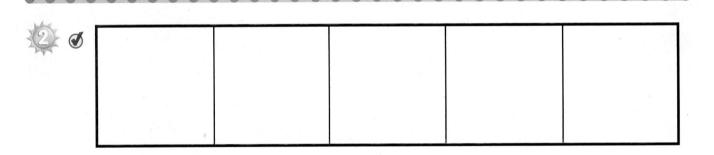

2 ✓

DIRECTIONS **1.** Look at the counters in the five frame. Trace the numbers to show the pair that makes 5. **2.** Use two colors of counters to show a different way to make 5. Write the numbers to show the pair that makes 5.

Name _____

3

⬤ and _ _ _ _ ⬤

4

⬤ and _ _ _ _ ⬤

DIRECTIONS **3–4.** Use two colors of counters to show a different
way to make 5. Write the numbers to show the pair that makes 5.

Chapter 1 • Lesson 7

thirty-nine **39**

Problem Solving • Applications

5

I ⬤ and _____ ⚪

6

_____ 🔲 and _____ 🔲

© Houghton Mifflin Harcourt Publishing Company

DIRECTIONS **5.** Austin has 5 counters. One counter is red. How many yellow counters does he have? Color the counters. **6.** Madison has 5 red and blue cubes. Color to show the cubes. Write the pair of numbers that make up Madison's cubes.

HOME ACTIVITY • Have your child use two colors of buttons to show all the different ways to make 5. Then have him or her write the number of each color used in the pairs to make 5.

40 forty

FOR MORE PRACTICE: Standards Practice Book

Name _____

Count and Order to 5

Essential Question How do you know that the order of numbers is the same as a set of objects that is one larger?

Counting and Cardinality—K.CC.4c
Also K.CC.4a, K.CC.5
MATHEMATICAL PRACTICES
MP.2, MP.5, MP.7

1   2   3   4   5

DIRECTIONS Use cubes to make cube towers that have 1 to 5 cubes. Place the cube towers in order to match the numbers 1 to 5. Draw the cube towers in order.

1

DIRECTIONS 1. Use cubes to make cube trains that have 1 to 5 cubes. Place the cube trains in order beginning with 1. Draw the cube trains and write the numbers in order. Tell a friend what you know about the numbers and the cube trains.

Name _____

DIRECTIONS **2.** Count the objects in each set. Write the number beside the set of objects. Write those numbers in order beginning with number 1.

Problem Solving • Applications

WRITE Math

3

4

© Houghton Mifflin Harcourt Publishing Company

DIRECTIONS   3. Paul has a set of blocks that is one larger than a set of 3 blocks. Circle Paul's blocks. Check to make sure your answer makes sense.   **4.** Draw to show what you know about the order of sets 1 to 5. Tell a friend about your drawing.

 HOME ACTIVITY • Show your child sets of objects from 1 to 5. Have him or her place the sets in order from 1 to 5.

FOR MORE PRACTICE:
Standards Practice Book

Name _____

Problem Solving • Understand 0

Essential Question How can you solve problems using the strategy *make a model*?

 Counting and Cardinality—K.CC.3

MATHEMATICAL PRACTICES
MP.1, MP.2, MP.4

 Unlock the Problem

zero

DIRECTIONS Use counters to model this problem. There are two horses in the pen. The horses leave the pen and go to the field. How many horses are in the pen now? Trace the number. Tell a friend what you know about that number.

Chapter 1 • Lesson 9

_____

- - - - - - -

_____

_____

- - - - - - -

_____

DIRECTIONS **1.** Use counters to model this problem. Three children each have one backpack on a peg. Draw counters to show the backpacks. How many backpacks are there? Write the number. **2.** Use counters to model a backpack on each peg. Three children each take one backpack. How many backpacks are there now? Write the number.

Name _____

3 ✓

4

DIRECTIONS Use counters to model these problems. **3.** Drew has one book. Adam has one fewer book than Drew. How many books does Adam have? Write the number. **4.** Bradley has no pencils. Matt has one more pencil than Bradley. How many pencils does Matt have? Write the number.

On Your Own

5

WRITE Math

_____

- - - - - - -

_____

6

_____

- - - - - - -

_____

DIRECTIONS **5.** Vera has 2 apples. She eats 1 apple and gives 1 apple to her friend. How many apples does Vera have now? Write the number. **6.** Amy has 3 crayons. She gives some away. Now she has no crayons. How many crayons did she give away? Write the number.

HOME ACTIVITY • Have your child place a set of up to five coins in a cup. Remove some or all of the coins and have him or her tell how many coins are in the cup and write the number.

© Houghton Mifflin Harcourt Publishing Company

FOR MORE PRACTICE:
Standards Practice Book

Name _____

Identify and Write 0

Essential Question How can you identify and write 0 with words and numbers?

Counting and Cardinality—K.CC.3

MATHEMATICAL PRACTICES
MP.2

Listen and Draw Real World

DIRECTIONS How many fish are in the bowl? Trace the numbers and the word. Tell a friend what you know about that number.

Chapter 1 • Lesson 10

DIRECTIONS **1.** How many fish are in the tank? Trace the number.
2–4. How many fish are in the tank? Write the number. Circle the tanks that have 0 fish.

Name _____

 5

_____

_ _ _ _ _ _ _

_____

 6

_____

_ _ _ _ _ _ _

_____

 7

_____

_ _ _ _ _ _ _

_____

 8

_____

_ _ _ _ _ _ _

_____

DIRECTIONS   5–8. How many fish are in the tank?
Write the number. Circle the tanks that have 0 fish.

Chapter 1 • Lesson 10

Problem Solving • Applications Real World

9

10

© Houghton Mifflin Harcourt Publishing Company

DIRECTIONS 9. Bryce has two fish. Chris has no fish. Circle to show which fish bowl belongs to Chris. **10.** Draw to show what you know about the number 0. Tell a friend about your drawing.

HOME ACTIVITY • Draw a five frame or use an egg carton that has just five sections. Have your child show a set of up to 3 or 4 objects and place the objects in the five frame. Then have him or her remove the objects and tell how many are in the five frame.

52 fifty-two

FOR MORE PRACTICE: Standards Practice Book

Name _____

 1

○ I
○ 2
○ one

 **2**

○ four
○ five
○ 5

 3

_____

– – – – – – –

_____

 4

_____

– – – – – – –

_____

5

_____

– – – – – – –

_____

DIRECTIONS 1–2. Choose all the answers that tell how many. **3.** How many eggs are in the nest? Write the number. 4–5. Count how many. Write the number.

_____   _____   _____   _____   _____

- - - - -   - - - - -   - - - - -   - - - - -   - - - - -

_____   _____   _____   _____   _____

_____   _____   _____   _____   _____

- - - - -   - - - - -   - - - - -   - - - - -   - - - - -

_____   _____   _____   _____   _____

DIRECTIONS **6.** Circle all sets that show 4. **7.** Count the cubes in each tower. Write the number. **8.** Write the numbers 1 to 5 in counting order.

54 fifty-four

9 THINK **SMARTER** +

4 2 1	○ Yes	○ No
3 4 5	○ Yes	○ No
1 2 3	○ Yes	○ No

10

_____

_ _ _ _ _ _ _ _

_____

11

12

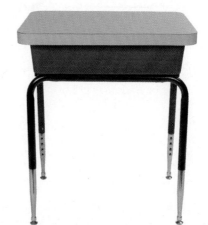

_____

_ _ _ _ _ _ _ _

_____

DIRECTIONS **9.** Are the numbers in counting order? Choose Yes or No.
10. Three children each bring one book to school. Draw counters to show
the books. Write the number. **11.** Sam has no apples in a basket. How many
apples does Sam have? Write the number. **12.** There are two apples on the
table. Kia takes the two apples to school. How many apples are on the table
now? Write the number.

13 **THINK** SMARTER +

____ and ____

____ and ____

14

DIRECTIONS **13.** Show 2 ways to make 5. Color some counters red. Color some yellow. Write the numbers. **14.** Write the number that comes after 3 in counting order. Draw counters to show the number.

56 fifty-six

© Houghton Mifflin Harcourt Publishing Company

Personal Math Trainer

Compare Numbers to 5

Curious About Math with Curious George

Butterflies have taste buds in their feet so they stand on their food to taste it!

• Are there more butterflies or more flowers in this picture?

Name _____

One-to-One Correspondence

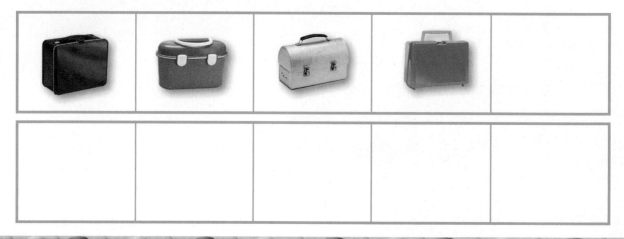

Model Numbers 0 to 5

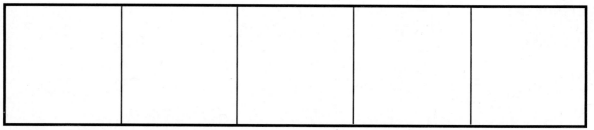

Write Numbers 0 to 5

This page checks understanding of important skills needed for success in Chapter 2.

DIRECTIONS **1.** Draw one apple for each lunch box. **2.** Place counters in the five frame to model the number. Draw the counters. Trace the number. **3–4.** Count and tell how many. Write the number.

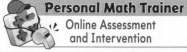

Personal Math Trainer
Online Assessment
and Intervention

© Houghton Mifflin Harcourt Publishing Company

Name _____

four

three

three

one

two

five

DIRECTIONS Circle the sets with the same number of animals. Count and tell how many trees. Draw a line below the word for the number of trees.

• **Interactive Student Edition**
• **Multimedia eGlossary**

Game

Counting to Blastoff

Player 1

5	4	3	2	1	0

Player 2

5	4	3	2	1	0

DIRECTIONS Each player tosses the number cube and finds that number on his or her board. The player covers the number with a counter. Players take turns in this way until they have covered all of the numbers on the board. Then they are ready for blastoff.

MATERIALS 6 counters for each player, number cube (0–5)

Name _____

Same Number

Essential Question How can you use matching and counting to compare sets with the same number of objects?

Counting and Cardinality—K.CC.6
Also K.CC.4b, K.CC.7
MATHEMATICAL PRACTICES
MP.3, MP.5

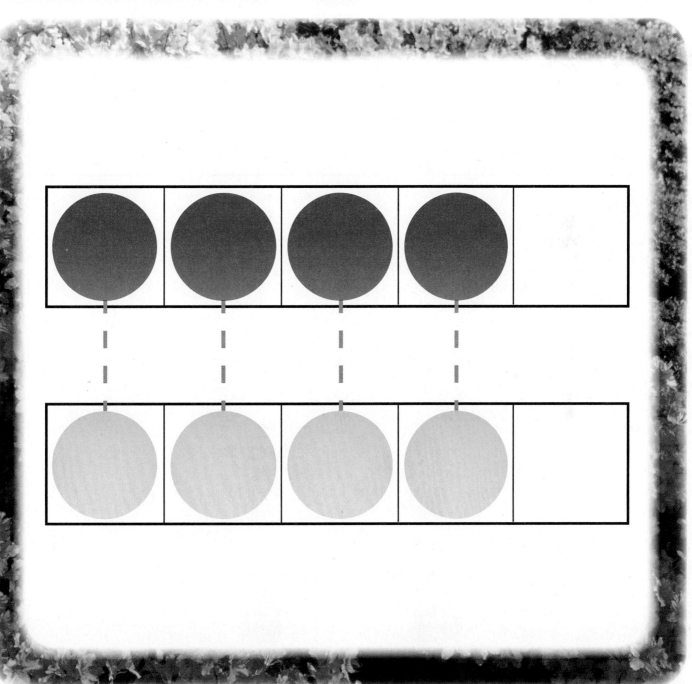

DIRECTIONS Place counters as shown. Trace the lines to match each counter in the top five frame to a counter below it in the bottom five frame. Count how many in each set. Tell a friend about the number of counters in each set.

Chapter 2 • Lesson 1

1

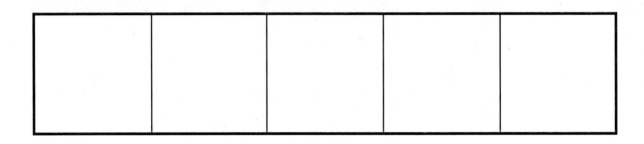

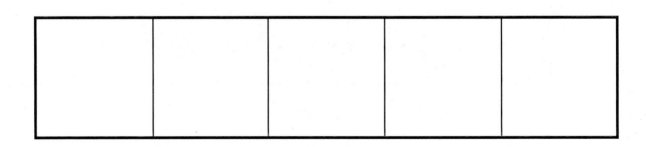

DIRECTIONS 1. Place a counter on each car in the set as you count them. Move the counters to the five frame below the cars. Draw the counters. Place a counter on each finger puppet in the set as you count them. Move the counters to the five frame above the puppets. Draw those counters. Is the number of objects in one set greater than, less than, or the same as the number of objects in the other set? Draw a line to match a counter in each set.

_____

- - - - - - - - -

_____

_____

- - - - - - - - -

_____

DIRECTIONS **2.** Compare the sets of objects. Is the number of hats greater than, less than, or the same as the number of juice boxes? Count how many hats. Write the number. Count how many juice boxes. Write the number. Tell a friend what you know about the number of objects in each set.

Problem Solving • Applications

DIRECTIONS **3.** Count how many buses. Write the number. Draw to show a set of counters that has the same number as the set of buses. Write the number. Draw a line to match the objects in each set. **4.** Draw two sets that have the same number of objects shown in different ways. Tell a friend about your drawing.

HOME ACTIVITY • Show your child two sets that have the same number of up to five objects. Have him or her identify whether the number of objects in one set is greater than, less than, or has the same number of objects as the other set.

FOR MORE PRACTICE:
Standards Practice Book

Name _____

Greater Than

Essential Question How can you compare sets when the number of objects in one set is greater than the number of objects in the other set?

Counting and Cardinality—K.CC.6
Also K.CC.7
MATHEMATICAL PRACTICES
MP.2, MP.3, MP.5

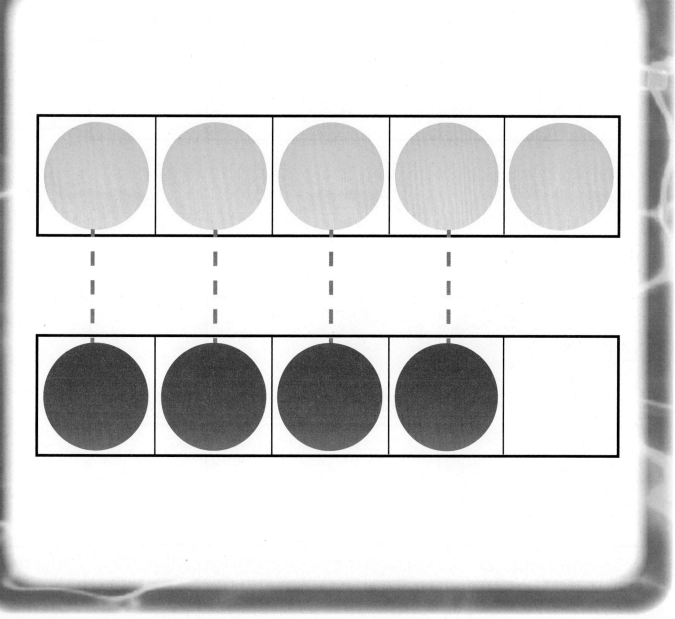

DIRECTIONS Place counters as shown. Trace the lines to match a counter in the top five frame to a counter below it in the bottom five frame. Count how many in each set. Tell a friend which set has a number of objects greater than the other set.

© Houghton Mifflin Harcourt Publishing Company • Image Credits: (bg) ©Image Plan/Corbis

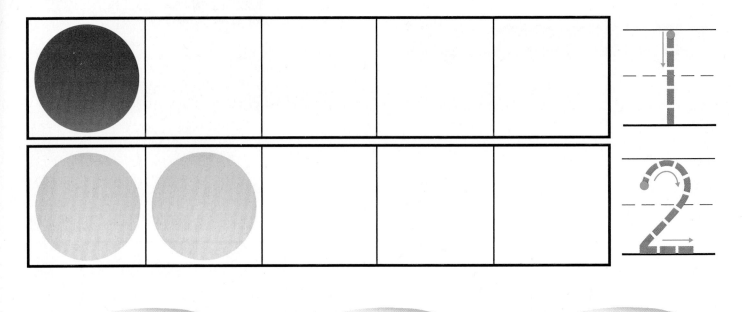

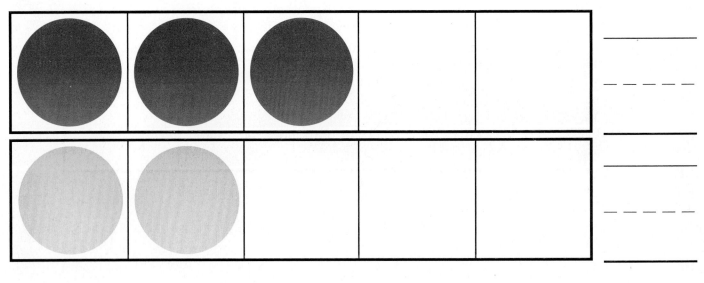

DIRECTIONS 1. Place counters as shown. Count and tell how many in each set. Trace the numbers. Compare the sets by matching. Circle the number that is greater. 2. Place counters as shown. Count and tell how many in each set. Write the numbers. Compare the sets by matching. Circle the number that is greater.

Name _____

_____

‒ ‒ ‒ ‒ ‒ ‒

━━━━━━━━

_____

‒ ‒ ‒ ‒ ‒ ‒

━━━━━━━━

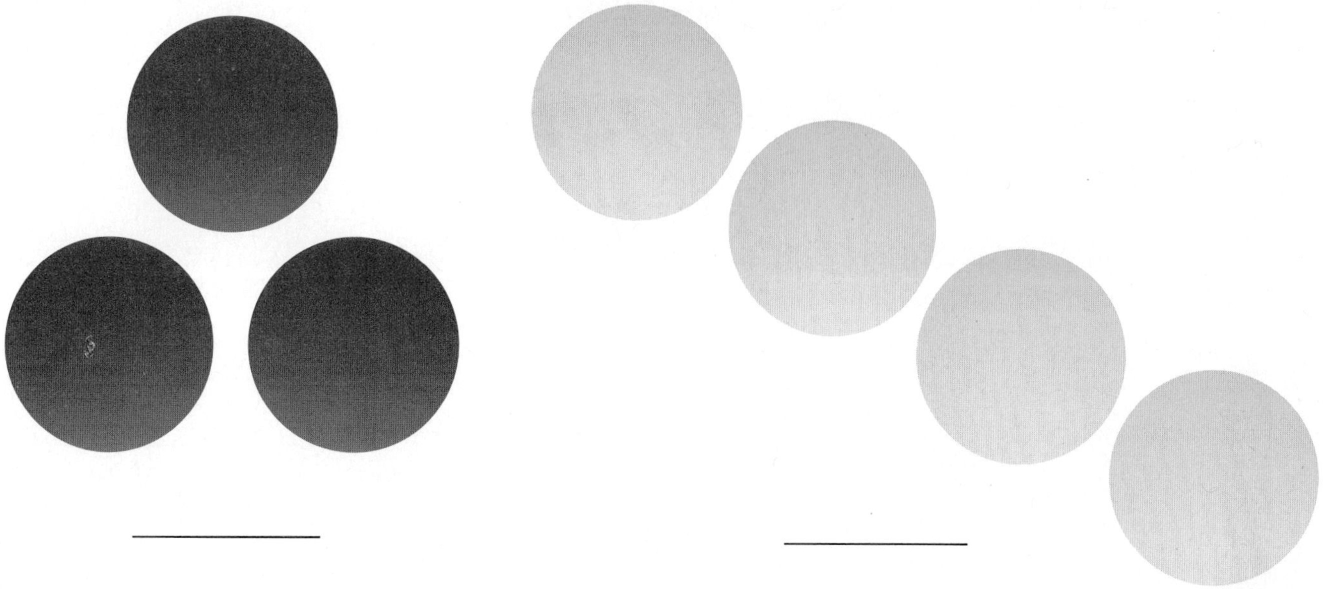

🌼 4

_____

‒ ‒ ‒ ‒ ‒ ‒

━━━━━━━━

_____

‒ ‒ ‒ ‒ ‒ ‒

━━━━━━━━

DIRECTIONS **3–4.** Place counters as shown. Count and tell how many in each set. Write the numbers. Compare the numbers. Circle the number that is greater.

Chapter 2 • Lesson 2

Problem Solving • Applications Real World

WRITE Math

❀ 5

DIRECTIONS 5. Brianna has a bag with three apples in it. Her friend has a bag with a number of apples that is one greater. Draw the bags. Write the numbers on the bags to show how many apples. Tell a friend what you know about the numbers.

HOME ACTIVITY • Show your child a set of up to four objects. Have him or her show a set with a number of objects greater than your set.

68 sixty-eight

FOR MORE PRACTICE:
Standards Practice Book

Name _____

Less Than

Essential Question How can you compare sets when the number of objects in one set is less than the number of objects in the other set?

 Listen and Draw

Counting and Cardinality—K.CC.6
Also K.CC.7
MATHEMATICAL PRACTICES
MP.2, MP.3, MP.5

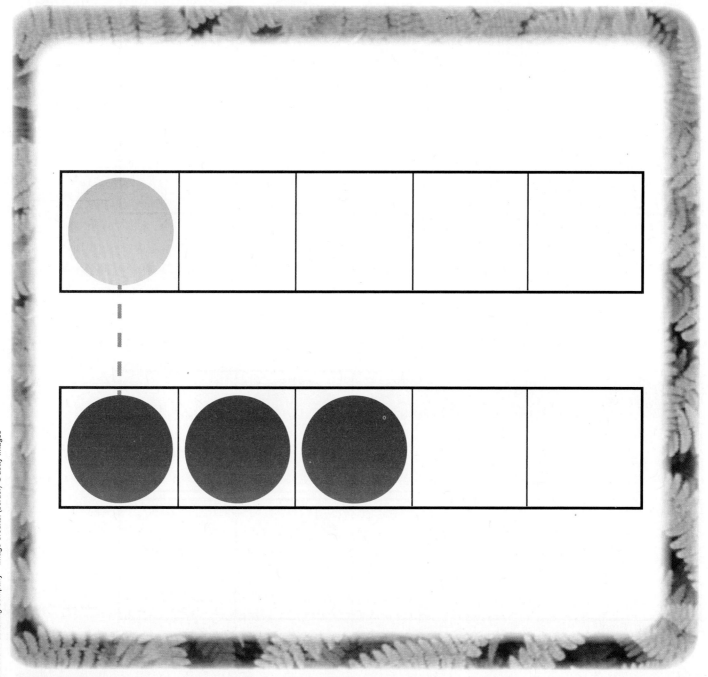

DIRECTIONS Place counters as shown. Trace the line to match a counter in the top five frame to a counter below it in the bottom five frame. Count how many in each set. Tell a friend which set has a number of objects less than the other set.

Chapter 2 • Lesson 3

sixty-nine **69**

Share and Show

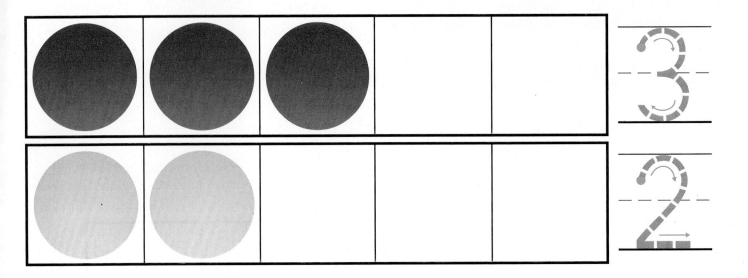

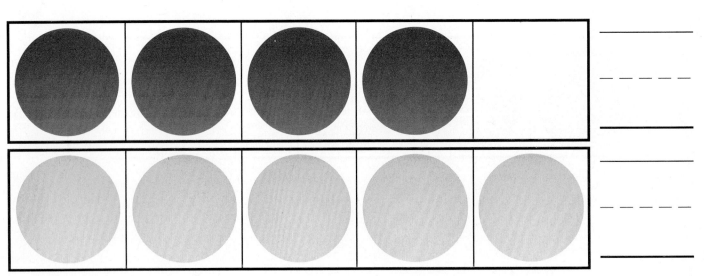

DIRECTIONS **I.** Place counters as shown. Count and tell how many in each set. Trace the numbers. Compare the sets by matching. Circle the number that is less. **2.** Count and tell how many in each set. Write the numbers. Compare the sets by matching. Circle the number that is less.

Name _____

_____

‐ ‐ ‐ ‐ ‐

_____

_____

‐ ‐ ‐ ‐ ‐

_____

DIRECTIONS 3–4. Count and tell how many in each set. Write the numbers. Compare the numbers. Circle the number that is less.

HOME ACTIVITY • Show your child a set of two to five objects. Have him or her show a set of objects that has a number of objects less than you have.

Chapter 2 • Lesson 3

FOR MORE PRACTICE:
Standards Practice Book

Concepts and Skills

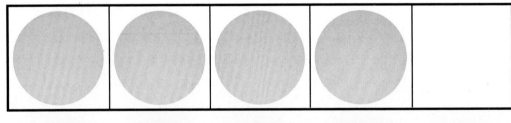

THINK SMARTER

DIRECTIONS **1.** Place a counter below each object to show the same number of objects. Draw and color each counter. Write how many objects in each row. (K.CC.6) **2.** Place counters as shown. Count and tell how many in each set. Write the numbers. Compare the sets by matching. Circle the number that is greater. (K.CC.6) **3.** Count the fish in the bowl at the beginning of the row. Circle all the bowls that have a number of fish less than the bowl at the beginning of the row. (K.CC.6)

Name _____

Problem Solving • Compare by Matching Sets to 5

Essential Question How can you make a model to solve problems using a matching strategy?

Counting and Cardinality—K.CC.6
Also K.CC.7
MATHEMATICAL PRACTICES
MP.3, MP.4, MP.5

 Unlock the Problem   Hands On

DIRECTIONS These are Brandon's toy cars. How many toy cars does Brandon have? Jay has a number of toy cars that is less than the number of toy cars Brandon has. Use cubes to show how many toy cars Jay might have. Draw the cubes. Use matching to compare the sets.

Chapter 2 • Lesson 4

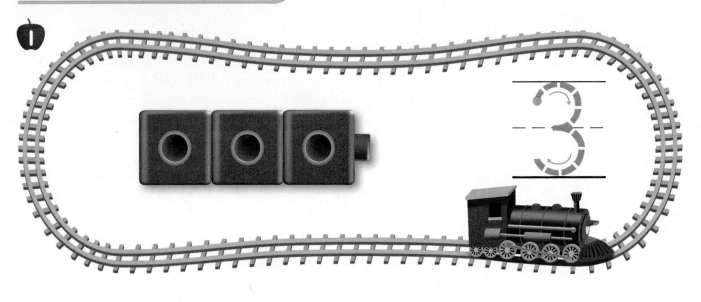

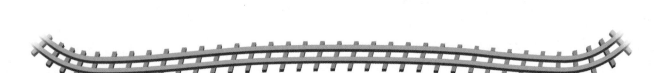

DIRECTIONS 1. How many cubes? Trace the number. 2–3. Model a cube train that has a number of cubes greater than 3. Draw the cube train. Write how many. Compare the cube train by matching with the model at the top of the page. Tell a friend about the cube trains.

Name _____

DIRECTIONS **4.** How many cubes? Write the number.   **5–6.** Model a cube train that has a number of cubes less than 5. Draw the cube train. Write how many. Compare the cube train by matching with the model at the top of the page. Tell a friend about the cube trains.

Chapter 2 • Lesson 4

seventy-five **75**

On Your Own Real World

7

8

DIRECTIONS **7.** Kendall has a set of three pencils. Her friend has a set with the same number of pencils. Draw to show the sets of pencils. Compare the sets by matching. Write how many in each set. **8.** Draw to show what you know about matching to compare two sets of objects. Write how many in each set.

 HOME ACTIVITY • Show your child two sets with a different number of objects in each set. Have him or her use matching to compare the sets.

FOR MORE PRACTICE: Standards Practice Book

Name _____

Compare by Counting Sets to 5

Essential Question How can you use a counting strategy to compare sets of objects?

Counting and Cardinality—K.CC.6
Also K.CC.7
MATHEMATICAL PRACTICES
MP.2, MP.3, MP.6

Listen and Draw *Real World*

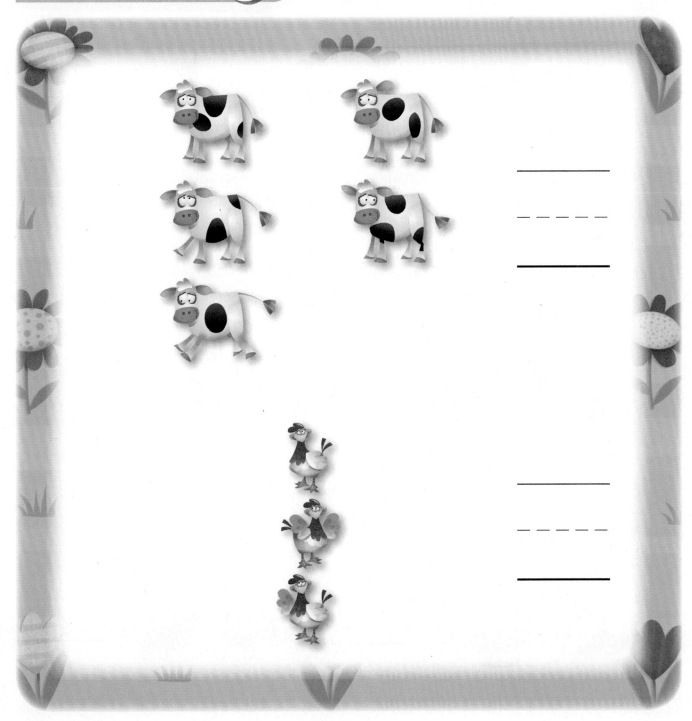

DIRECTIONS Look at the sets of objects. Count how many objects in each set. Write the numbers. Compare the numbers and tell a friend which number is greater and which number is less.

Chapter 2 • Lesson 5

1

_____

_____

2

_____

_____

3 ✓

_____

_____

DIRECTIONS   1–3. Count how many objects in each set.
Write the numbers. Compare the numbers. Circle the number
that is greater.

78 seventy-eight

4

_____

– – – – – – – – –

_____

5

_____

– – – – – – – – –

_____

6

_____

– – – – – – – – –

_____

DIRECTIONS 4–6. Count how many objects in each set.
Write the numbers. Compare the numbers. Circle the number
that is less.

Chapter 2 • Lesson 5

Problem Solving • Applications

WRITE Math

❤ 7

_____

— — — — —

_____

_____

— — — — —

_____

🐟 8

_____

— — — — —

_____

_____

— — — — —

_____

DIRECTIONS **7.** Tony has stuffed toy frogs. His friend has stuffed toy turkeys. Count how many objects in each set. Write the numbers. Compare the numbers. Tell a friend what you know about the sets. **8.** Draw to show what you know about counting to compare two sets of objects. Write how many in each set.

 HOME ACTIVITY • Draw a domino block with up to three dots on one end. Ask your child to draw on the other end a number of dots greater than the set you drew.

FOR MORE PRACTICE:
Standards Practice Book

 **Chapter 2 Review/Test**

1

_____

- - - - - - - - - - - - - -

_____

_____

- - - - - - - - - - - - - -

_____

2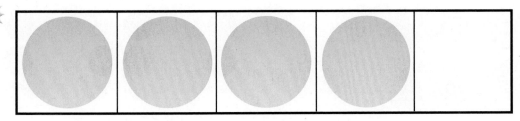

_____

- - - - - - - - - - - - - -

_____

_____

- - - - - - - - - - - - - -

_____

DIRECTIONS 1. Draw a counter below each finger puppet to show the same number of counters as puppets. Write how many puppets. Write how many counters. **2.** How many counters are there in each row? Write the numbers. Compare the sets by matching. Circle the number that is greater.

 GO DIGITAL Assessment Options
Chapter Test

Chapter 2

3

○   ○   ○

4

○   ○   ○

5

○   ○   ○

6

○ **I**   ○ **2**   ○ **3**

DIRECTIONS **3.** Mark under all the sets that have the same number of counters as the number of cars.   **4.** Mark under all the sets that have a number of counters greater than the number of turtles.   **5.** Mark under all the sets that have a number of counters less than the number of vans.   **6.** Mark all the numbers less than 3.

Name _____

_____

— — — — — — —

_____

_____

— — — — — — —

_____

Personal Math Trainer

8 🐟 THINK SMARTER ➕

_____

— — — — — — —

_____

© Houghton Mifflin Harcourt Publishing Company

DIRECTIONS **7.** Maria has these apples. Draw a set of oranges below the apples that has the same number. Compare the sets by matching. Write how many pieces of fruit in each set. **8.** Amy has two crayons. Draw Amy's crayons. Brad has 1 more crayon than Amy. How many crayons does Brad have? Draw Brad's crayons. Write how many in each set.

9 THINK SMARTER ✚

• same number

• greater than

• less than

10

_____
_ _ _ _ _
_____

_____
_ _ _ _ _
_____

DIRECTIONS **9.** Compare the number of red counters in each set to the number of blue counters. Draw lines from the sets of counters to the words that show *same number*, *greater than*, or *less than*. **10.** Draw four counters. Now draw a set that has a greater number of counters. How many are in each set? Write the numbers. Use green to color the set with a greater number of counters. Use blue to color the set with a number of counters that is less than the green set.

Represent, Count, and Write Numbers 6 to 9

Curious About Math with

Curious George

Rides are popular at fairs.

- What can you tell me about this ride?

Name _____

Explore Numbers to 5

Compare Numbers to 5

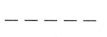

Write Numbers to 5

0

This page checks understanding of important skills needed for success in Chapter 3.

DIRECTIONS 1. Circle the dot cards that show 3. 2. Circle the dot cards that show 5. 3. Write the number of cubes in each set. Circle the greater number. 4. Write the numbers 1 to 5 in order.

 **Personal Math Trainer**
Online Assessment and Intervention

© Houghton Mifflin Harcourt Publishing Company

Name _____

same number

more

fewer

DIRECTIONS Point to sets of objects as you count. Circle two sets that have the same number of objects. Tell what you know about sets that have more objects or fewer objects than other sets on this page.

• **Interactive Student Edition**
• **Multimedia eGlossary**

Game

Number Line Up

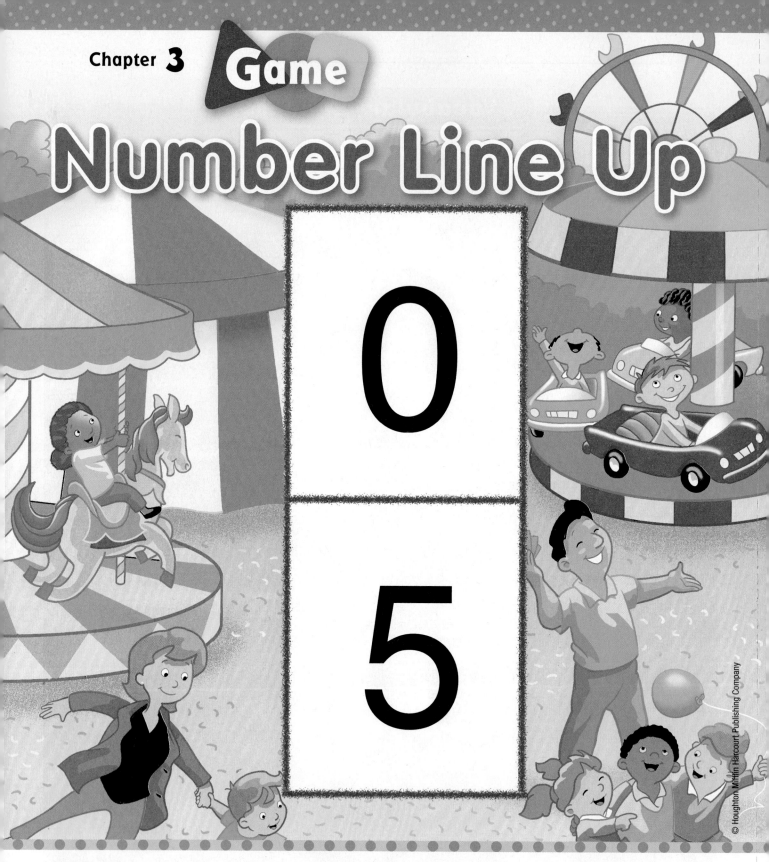

DIRECTIONS Play with a partner. Place numeral cards as shown on the board. Shuffle the remaining cards and place them face down in a stack. Players take turns picking one card from the stack. They place the card to the right to form a number sequence without skipping any numbers. The number sequence can be forward from 0 or backward from 5. If a player picks a card that is not next in either number sequence, the card is returned to the bottom of the stack. The first player to complete a number sequence wins the game.

MATERIALS 2 sets of numeral cards 0–5

Name _____

Model and Count 6

Essential Question How can you show and count 6 objects?

Counting and Cardinality—K.CC.5
Also K.CC.4a, K.CC.4b
MATHEMATICAL PRACTICES
MP.4, MP.5, MP.7

Listen and Draw *Real World*   *Hands On*

DIRECTIONS Place a counter on each ticket in the set as you count them. Move the counters to the ten frame. Draw the counters.

Chapter 3 • Lesson 1

six

DIRECTIONS 1. Place a counter on each car in the set as you count them. Move the counters to the parking lot. Draw the counters. Say the number as you trace it.

6

six

____ ____ and ____ ____

____ ____ and ____ ____

____ ____ and ____ ____

____ ____ and ____ ____

DIRECTIONS 2. Trace the number 6. Use two-color counters to model the different ways to make 6. Write to show some pairs of numbers that make 6.

Problem Solving • Applications (Real World)

WRITE Math

3

4

© Houghton Mifflin Harcourt Publishing Company

DIRECTIONS 3. Six people each bought a bucket of popcorn. Count the buckets of popcorn in each set. Circle all the sets that show six buckets. **4.** Draw to show a set of six objects. Tell about your drawing.

HOME ACTIVITY • Ask your child to show a set of five objects. Have him or her show one more object and tell how many objects are in the set.

FOR MORE PRACTICE:
Standards Practice Book

Name _____

Count and Write to 6

Essential Question How can you count and write up to 6 with words and numbers?

Counting and Cardinality—K.CC.3
Also K.CC.4b, K.CC.5
MATHEMATICAL PRACTICES
MP.2

Listen and Draw

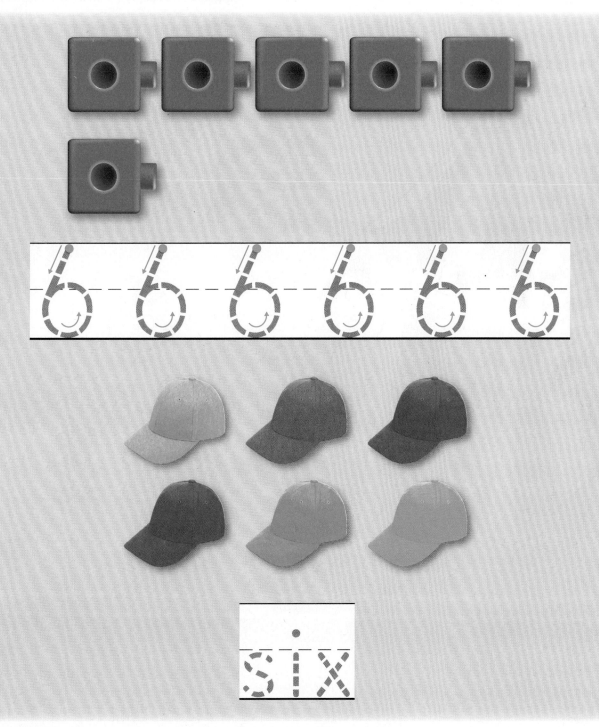

DIRECTIONS Count and tell how many cubes. Trace the numbers. Count and tell how many hats. Trace the word.

Chapter 3 • Lesson 2

DIRECTIONS I. Look at the picture. Circle all the sets of six objects. Circle the group of six people.

6
six

3

_____

– – – – –

_____

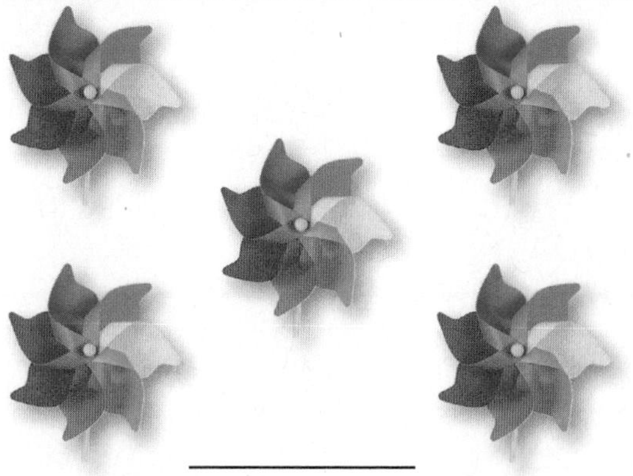

4

_____

– – – – –

_____

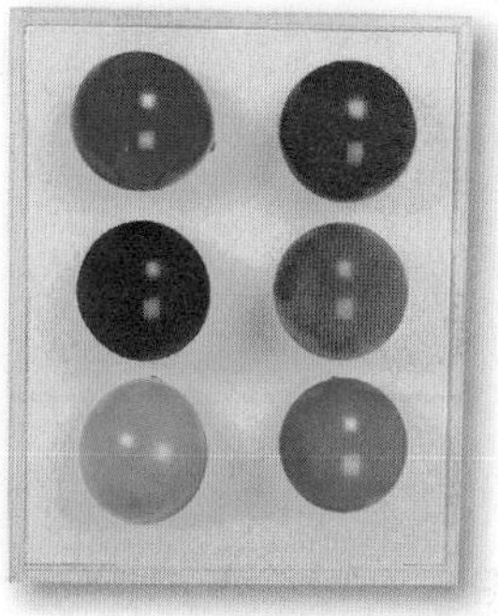

5

_____

– – – – –

_____

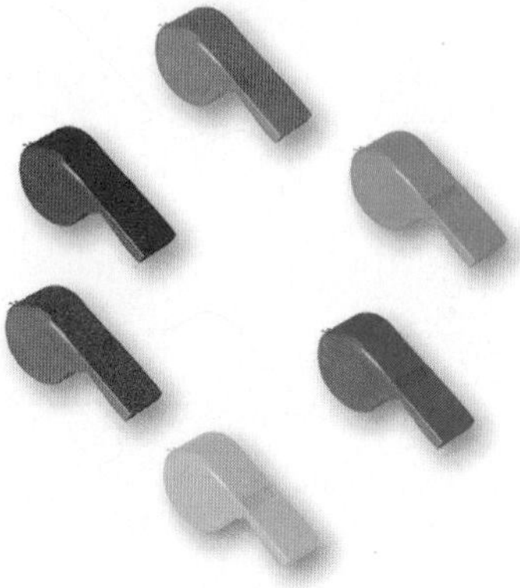

6

_____

– – – – –

_____

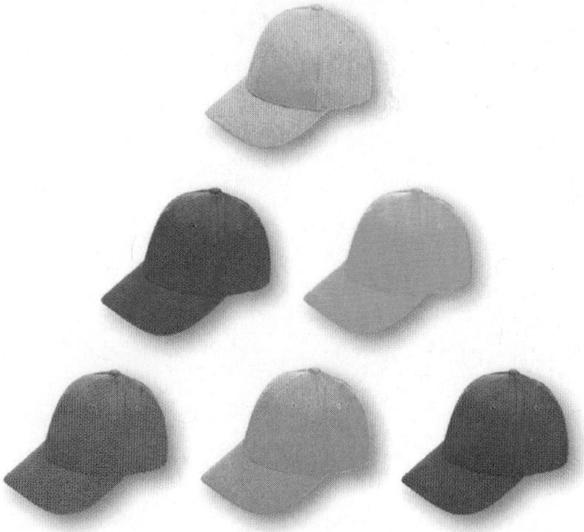

DIRECTIONS 2. Say the number. Trace the numbers.
3–6. Count and tell how many. Write the number.

Problem Solving • Applications

WRITE Math

 7

 8

_____

- - - - - -

_____

DIRECTIONS **7.** Marta has a number of whistles that is two less than 6. Count the whistles in each set. Circle the set that shows a number of whistles two less than 6. **8.** Draw a set of objects that has a number of objects one greater than 5. Tell about your drawing. Write how many objects.

HOME ACTIVITY • Show six objects. Have your child point to each object as he or she counts it. Then have him or her write the number on paper to show how many.

FOR MORE PRACTICE:
Standards Practice Book

Name _____

Model and Count 7

Essential Question How can you show and count 7 objects?

Listen and Draw

Counting and Cardinality—K.CC.5
Also K.CC.4a, K.CC.4b, K.CC.4c
MATHEMATICAL PRACTICES
MP.5, MP.7, MP.8

DIRECTIONS Model 6 objects. Show one more object. How many are there now? Tell a friend how you know. Draw the objects.

Chapter 3 • Lesson 3

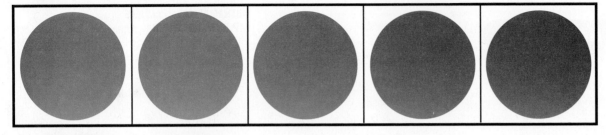

seven

5 and ____ more

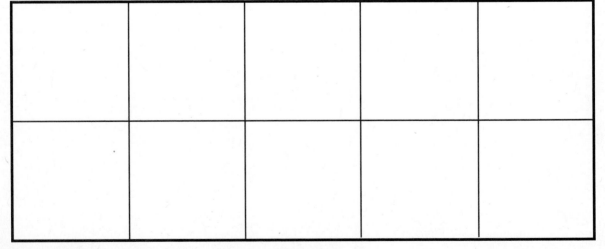

DIRECTIONS 1. Place counters as shown. Count and tell how many counters. Trace the number. 2. How many more than 5 is 7? Write the number. 3. Place counters in the ten frame to model seven. Tell a friend what you know about the number 7.

🌸 4

7
seven

_ _ _ _ _ _
_____
⚪ and ⚫

_ _ _ _ _ _
_____
⚪ and ⚫

_ _ _ _ _ _
_____
⚪ and ⚫

_ _ _ _ _ _
_____
⚪ and ⚫

DIRECTIONS 4. Use two-color counters to model the different ways to make 7. Write to show some pairs of numbers that make 7.

Problem Solving • Applications

5

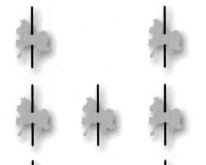

6

DIRECTIONS 5. A carousel needs seven horses. Count the horses in each set. Which sets show seven horses? Circle those sets. **6.** Draw to show what you know about the number 7. Tell a friend about your drawing.

HOME ACTIVITY • Ask your child to show a set of six objects. Have him or her show one more object and tell how many objects are in the set.

FOR MORE PRACTICE:
Standards Practice Book

Name _____

Count and Write to 7

Essential Question How can you count
and write up to 7 with words and numbers?

Counting and Cardinality—K.CC.3
Also K.CC.4b, K.CC.5
MATHEMATICAL PRACTICES
MP.2

Listen and Draw Real World

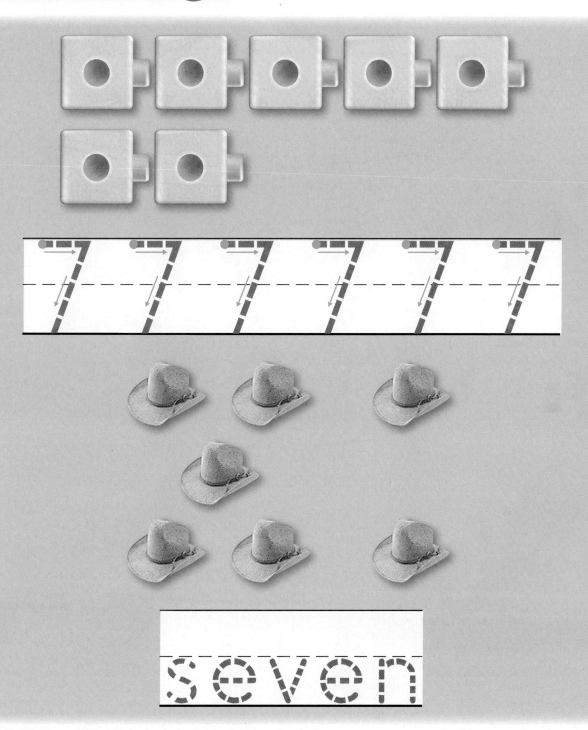

seven

DIRECTIONS Count and tell how many cubes. Trace the
numbers. Count and tell how many hats. Trace the word.

Chapter 3 • Lesson 4

one hundred one **101**

DIRECTIONS I. Look at the picture. Circle all the sets of seven objects.

Name _____

 7

seven

7 7 7 7 7

3 ✓

_____

- - - - - - - - - - - - - - - - - - - -

_____

4

_____

- - - - - - - - - - - - - - - - - - - -

_____

5

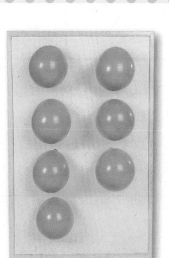

_____

- - - - - - - - - - - - - - - - - - - -

_____

6

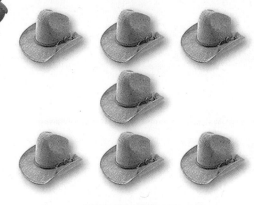

_____

- - - - - - - - - - - - - - - - - - - -

_____

DIRECTIONS **2.** Say the number. Trace the numbers. **3–6.** Count and tell how many. Write the number.

HOME ACTIVITY • Show your child seven objects. Have him or her point to each object as he or she counts it. Then have him or her write the number on paper to show how many objects.

FOR MORE PRACTICE: Standards Practice Book

© Houghton Mifflin Harcourt Publishing Company • Image Credits: (bl) ©Stockbyte/Getty Images (br) ©PhotoDisc/Getty Images

Concepts and Skills

🍎 **1**

					_____
					- - - - - - - -
					_____

☀️ **2**

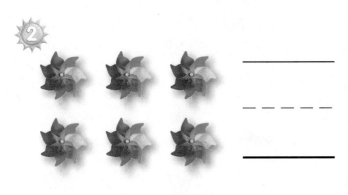

_____

- - - - - - - -

_____

🍂 **3**

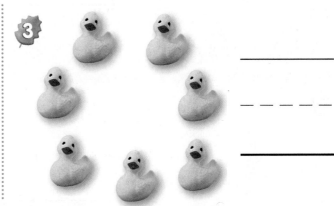

_____

- - - - - - - -

_____

🌸 **4** **THINK SMARTER**

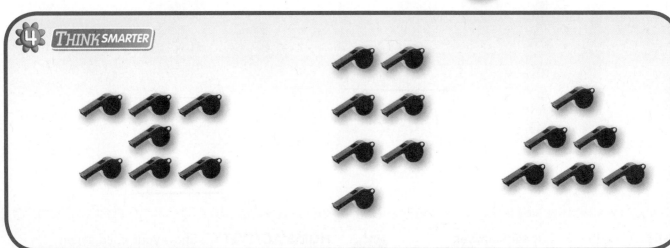

DIRECTIONS 1. Use counters to model the number 7. Draw the counters. Write the number. (K.CC.5) **2–3.** Count and tell how many. Write the number. (K.CC.3) **4.** Circle all the sets of 7 whistles. (K.CC.3)

© Houghton Mifflin Harcourt Publishing Company • Image Credits: (cr) ©Lawrence Manning/Corbis

Name _____

Model and Count 8

Essential Question How can you show and count
8 objects?

Listen and Draw Hands On

Counting and Cardinality—K.CC.5
Also K.CC.4a, K.CC.4b, K.CC.4c
MATHEMATICAL PRACTICES
MP.5, MP.7, MP.8

DIRECTIONS Model 7 objects. Show one more object. How
many are there now? Tell a friend how you know. Draw the objects.

Chapter 3 • Lesson 5

1

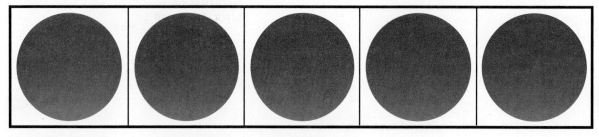

eight

2

5 and ___ more

3 ✓

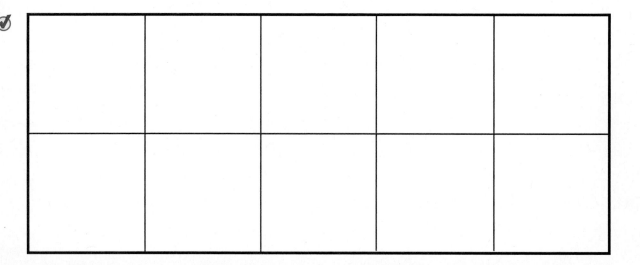

DIRECTIONS 1. Place counters as shown. Count and tell how many counters. Trace the number. **2.** How many more than 5 is 8? Write the number. **3.** Place counters in the ten frame to model eight. Tell a friend what you know about the number 8.

106 one hundred six

4

<table>
<tr><td></td><td></td><td></td><td></td><td></td></tr>
<tr><td></td><td></td><td></td><td></td><td></td></tr>
</table>

8
eight

_ _ _ _ _ _ _

_____ and _____

_____ and _____

_____ and _____

_____ and _____

DIRECTIONS 4. Use two-color counters to model the different ways to make 8. Write to show some pairs of numbers that make 8.

Problem Solving • Applications

5

6

DIRECTIONS 5. Dave sorted sets of balls by color. Count the balls in each set. Which sets show eight balls? Circle those sets. 6. Draw to show what you know about the number 8. Tell a friend about your drawing.

 HOME ACTIVITY • Ask your child to show a set of seven objects. Have him or her show one more object and tell how many.

108 one hundred eight

FOR MORE PRACTICE:
Standards Practice Book

Name _____

Count and Write to 8

Essential Question How can you count and write up to 8 with words and numbers?

Counting and Cardinality—K.CC.3
Also K.CC.4b, K.CC.5
MATHEMATICAL PRACTICES
MP.2

Listen and Draw *Real World*

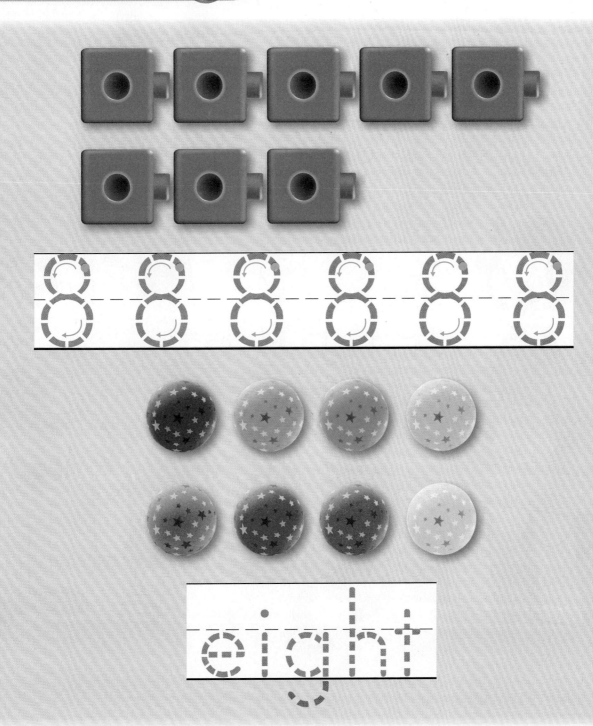

DIRECTIONS Count and tell how many cubes. Trace the numbers. Count and tell how many balls. Trace the word.

Chapter 3 • Lesson 6

1

DIRECTIONS I. Look at the picture. Circle all the sets of eight objects.

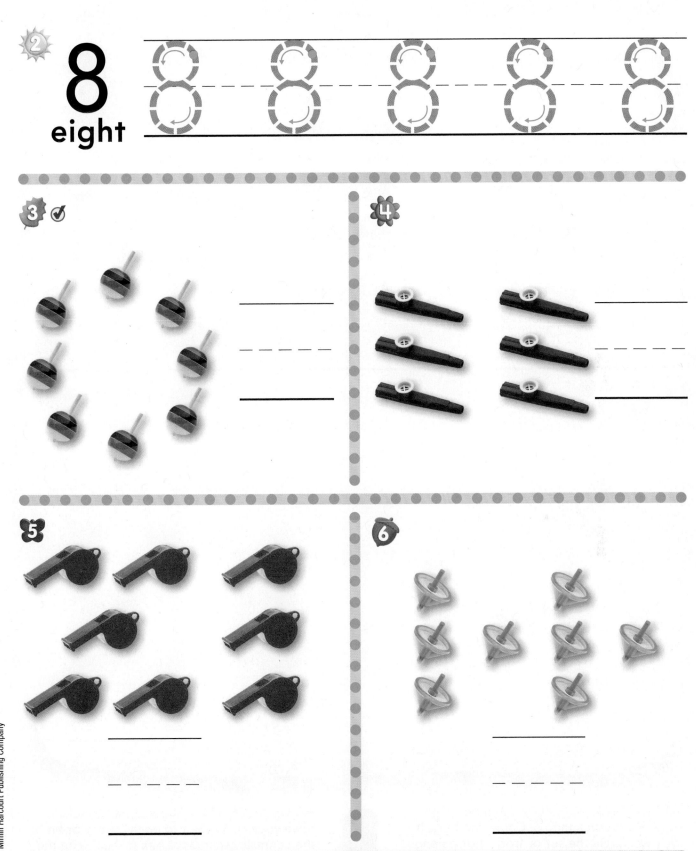

8 eight

DIRECTIONS 2. Say the number. Trace the numbers.
3–6. Count and tell how many. Write the number.

Chapter 3 • Lesson 6

one hundred eleven **111**

Problem Solving • Applications Real World

WRITE Math

7

8

© Houghton Mifflin Harcourt Publishing Company

DIRECTIONS **7.** Ed has a number of toy frogs two greater than 6. Count the frogs in each set. Circle the set of frogs that belongs to Ed. **8.** Robbie won ten prizes at the fair. Marissa won a number of prizes two less than Robbie. Draw to show Marissa's prizes. Write how many.

HOME ACTIVITY • Show eight objects. Have your child point to each object as he or she counts it. Then have him or her write the number on paper to show how many objects.

FOR MORE PRACTICE:
Standards Practice Book

Name _____

Model and Count 9

Essential Question How can you show and count 9 objects?

Counting and Cardinality—K.CC.5
Also K.CC.4a, K.CC.4b, K.CC.4c
MATHEMATICAL PRACTICES
MP.5, MP.7, MP.8

DIRECTIONS Model 8 objects. Show one more object. How many are there now? Tell a friend how you know. Draw the objects.

1

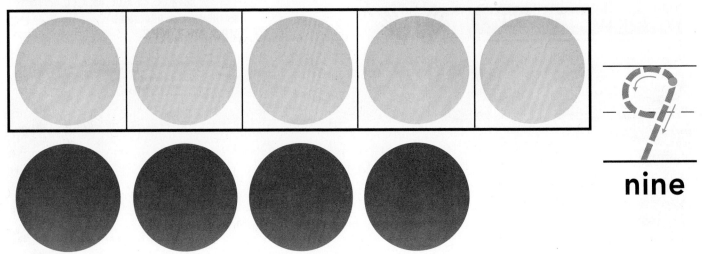

9
nine

2 ☑

5 and ___ more

3 ☑

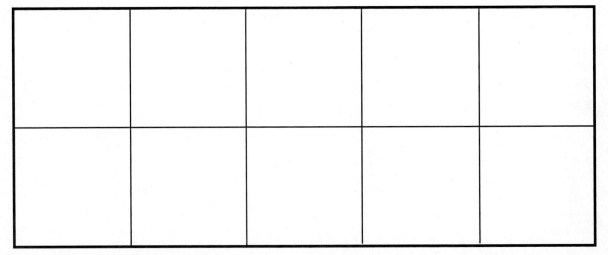

DIRECTIONS 1. Place counters as shown. Count and tell how many counters. Trace the number. **2.** How many more than 5 is 9? Write the number. **3.** Place counters in the ten frame to model nine. Tell a friend what you know about the number 9.

Name _____

nine

____ and ____

and

and

and

and

DIRECTIONS 4. Use two-color counters to model the different ways to make 9. Write to show some pairs of numbers that make 9.

Chapter 3 • Lesson 7

one hundred fifteen 115

Problem Solving • Applications Real World

5

6

DIRECTIONS 5. Mr. Lopez is making displays using sets of nine flags. Count the flags in each set. Which sets show nine flags? Circle those sets. 6. Draw to show what you know about the number 9. Tell a friend about your drawing.

HOME ACTIVITY • Ask your child to show a set of eight objects. Have him or her show one more object and tell how many.

FOR MORE PRACTICE:
Standards Practice Book

DIRECTIONS I. Look at the picture. Circle all the sets of nine objects.

Name _____

Count and Write to 9

Essential Question How can you count and write up to 9 with words and numbers?

Counting and Cardinality—K.CC.3
Also K.CC.4b, K.CC.5
MATHEMATICAL PRACTICES
MP.2

Listen and Draw Real World

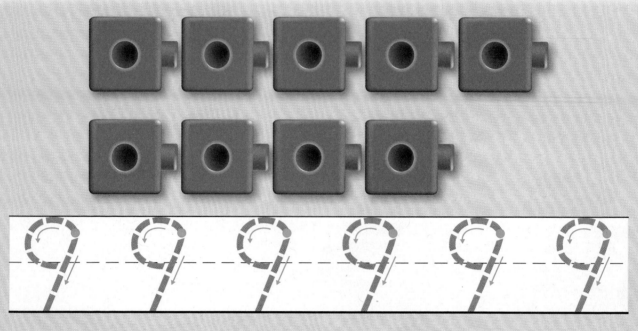

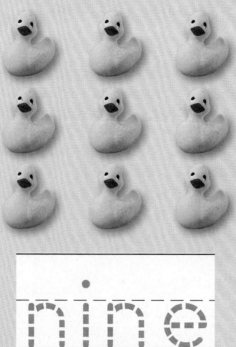

© Houghton Mifflin Harcourt Publishing Company • Image Credits: (bc) ©Lawrence Manning/Corbis

DIRECTIONS Count and tell how many cubes. Trace the numbers. Count and tell how many ducks. Trace the word.

Chapter 3 • Lesson 8

9

nine

DIRECTIONS **2.** Say the number. Trace the numbers.
3–6. Count and tell how many. Write the number.

Chapter 3 • Lesson 8

one hundred nineteen **119**

Problem Solving • Applications Real World

WRITE Math

7

8

DIRECTIONS 7. Eva wants to find the set that has a number of bears one less than 10. Circle that set.   8. Draw a set that has a number of objects two greater than 7. Write how many.

HOME ACTIVITY • Ask your child to find something in your home that has the number 9 on it, such as a clock or a phone.

FOR MORE PRACTICE:
Standards Practice Book

Name _____

Problem Solving • Numbers to 9

Essential Question How can you solve problems using the strategy *draw a picture*?

Counting and Cardinality—K.CC.6
Also K.CC.7
MATHEMATICAL PRACTICES
MP.1, MP.3, MP.4

Unlock the Problem Real World

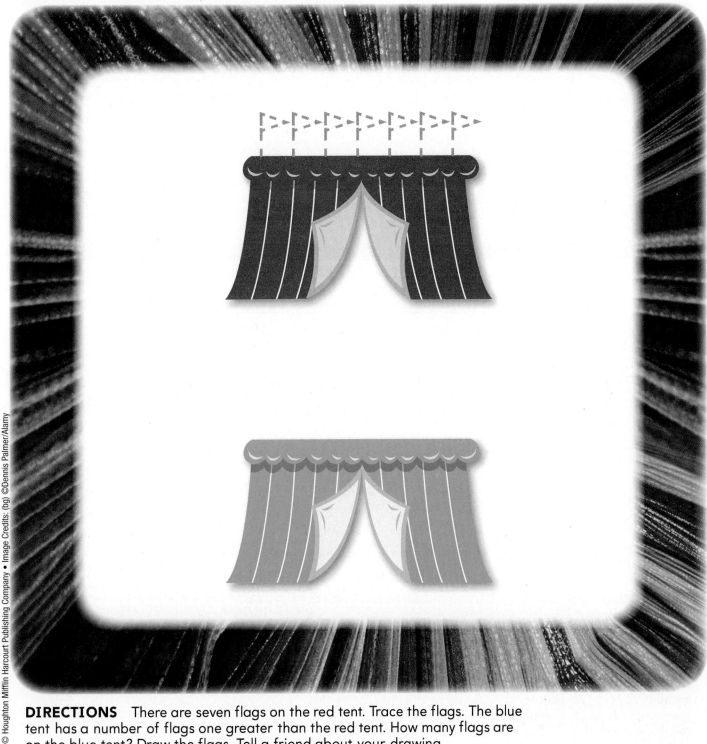

DIRECTIONS There are seven flags on the red tent. Trace the flags. The blue tent has a number of flags one greater than the red tent. How many flags are on the blue tent? Draw the flags. Tell a friend about your drawing.

Chapter 3 • Lesson 9

one hundred twenty-one **121**

1

2

DIRECTIONS **1.** Bianca buys five hats. Leigh buys a number of hats two greater than 5. Draw the hats. Write the numbers. **2.** Donna wins nine tokens. Jackie wins a number of tokens two less than 9. Draw the tokens. Write the numbers.

Share and Show

DIRECTIONS **3.** Gary has eight tickets. Four of the tickets are red. The rest are blue. How many are blue? Draw the tickets. Write the number beside each set of tickets. **4.** Ann has seven balloons. Molly has a set of balloons less than seven. How many balloons does Molly have? Draw the balloons. Write the number beside each set of balloons.

On Your Own

5

_____

- - - - - - -

_____

6

DIRECTIONS **5.** There are six seats on a teacup ride. The number of seats on a train ride is two less than 8. How many seats on the train ride? Draw the seats. Write the number. **6.** Pick two numbers between 0 and 9. Draw to show what you know about those numbers.

HOME ACTIVITY • Have your child say two different numbers from 0–9 and tell what he or she knows about them.

124 one hundred twenty-four

FOR MORE PRACTICE: Standards Practice Book

Chapter 3 Review/Test

 1

 2

3

_____

_ _ _ _ _ _

_____

 4

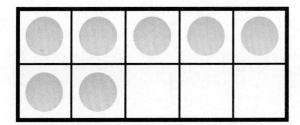

_____

_ _ _ _ _ _

_____

DIRECTIONS 1. Circle all the sets that show 6.   2. Circle all the sets that show 7.   3–4. Count and tell how many. Write the number.

GO DIGITAL Assessment Options **Chapter Test**

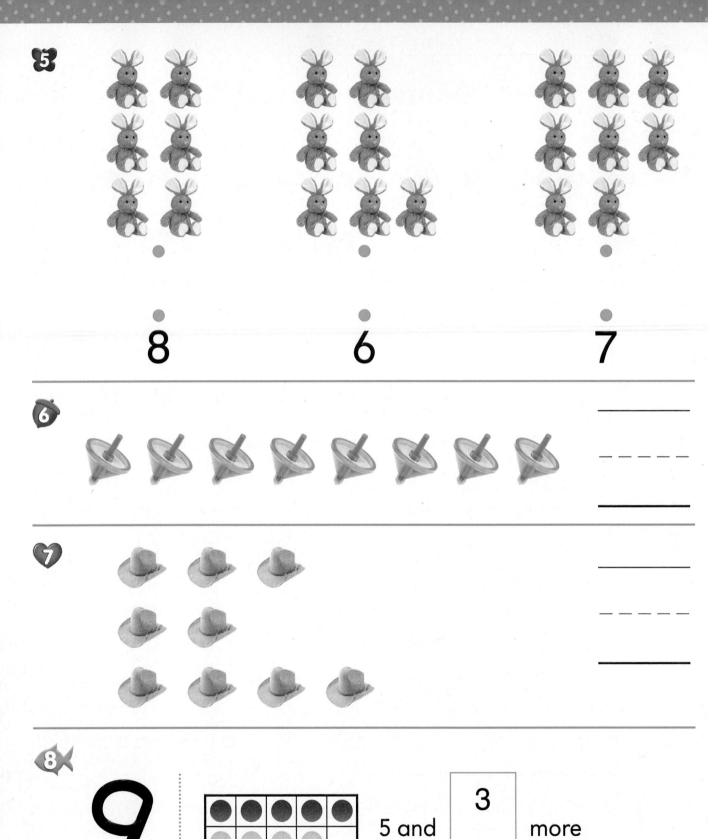

5   8   6   7

8

9   5 and   3   more
                 4

DIRECTIONS   **5.** Match each set to the number that tells how many.   **6–7.** Count to tell how many. Write the number.   **8.** The ten frame shows 5 red counters and some yellow counters. Five and how many more make 9? Choose the number.

Personal Math Trainer

9 THINK SMARTER +

_____

- - - - - - - -

_____

_____

- - - - - - - -

_____

10

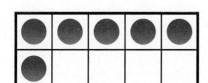   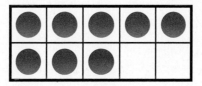   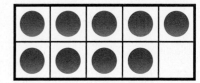

○   ○   ○

DIRECTIONS 9. Jeffrey has 8 marbles. Sarah has a number of marbles that is one greater than 8. Draw the marbles. Write the number for each set of marbles. **10.** Choose all the ten frames that have a number of counters greater than 6.

THINK SMARTER +

_____

— — — — —

_____

_____

— — — — —

_____

DIRECTIONS 11. The number of turtles in a pond is 2 less than 9. Draw counters to show the turtles. Write the number. 12. Draw a set that has a number of objects that is 2 more than 6. Write the number.

Represent and Compare Numbers to 10

Curious About Math with
Curious George

Apple trees grow from a small seed.

• About how many seeds are in an apple?

Name _____

Show What You Know ✓

Draw Objects to 9

 1

9

 2

7

Write Numbers to 9

3  _____

4  _____

---

5  _____

6 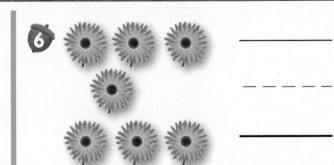 _____

This page checks understanding of important skills needed for success in Chapter 4.

DIRECTIONS 1. Draw 9 flowers. 2. Draw 7 flowers.
3–6. Count and tell how many. Write the number.

Personal Math Trainer
Online Assessment
and Intervention

Name _____

greater

less

same number

DIRECTIONS Circle the words that describe the number of carrots and the number of celery sticks. Use *greater* and *less* to describe the number of trees and the number of bushes.

 • **Interactive Student Edition**
• **Multimedia eGlossary**

Game

Spin and Count!

START

END

DIRECTIONS Play with a partner. Place game markers on START. Use a pencil and a paper clip to spin for a number. Take turns spinning. Each player moves his or her marker to the next space that has the same number of objects as the number on the spinner. The first player to reach END wins.

MATERIALS two game markers, pencil, paper clip

Name _____

Model and Count 10

Essential Question How can you show and count 10 objects?

Counting and Cardinality—K.CC.5
Also K.CC.4a, K.CC.4b, K.CC.4c
MATHEMATICAL PRACTICES
MP.4, MP.5

Listen and Draw *Real World*   Hands On

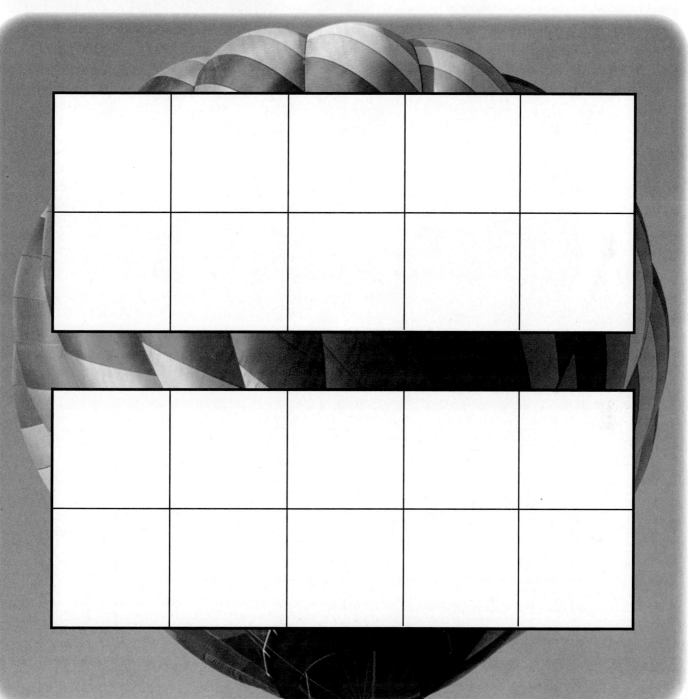

DIRECTIONS Use counters to model 9 in the top ten frame. Use counters to model 10 in the bottom ten frame. Draw the counters. Tell about the ten frames.

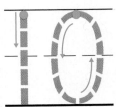

ten

DIRECTIONS 1. Place a counter on each balloon. 2. Move the counters to the ten frame. Draw the counters. Point to each counter as you count it. Trace the number.

3

10

ten

_____ _____ **and** _____ _____

_____ _____ **and** _____ _____

_____ _____ **and** _____ _____

_____ _____ **and** _____ _____

DIRECTIONS 3. Trace the number. Use counters to model the different ways to make 10. Write to show some pairs of numbers that make 10.

Problem Solving • Applications

WRITE Math

4.

5.

DIRECTIONS 4. Michelle puts her star stickers in sets of 10. Circle all the sets of star stickers that belong to Michelle. 5. Draw to show what you know about the number 10. Tell a friend about your drawing.

HOME ACTIVITY • Ask your child to show a set of nine objects. Then have him or her show one more object and tell how many objects are in the set.

136 one hundred thirty-six

FOR MORE PRACTICE:
Standards Practice Book

Name _____

Count and Write to 10

Essential Question How can you count and write up to 10 with words and numbers?

Counting and Cardinality—K.CC.3
Also K.CC.4b, K.CC.5
MATHEMATICAL PRACTICES
MP.2

Listen and Draw Real World

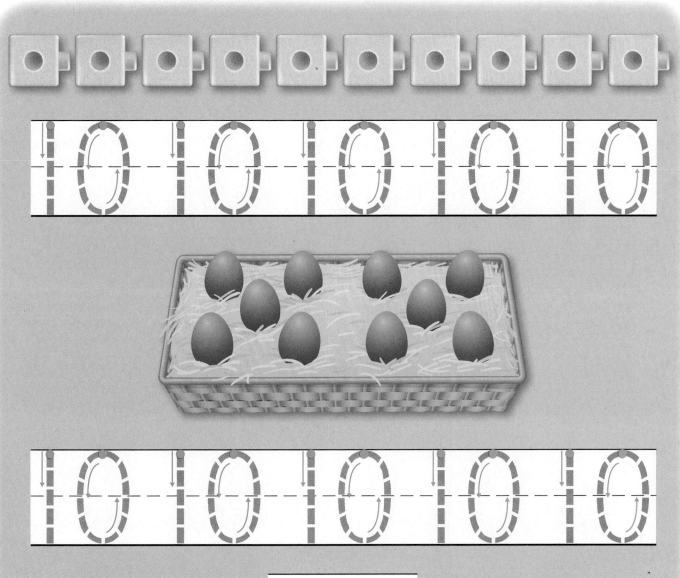

DIRECTIONS Count and tell how many cubes. Trace the numbers. Count and tell how many eggs. Trace the numbers and the word.

Chapter 4 • Lesson 2

1 # 10
ten

2

_____

- - - - -

_____

3

_____

- - - - -

_____

4 ✓

_____

- - - - -

_____

5 ✓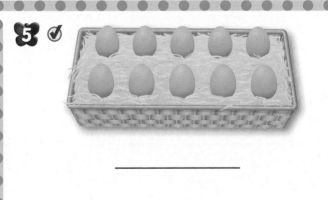

_____

- - - - -

_____

DIRECTIONS **1.** Count and tell how many eggs. Trace the number. **2–5.** Count and tell how many eggs. Write the number.

Name _____

10
ten

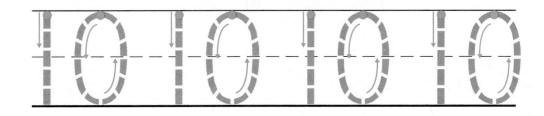

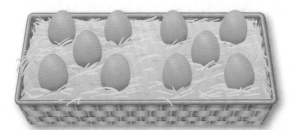

_____

- - - - - - - - - - - - -

_____

_____

- - - - - - - - - - - - -

_____

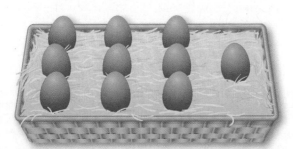

_____

- - - - - - - - - - - - -

_____

DIRECTIONS 6. Say the number. Trace the numbers.
7–9. Count and tell how many. Write the number.

Chapter 4 • Lesson 2

Problem Solving • Applications

WRITE Math

10

DIRECTIONS 10. Draw to show a set that has a number of objects one greater than 9. Write how many objects. Tell a friend about your drawing.

HOME ACTIVITY • Show ten objects. Have your child point to each object in the set as he or she counts them. Then have him or her write the number on paper to show how many objects.

FOR MORE PRACTICE: Standards Practice Book

Name _____

Algebra • Ways to Make 10

Essential Question How can you use a drawing to make 10 from a given number?

Operations and Algebraic Thinking—K.OA.4
Also K.OA.3
MATHEMATICAL PRACTICES
MP.4, MP.7

Listen and Draw

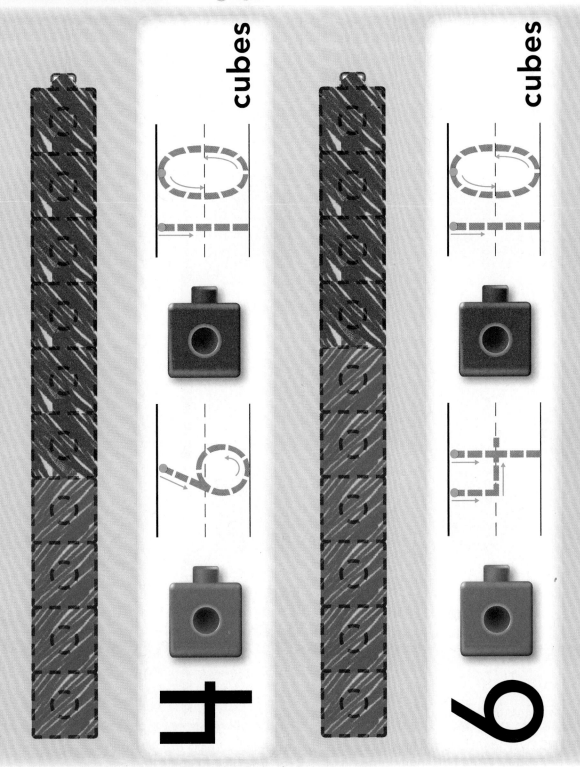

cubes

cubes

DIRECTIONS Use cubes of two colors to show different ways to make 10. Trace the number of red cubes. Trace the number of cubes in all.

Chapter 4 • Lesson 3

1.

cubes

_____

9

cubes

8

cubes

7

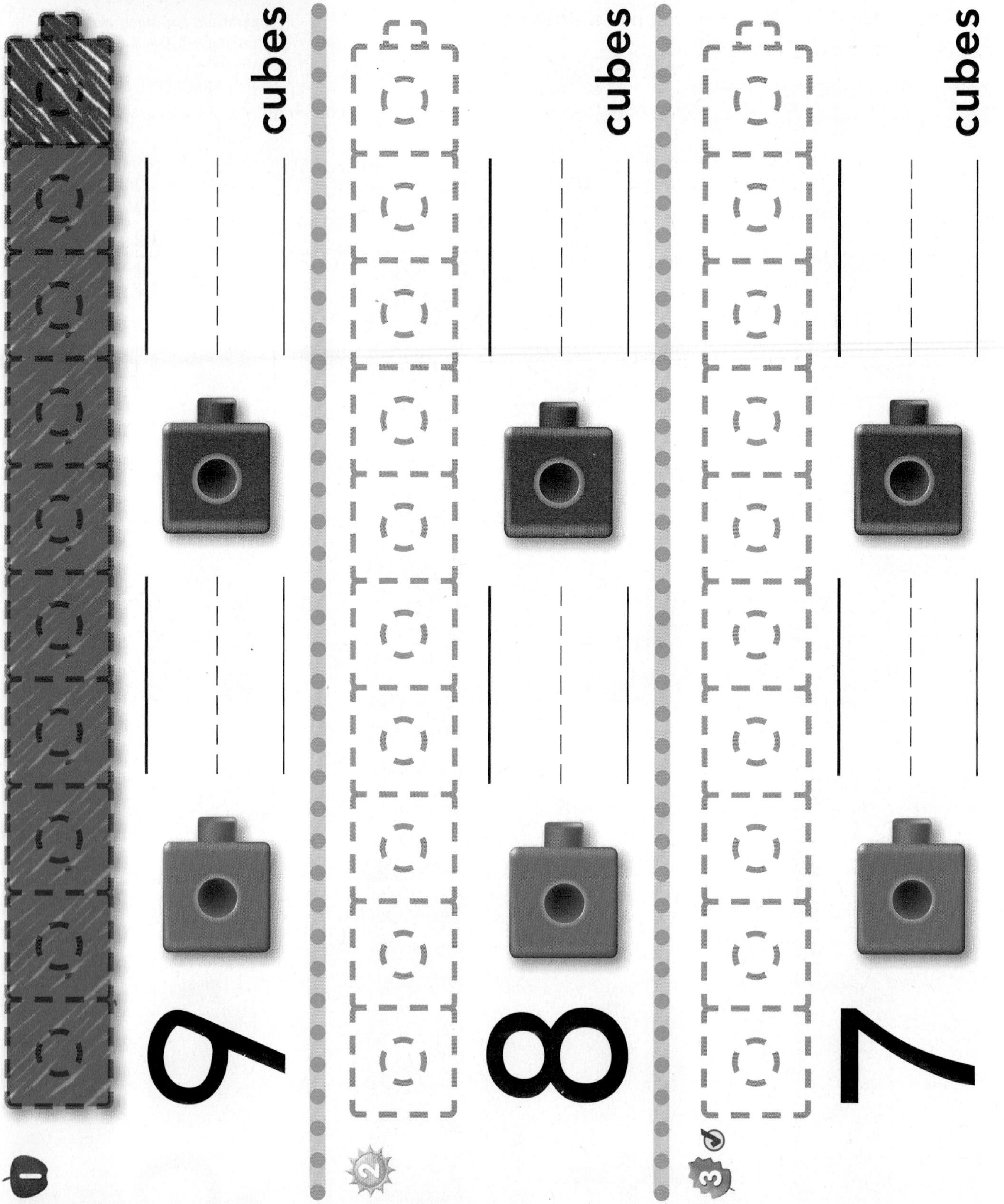

DIRECTIONS 1. Count and tell how many cubes of each color there are. Write how many red cubes. Write how many cubes in all.   **2–3.** Use blue to color the cubes to match the number. Use red to color the other cubes. Write how many red cubes. Write how many cubes in all.

142 one hundred forty-two

cubes

cubes

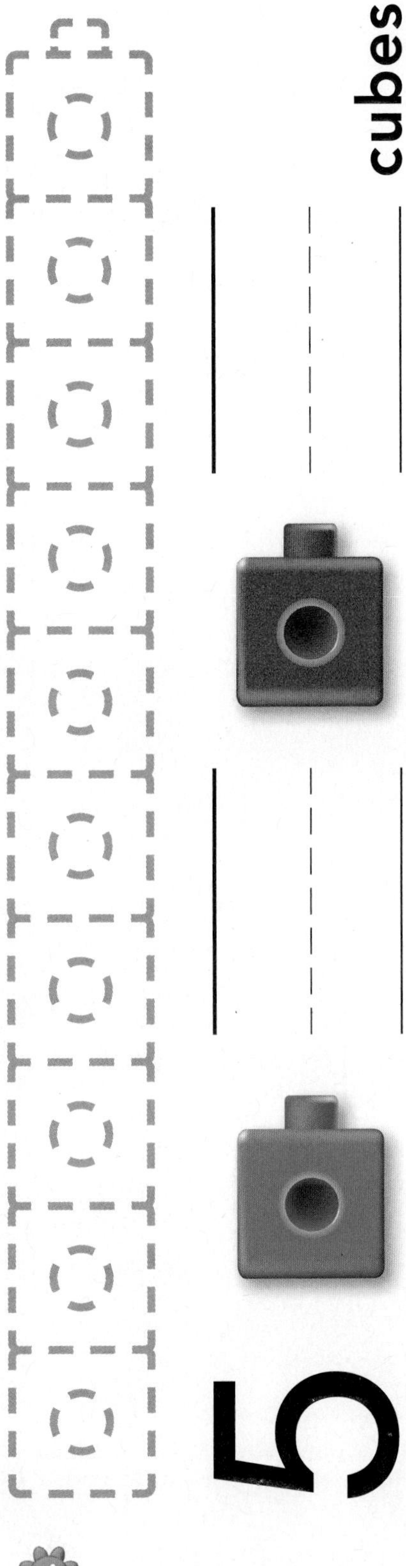

cubes

5

3

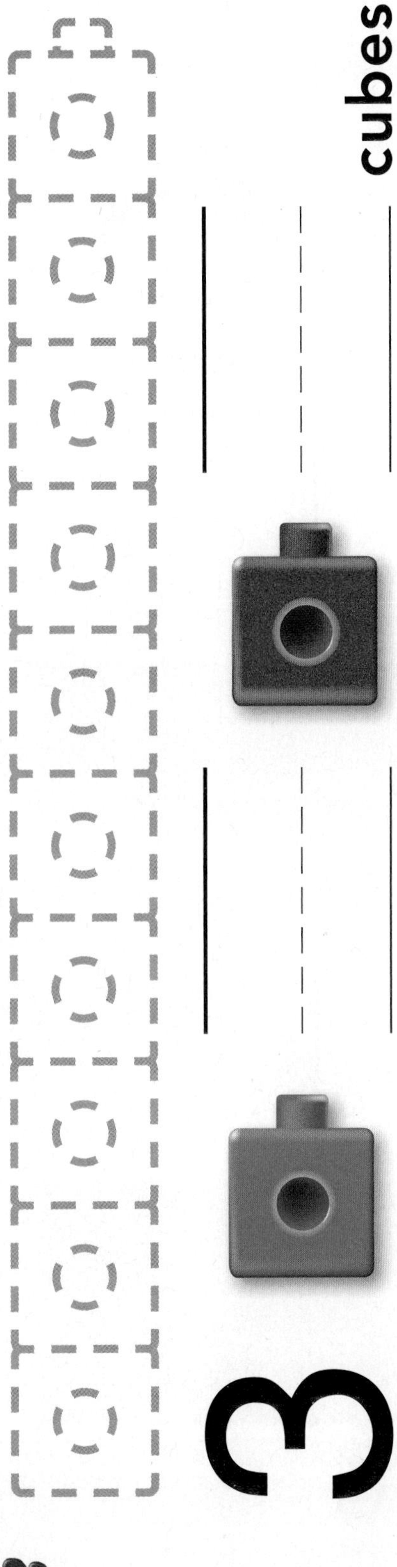

2

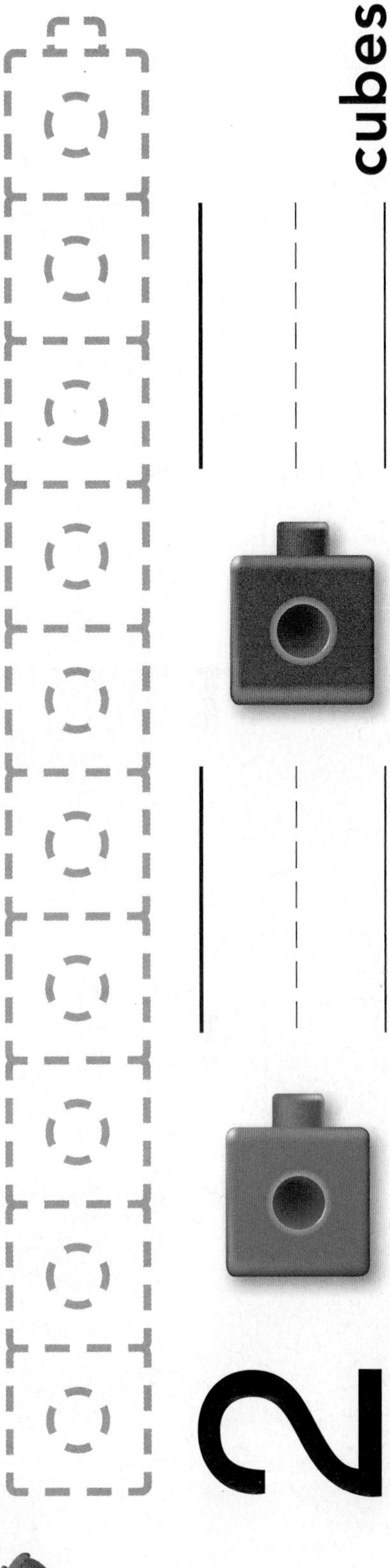

4

5

6

DIRECTIONS 4–6. Use blue to color the cubes to match the number. Use red to color the other cubes. Write how many red cubes. Write how many cubes in all.

Chapter 4 • Lesson 3

Problem Solving • Applications

 Real World

10

10

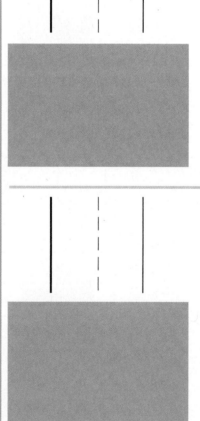

10

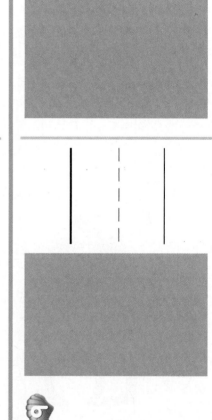

10

DIRECTIONS 7–9. Jill uses the dot side of two Number Tiles to make 10. Draw the dots on each Number Tile to show a way Jill can make 10. Write the numbers.

HOME ACTIVITY • Ask your child to show a set of 10 objects, using objects of the same kind that are different in one way; for example, large and small paper clips. Then have him or her write the numbers that show how many of each kind are in the set.

144 one hundred forty-four

FOR MORE PRACTICE: Standards Practice Book

Name _____

Count and Order to 10

Essential Question How can you count forward to 10 from a given number?

Counting and Cardinality—K.CC.2

MATHEMATICAL PRACTICES
MP.2

Listen and Draw

1 2 3 4 5 6 7 8 9 10

2   3 4 ___   6 7 ___   9 10

DIRECTIONS Point to the numbers in the top workspace as you count forward to 10. Trace and write the numbers in order in the bottom workspace as you count forward to 10.

Chapter 4 • Lesson 4

one hundred forty-five **145**

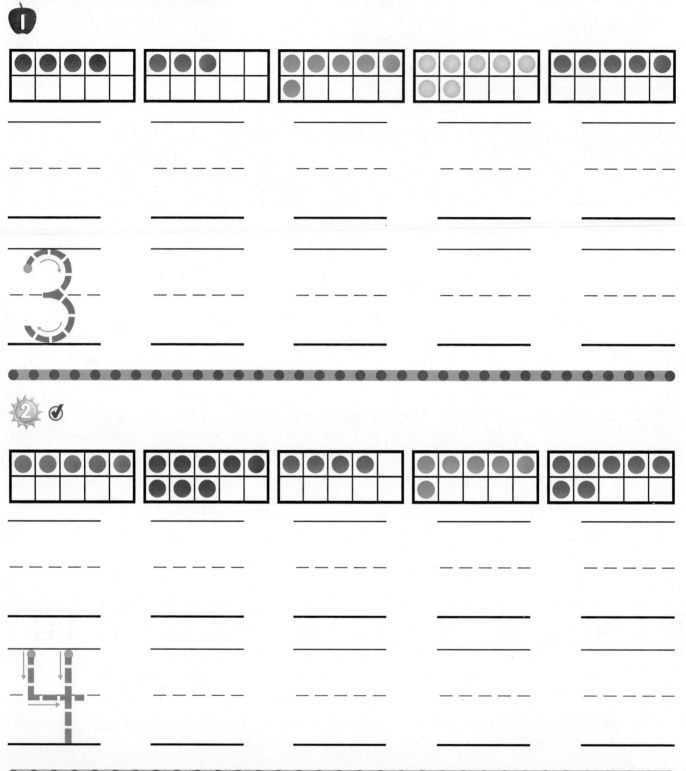

DIRECTIONS 1–2. Count the dots of each color in the ten frames. Write the numbers. Look at the next line. Write the numbers in order as you count forward from the dashed number.

Name _____

_____   _____   _____   _____   _____

- -

_____   _____   _____   _____   _____

5   _____   _____   _____   _____

●●

_____   _____   _____   _____   _____

- -

_____   _____   _____   _____   _____

6   _____   _____   _____   _____

●●

DIRECTIONS **3–4.** Count the dots of each color in the ten frames. Write the numbers. Look at the next line. Write the numbers in order as you count forward from the dashed number.

HOME ACTIVITY • Write the numbers 1 to 10 in order on a piece of paper. Ask your child to point to each number as he or she counts to 10. Repeat beginning with a number other than 1 when counting.

Chapter 4 • Lesson 4

FOR MORE PRACTICE:
Standards Practice Book

one hundred forty-seven   **147**

Concepts and Skills

❶

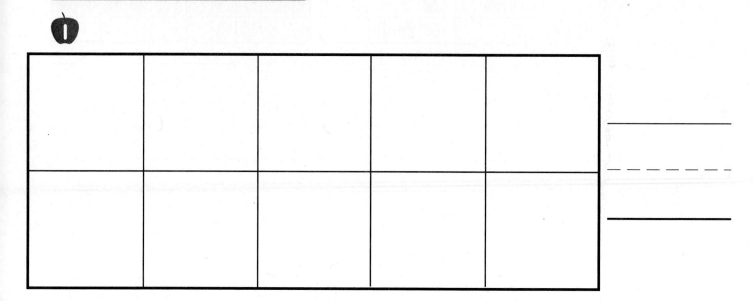

②

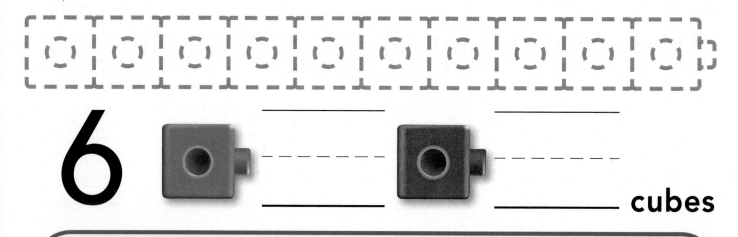

cubes

③ **THINK SMARTER**

7 8 ___ 10

DIRECTIONS 1. Place counters in the ten frame to model ten. Draw the counters. Write the number. (K.CC.5) 2. Use blue to color the cubes to match the number. Use red to color the other cubes. Write how many red cubes. Write how many cubes in all. (K.OA.4) 3. Count forward. Write the number to complete the counting order. (K.CC.2)

Name _____

Problem Solving • Compare by Matching Sets to 10

Essential Question How can you solve problems using the strategy *make a model*?

Counting and Cardinality—K.CC.6
Also K.CC.7
MATHEMATICAL PRACTICES
MP.4, MP.5, MP.8

Unlock the Problem

DIRECTIONS Break a ten-cube train into two parts. How can you use matching to compare the parts? Tell a friend about the cube trains. Draw the cube trains.

Chapter 4 • Lesson 5

one hundred forty-nine **149**

Try Another Problem

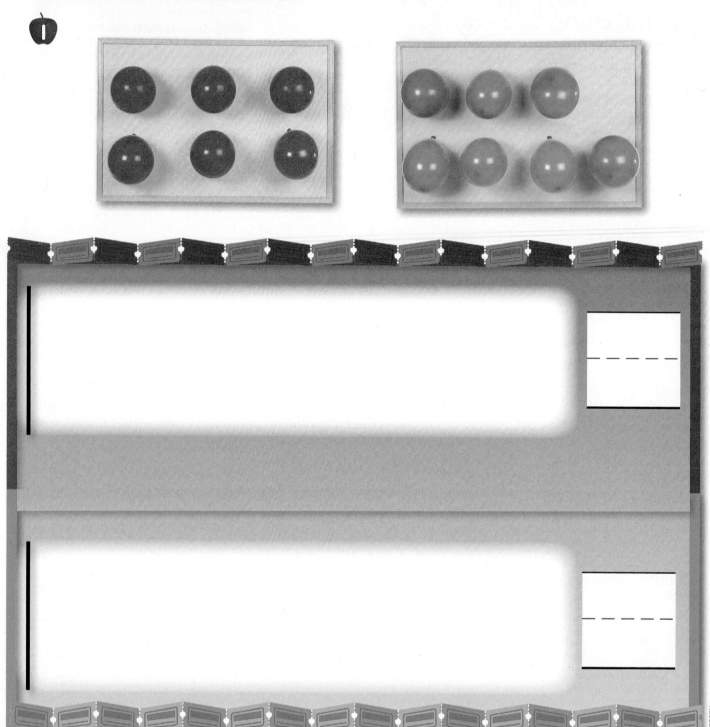

DIRECTIONS 1. Malia has the red balloons. Andrew has the blue balloons. Who has more balloons? Use red and blue cube trains to model the sets of balloons. Compare the cube trains by matching. Draw and color the cube trains. Write how many in each set. Which number is greater? Circle that number.

Name _____

② ✓

_____
- - - - - - -
_____

_____
- - - - - - -
_____

③

_____
- - - - - - -

_____
- - - - - - -

_____

DIRECTIONS 2. Kyle has 9 tickets. Jared has 7 tickets. Who has fewer tickets? Use cube trains to model the sets of tickets. Compare the cube trains by matching. Draw and color the cube trains. Write how many. Circle the number that is less. **3.** Phil won 8 prizes. Naomi won 5 prizes. Who won fewer prizes? Use cube trains to model the sets of prizes. Compare the cube trains by matching. Draw and color the cube trains. Write how many. Circle the number that is less.

On Your Own

④

_____

_ _ _ _ _ _

_____

_____

_ _ _ _ _ _

_____

DIRECTIONS 4. Ryan has a cube train with red and blue cubes. Does his cube train have more blue cubes or more red cubes? Make cube trains of each color from the cubes in Ryan's cube train. Compare the cube trains by matching. Draw and color the cube trains. Write how many cubes are in each train. Circle the greater number.

HOME ACTIVITY • Ask your child to show two sets of up to 10 objects each. Then have him or her compare the sets by matching and tell which set has more objects.

© Houghton Mifflin Harcourt Publishing Company

FOR MORE PRACTICE:
Standards Practice Book

Name _____

Compare by Counting Sets to 10

Essential Question How can you use counting strategies to compare sets of objects?

Counting and Cardinality—K.CC.6
Also K.CC.5, K.CC.7
MATHEMATICAL PRACTICES
MP.6, MP.8

Listen and Draw *Real World*

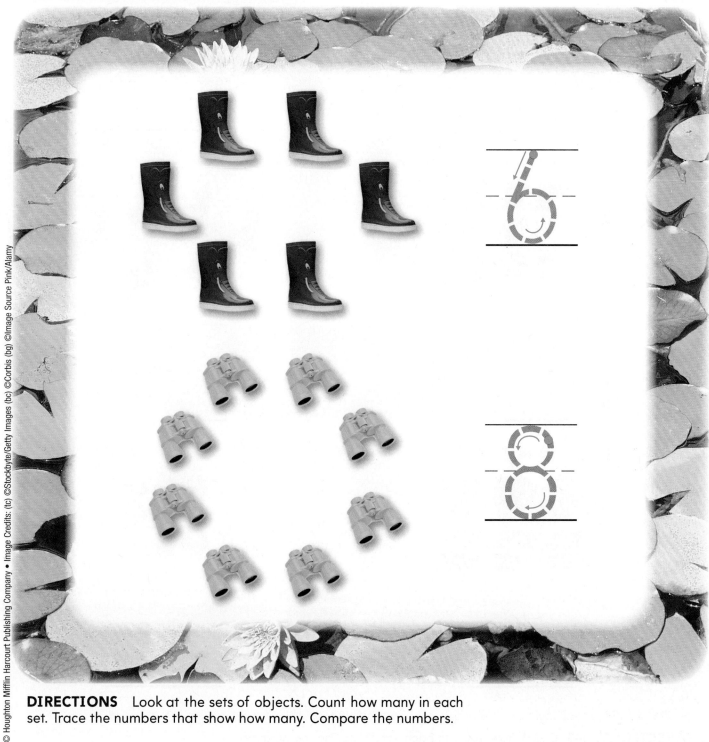

DIRECTIONS Look at the sets of objects. Count how many in each set. Trace the numbers that show how many. Compare the numbers.

Chapter 4 • Lesson 6

1

_____

– – – – – – – –

_____

_____

– – – – – – – –

_____

2 ✓

_____

– – – – – – – –

_____

_____

– – – – – – – –

_____

3 ✓

_____

– – – – – – – –

_____

_____

– – – – – – – –

_____

DIRECTIONS 1–3. Count how many in each set. Write the number of objects in each set. Compare the numbers. Circle the greater number.

Name _____

 4

_____

- - - - - - - - - - - - -

_____

 5

_____

- - - - - - - - - - - - -

_____

 6

_____

- - - - - - - - - - - - -

_____

DIRECTIONS 4–6. Count how many in each set. Write the number of objects in each set. Compare the numbers. Circle the number that is less.

Problem Solving • Applications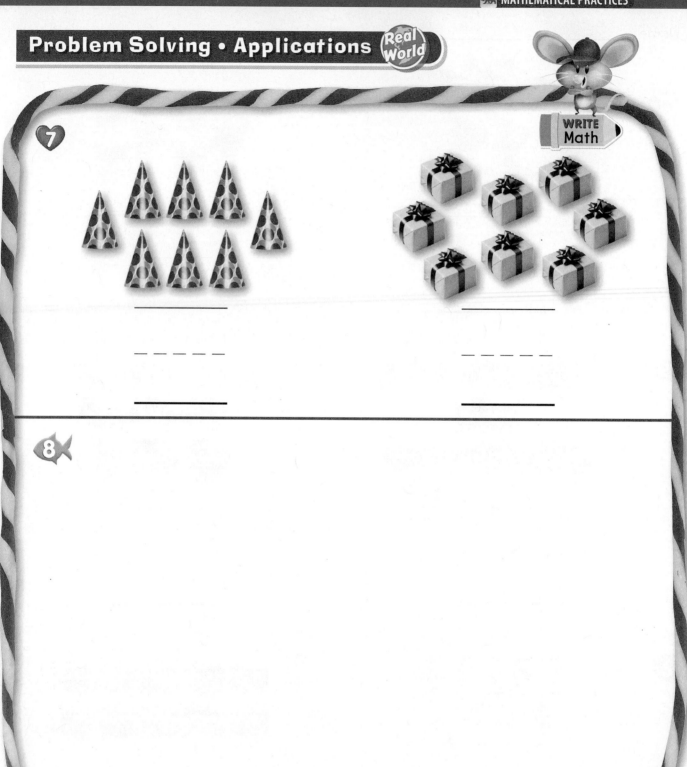

7

_____   _____

_ _ _ _ _ _ _ _   _ _ _ _ _ _ _ _

_____   _____

8

DIRECTIONS 7. Megan bought hats and gifts for a party. How many hats did she buy? How many gifts did she buy? Write the number of objects in each set. Compare the numbers. Tell a friend about the sets. **8.** Draw to show what you know about counting sets to 10 with the same number of objects.

HOME ACTIVITY • Show your child two sets of up to 10 objects. Have him or her count the objects in each set. Then have him or her compare the numbers of objects in each set, and tell what he or she knows about those numbers.

FOR MORE PRACTICE:
Standards Practice Book

Name _____

Compare Two Numbers

Essential Question How can you compare two numbers between 1 and 10?

Counting and Cardinality—
K.CC.7
MATHEMATICAL PRACTICES
MP.6, MP.8

Listen and Draw Real World

7

7 is less than 8

7 is greater than 8

8

8 is less than 7

8 is greater than 7

DIRECTIONS Look at the numbers. As you count forward does 7 come before or after 8? Is it greater or less than 8? Circle the words that describe the numbers when comparing them.

Chapter 4 • Lesson 7

1

3   8

2

10   5

3

6   4

4 ✓

7   9

5 ✓

10   8

DIRECTIONS 1. Look at the numbers. Think about the counting order as you compare the numbers. Trace the circle around the greater number. 2–5. Look at the numbers. Think about the counting order as you compare the numbers. Circle the greater number.

6

2   4

7

5   3

8

8   9

9

10   7

10

6   8

DIRECTIONS   6–10. Look at the numbers. Think about the counting order as you compare the numbers. Circle the number that is less.

Problem Solving • Applications

WRITE Math

11.

_____

- - - - -

_____

_____

- - - - -

_____

12.

_____

- - - - -

_____

_____

- - - - -

_____

DIRECTIONS **11.** John has a number of apples that is greater than 5 and less than 7. Cody has a number of apples that is two less than 8. Write how many apples each boy has. Compare the numbers. Tell a friend about the numbers. **12.** Write two numbers between 1 and 10. Tell a friend about the two numbers.

HOME ACTIVITY • Write the numbers 1 to 10 on individual pieces of paper. Select two numbers and ask your child to compare the numbers and tell which number is greater and which number is less.

FOR MORE PRACTICE:
Standards Practice Book

Name _____

 Chapter 4 Review/Test

1

2

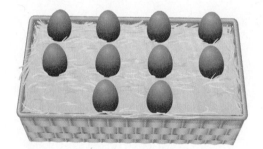

_____

_ _ _ _ _ _ _ _ _ _ _ _ _ _

_____

3

10

nine

ten

DIRECTIONS 1. Circle all the sets that have 10 stars.
2. How many eggs are shown? Write the number.
3. What is another way to write 10? Circle the word.

Chapter 4

 Assessment Options
Chapter Test

4

_____

_ _ _ _ _ _ _ _

_____ cubes

_____   _____

_ _ _ _ _ _ _ _   _ _ _ _ _ _ _ _

_____   _____

5

3   7

---

6 THINK SMARTER ➕

5 6 7 8	○ Yes ○ No
8 10 9 7	○ Yes ○ No
7 8 9 10	○ Yes ○ No

DIRECTIONS **4.** Write how many red cubes. Write how many blue cubes. Write how many cubes in all. **5.** Look at the numbers. Think about the counting order as you compare the numbers. Circle the number that is less. **6.** Are the numbers in counting order? Choose Yes or No.

7

● ● ● ● ● ● ● ●

_____

- - - - - - - - - - - - - - -

_____

- - - - - - - - - - - - - - -

_____

8

_____   _____

- - - - - - - - - - -   - - - - - - - - - - -

_____   _____

9

7   8   9

○   ○   ○

DIRECTIONS **7.** Write how many counters are in the set. Use matching lines to draw a set of counters less than the number of counters shown. Circle the number that is less.   **8.** Count how many in each set. Write the numbers. Circle the greater number.   **9.** Think about counting order. Choose the number that is less than 8.

10

_____

- - - - - - -

_____

11 THINK SMARTER +

_____

- - - - - - -

_____

_____

- - - - - - -

_____

12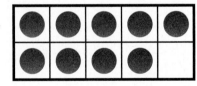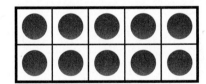

•   •   •

•   •   •

10   9   7

DIRECTIONS **10.** How many cans of paint are there? Write the number. **11.** Seth has 10 buttons. Draw Seth's buttons. The number of buttons Tina has is one less than Seth's. Draw Tina's buttons. How many buttons does Tina have? Write how many in each set. Circle the number that is less. **12.** Match sets to the numbers that show how many counters.

164 one hundred sixty-four

Curious About Math with

Curious George

Most ladybugs have red, orange, or yellow wing covers and black spots.

- How many ladybugs do you see?

Show What You Know

More

 1

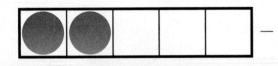

_____

- - - - - - -

_____

 2

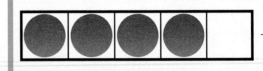

_____

- - - - - - -

_____

Compare Numbers to 10

 3

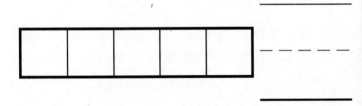

_____

- - - - - - -

_____

- - - - - - -

_____

This page checks understanding of important skills needed for success in Chapter 5.

DIRECTIONS **1–2.** Count and tell how many. Draw a set with one more counter. Write how many in each set. **3.** Write the number of cubes in each set. Circle the number that is greater than the other number.

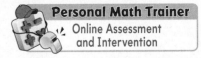

Personal Math Trainer
Online Assessment and Intervention

© Houghton Mifflin Harcourt Publishing Company

Vocabulary Builder

ten

DIRECTIONS Count and tell how many birds are on the ground. Count and tell how many birds are flying. Write these numbers to show a pair of numbers that make ten.

• **Interactive Student Edition**
• **Multimedia *eGlossary***

Game Pairs That Make 7

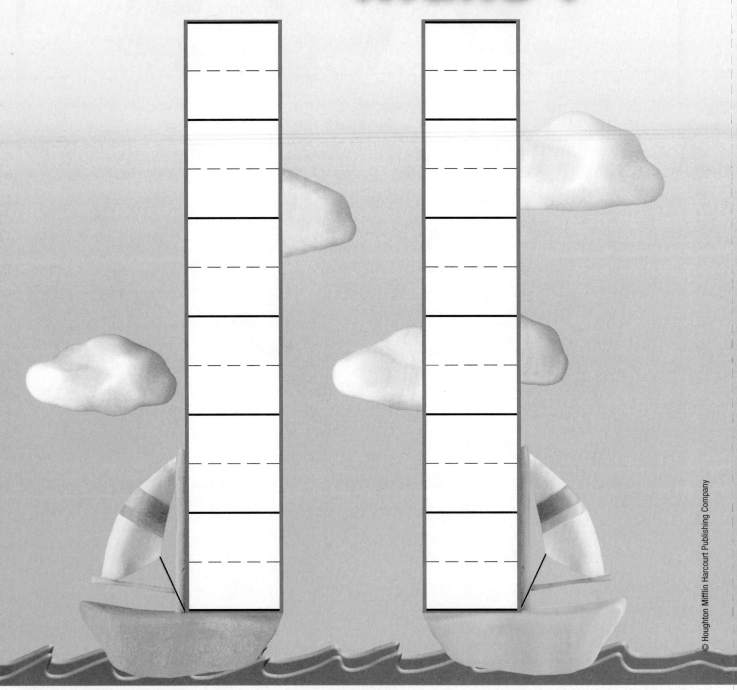

DIRECTIONS Play with a partner. The first player rolls the number cube and writes the number on the yellow boat. Partners determine what number makes 7 when paired with the number on the yellow boat. Players take turns rolling the number cube until that number is rolled. Write the number beside it on the green boat. Partners continue to roll the number cube finding pairs of numbers that make 7.

MATERIALS number cube (1–6)

© Houghton Mifflin Harcourt Publishing Company

Addition: Add To

Essential Question How can you show addition as adding to?

Operations and Algebraic Thinking—K.OA.1
MATHEMATICAL PRACTICES
MP.1, MP.2

Listen and Draw Real World

2 and 1

3

DIRECTIONS Listen to the addition word problem. Trace the number that shows how many children are on the swings. Trace the number that shows how many children are being added to the group. Trace the number that shows how many children there are now.

Chapter 5 • Lesson 1

 **and** _____

_____

DIRECTIONS   1. Listen to the addition word problem. Trace the number that shows how many children are sitting eating lunch. Write the number that shows how many children are being added to the group. Write the number that shows how many children are having lunch now.

——————   ——————

- - - - -   - - - - -

___ **and** ___

———

- - - - -

———

DIRECTIONS   2. Listen to the addition word problem. Write the number that shows how many children are playing with the soccer ball. Write the number that shows how many children are being added to the group. Write the number that shows how many children there are now.

Problem Solving • Applications

3

_____ _____

and

_____ _____

4

_____

_____

© Houghton Mifflin Harcourt Publishing Company

DIRECTIONS **3.** Two sheep are in a pen. Two sheep are added to the pen. How can you write the numbers to show the sheep in the pen and the sheep being added? **4.** Write how many sheep are in the pen now.

HOME ACTIVITY • Show your child a set of four objects. Have him or her add one object to the set and tell how many there are now.

172 one hundred seventy-two

FOR MORE PRACTICE:
Standards Practice Book

Name _____

Addition: Put Together

Essential Question How can you show addition as putting together?

Operations and Algebraic Thinking—K.OA.1
MATHEMATICAL PRACTICES
MP.2, MP.4, MP.5

Listen and Draw Real World   Hands On

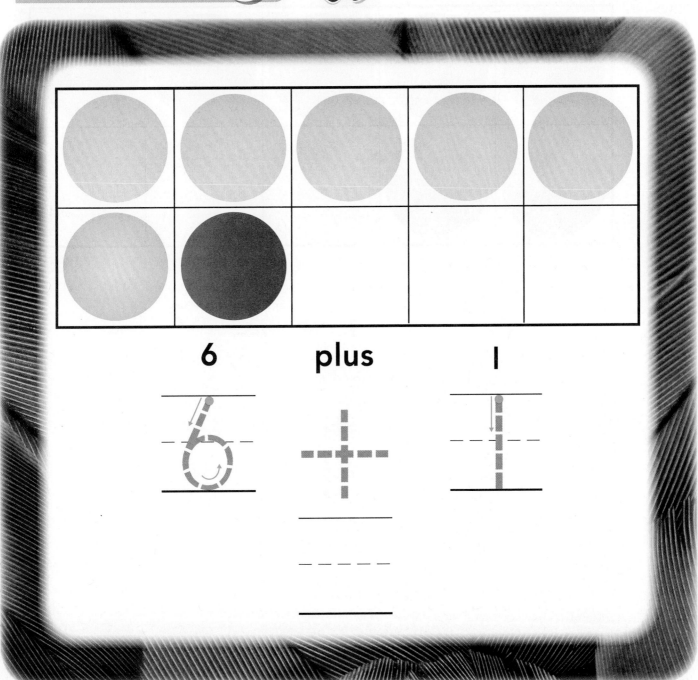

6   plus   1

DIRECTIONS Listen to the addition word problem. Place red and yellow counters in the ten frame as shown. Trace the numbers and the symbol to show the sets that are put together. Write the number that shows how many in all.

Chapter 5 • Lesson 2

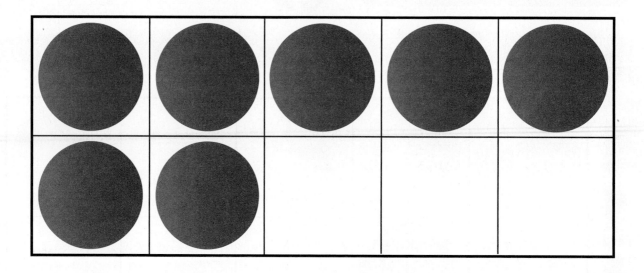

7   plus   2

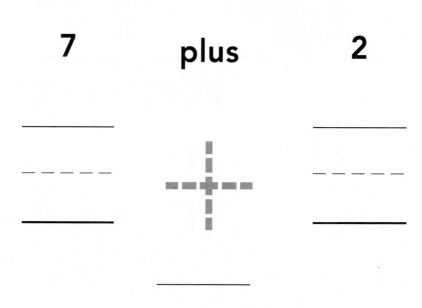

DIRECTIONS I. Listen to the addition word problem. Place red counters in the ten frame as shown. Place yellow counters to model the sets that are put together. Write the numbers and trace the symbol. Write the number to show how many in all.

174 one hundred seventy-four

2   plus   8

_____   _____

- - - - -   ┼   - - - - -

_____   _____

_____

- - - - -

_____

DIRECTIONS 2. Listen to the addition word problem. Place counters in the ten frame to model the sets that are put together. How many are there of each color counter? Write the numbers and trace the symbol. Write the number to show how many in all.

Chapter 5 • Lesson 2   one hundred seventy-five **175**

Problem Solving • Applications Real World

WRITE
Math

3

———————   ———————

- - - - -   +   - - - - -

———————   ———————

4

———————

- - - - -

———————

DIRECTIONS 3. Four red apples and two green apples are on the table. Write the numbers and trace the symbol to show the apples being put together. **4.** Write the number to show how many apples in all.

HOME ACTIVITY • Show your child two sets of 4 objects. Have him or her put the sets of objects together and tell how many in all.

FOR MORE PRACTICE:
Standards Practice Book

Name _____

Problem Solving • Act Out Addition Problems

Essential Question How can you solve problems using the strategy *act it out*?

Operations and Algebraic Thinking—K.OA.1
MATHEMATICAL PRACTICES
MP.1, MP.2, MP.4

 Unlock the Problem Real World

$$2 + 2 = 4$$

DIRECTIONS Listen to and act out the addition word problem. Trace the addition sentence. Tell a friend how many children in all.

Chapter 5 • Lesson 3

one hundred seventy-seven **177**

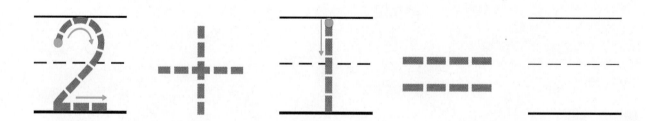

DIRECTIONS I. Listen to and act out the addition word problem. Trace the numbers and the symbols. Write the number that shows how many children in all.

178 one hundred seventy-eight

Name _____

DIRECTIONS 2. Listen to and act out the addition word problem.
Trace the numbers and the symbols. Write the number that shows how
many children in all.

Chapter 5 • Lesson 3   one hundred seventy-nine 179

On Your Own (Real World)

3

WRITE
Math

$$3 + 1 = \underline{}$$

4

$$1 + 4 = \underline{}$$

DIRECTIONS **3.** Tell an addition word problem about the puppies. Trace the numbers and the symbols. Write the number that shows how many puppies there are now. **4.** Draw a picture to match this addition sentence. Write how many in all. Tell a friend about your drawing.

HOME ACTIVITY • Tell your child a short word problem about adding three objects to a set of two objects. Have your child use toys to act out the word problem.

180 one hundred eighty

FOR MORE PRACTICE:
Standards Practice Book

Algebra • Model and Draw Addition Problems

Essential Question How can you use objects and drawings to solve addition word problems?

Operations and Algebraic Thinking—K.OA.5
Also K.OA.1, K.OA.2
MATHEMATICAL PRACTICES
MP.1, MP.2, MP.4

Listen and Draw Real World

$$1 + 1 = 2$$

DIRECTIONS Place cubes as shown. Listen to the addition word problem. Model to show the cubes put together in a cube train. Color to show how the cube train looks. Trace to complete the addition sentence.

Chapter 5 • Lesson 4

1

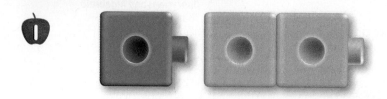

$$1 + 2 = 3$$

2 ✓

$$1 + 3 = \underline{}$$

DIRECTIONS **1–2.** Place cubes as shown. Listen to the addition word problem. Model to show the cubes put together. Draw the cube train. Trace and write to complete the addition sentence.

Name _____

4

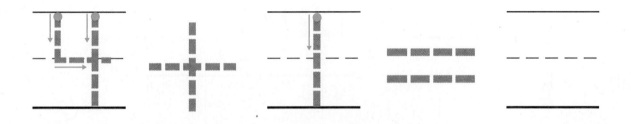

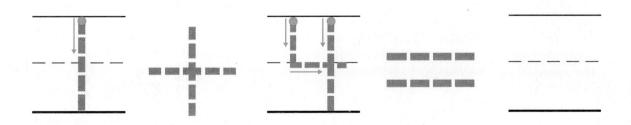

DIRECTIONS 3–4. Place cubes as shown. Listen to the addition word problem. Model to show the cubes put together. Draw the cube train. Trace and write to complete the addition sentence.

Chapter 5 • Lesson 4

FOR MORE PRACTICE:
Standards Practice Book

one hundred eighty-three **183**

© Houghton Mifflin Harcourt Publishing Company

Concepts and Skills

 1

_____

_____ **and** _____

2

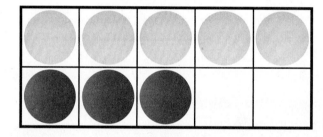

_ _ _ _   _ _ _ _

_ _ _ _ ✚ _ _ _ _

 3

1 plus 3

1 + 2

1 plus 2

DIRECTIONS **1.** Write the number that shows how many puppies are sitting. Write the number that shows how many puppies are being added to them. (K.OA.1) **2.** Write the numbers and trace the symbol to show the sets that are put together. (K.OA.1) **3.** Circle all the ways that show how many in all. (K.OA.1)

Name _____

Algebra • Write Addition Sentences for 10

Essential Question How can you use a drawing to find the number that makes a ten from a given number?

Operations and Algebraic Thinking—K.OA.4
Also K.OA.1, K.OA.2
MATHEMATICAL PRACTICES
MP.2, MP.7, MP.8

Listen and Draw

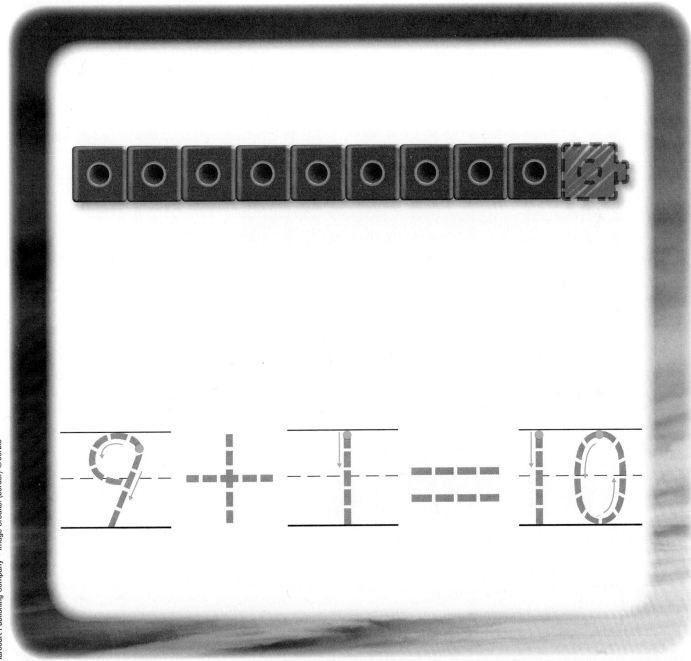

$$9 + 1 = 10$$

DIRECTIONS Look at the cube train. How many red cubes do you see? How many blue cubes do you need to add to make 10? Trace the blue cube. Trace to show this as an addition sentence.

Chapter 5 • Lesson 5

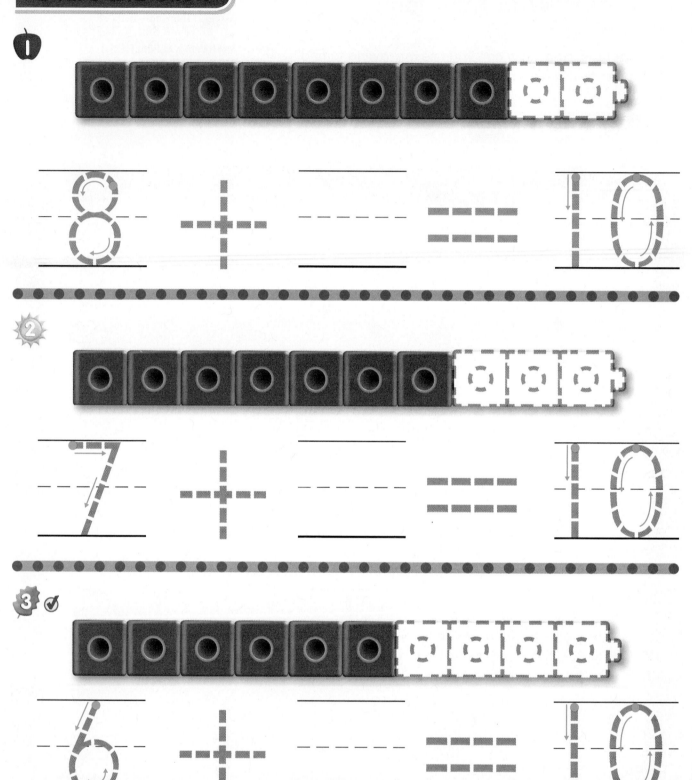

1

8 + ___ === 10

2

7 + ___ === 10

3

6 + ___ === 10

DIRECTIONS 1-3. Look at the cube train. How many red cubes do you see? How many blue cubes do you need to add to make 10? Use blue to color those cubes. Write and trace to show this as an addition sentence.

Name _____

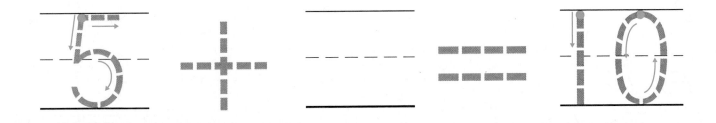

5 + ___ === 10

4 + ___ === 10

3 + ___ === 10

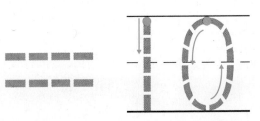

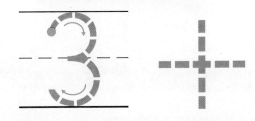

DIRECTIONS **4–6.** Look at the cube train. How many red cubes do you see? How many blue cubes do you need to add to make 10? Use blue to draw those cubes. Write and trace to show this as an addition sentence.

© Houghton Mifflin Harcourt Publishing Company

Chapter 5 • Lesson 5

Problem Solving • Applications

WRITE Math

7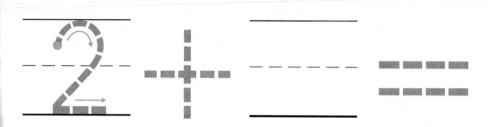

$$2 + \_\_\_ = 10$$

8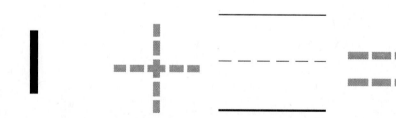

$$1 + \_\_\_ = 10$$

 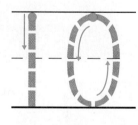

DIRECTIONS **7.** Troy has 2 ducks. How many more ducks does he need to get to have 10 ducks in all? Draw to solve the problem. Trace and write to show this as an addition sentence. **8.** Draw to find the number that makes 10 when put together with the given number. Trace and write to show this as an addition sentence.

HOME ACTIVITY • Show your child a number from 1 to 9. Ask him or her to find the number that makes 10 when put together with that number. Then have him or her tell a story to go with the problem.

FOR MORE PRACTICE:
Standards Practice Book

Name _____

Algebra • Write Addition Sentences

Essential Question How can you solve addition word problems and complete the addition sentence?

Operations and Algebraic Thinking—K.OA.5
Also K.OA.1, K.OA.2
MATHEMATICAL PRACTICES
MP.1, MP.2

Listen and Draw Real World

$$2 + 1 = 3$$

DIRECTIONS Listen to the addition word problem. Circle the set you start with. How many are being added to the set? How many are there now? Trace the addition sentence.

Chapter 5 • Lesson 6

one hundred eighty-nine **189**

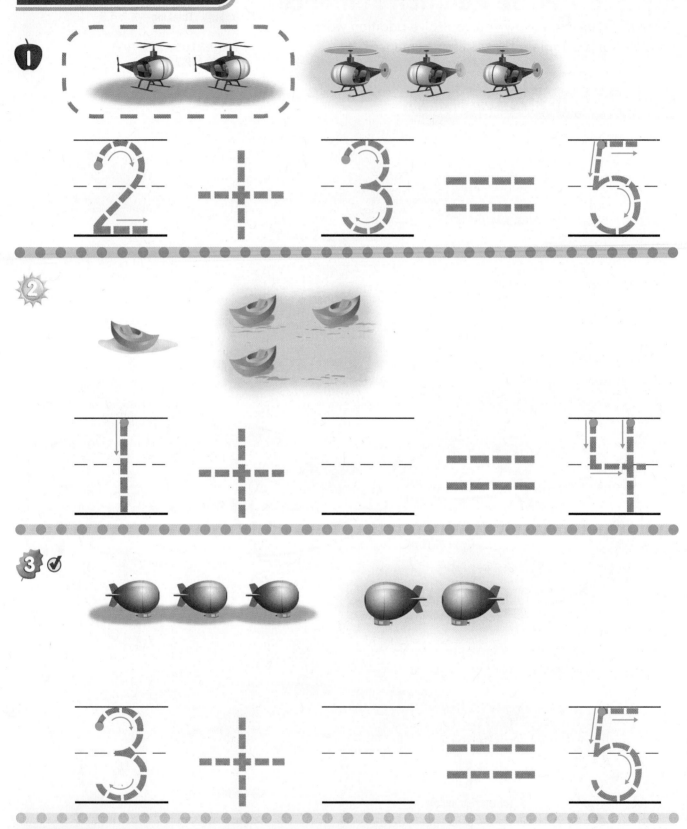

1

$$2 + 3 = 5$$

2

$$1 + \underline{} = 4$$

3 ✓

$$3 + \underline{} = 5$$

DIRECTIONS **I.** Listen to the addition word problem. Trace the circle around the set you start with. How many are being added to the set? How many are there now? Trace the addition sentence. **2–3.** Listen to the addition word problem. Circle the set you start with. How many are being added to the set? How many are there now? Write and trace the numbers to complete the addition sentence.

190 one hundred ninety

Name _____

4

$$1 + 4 = 5$$

5

$$3 + 1 = 4$$

6

$$2 + 3 = 5$$

DIRECTIONS 4–6. Tell an addition word problem about the sets.
Circle the set you start with. How many are being added to the set?
How many are there now? Write and trace the numbers to complete the
addition sentence.

Problem Solving • Applications Real World

7

WRITE
Math

$2 + \_\_\_ = \_\_\_$

8

$\_\_\_ + \_\_\_ = \_\_\_$

DIRECTIONS **7.** Bill catches two fish. Jake catches some fish. They catch four fish in all. How many fish does Jake catch? Draw to show the fish. Trace and write to complete the addition sentence. **8.** Tell a different addition word problem about fish. Draw to show the fish. Tell about your drawing. Complete the addition sentence.

HOME ACTIVITY • Have your child show three fingers. Have him or her show more fingers to make five fingers in all. Then have him or her tell how many more fingers he or she showed.

© Houghton Mifflin Harcourt Publishing Company

FOR MORE PRACTICE:
Standards Practice Book

Name _____

Algebra • Write More Addition Sentences

Essential Question How can you solve addition word problems and complete the addition sentence?

Operations and Algebraic Thinking—K.OA.2
Also K.OA.1
MATHEMATICAL PRACTICES
MP.1, MP.2

Listen and Draw *Real World*

DIRECTIONS Listen to the addition word problem about the birds. Circle the bird joining the other birds. How many birds did you start with? Trace the circle around that number. Trace the addition sentence.

Chapter 5 • Lesson 7

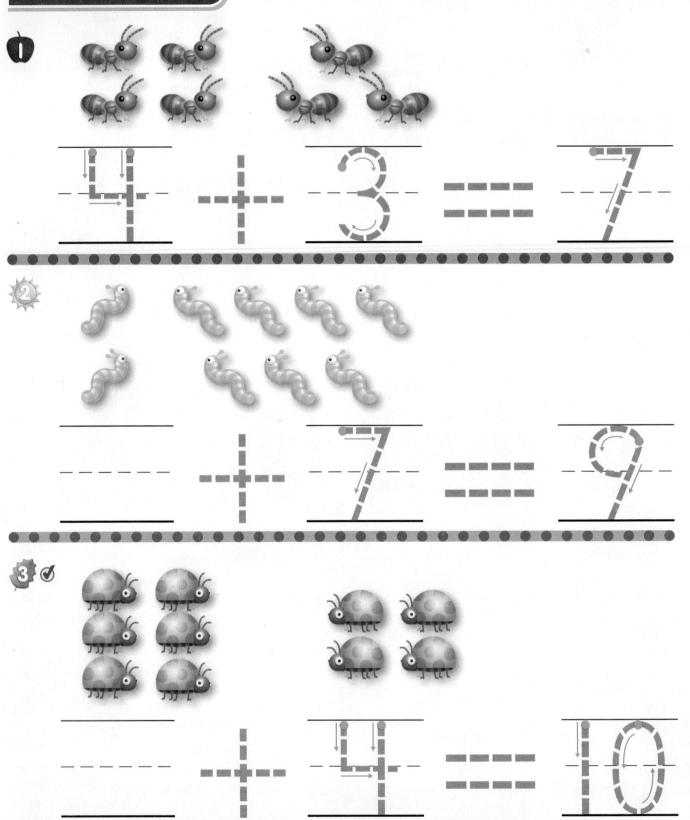

1. $4 + 3 = 7$

2. ___ $+ 7 = 9$

3. ___ $+ 4 = 10$

DIRECTIONS 1. Listen to the addition word problem. Circle the set being added. How many are in the set to start with? Trace to complete the addition sentence. 2-3. Listen to the addition word problem. Circle the set being added. How many are in the set to start with? Write and trace to complete the addition sentence.

❀ **4**

_____
_ _ _ _ _ + 5 === 8
_____

5

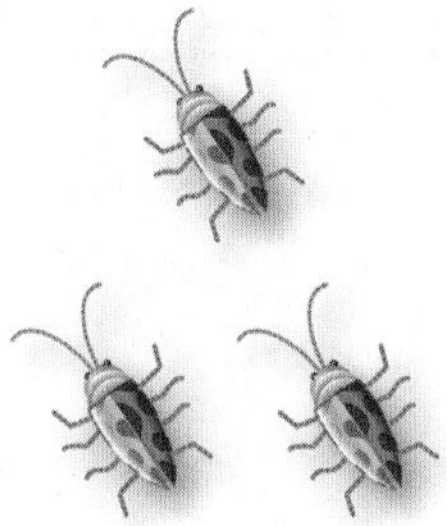

_ _ _ _ _ + 3 === 9

6

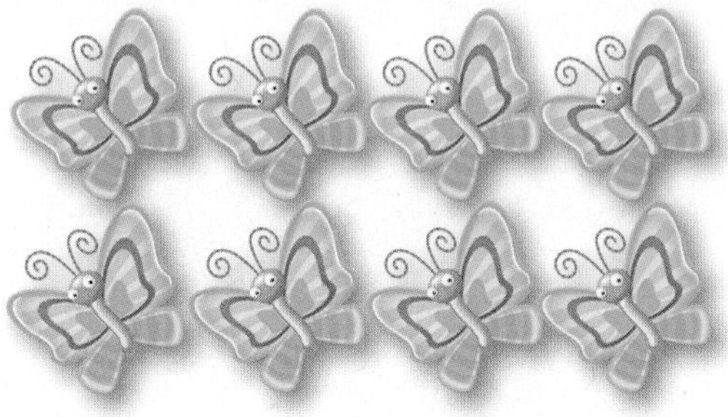

_ _ _ _ _ + 8 === 10

DIRECTIONS **4–6.** Tell an addition word problem. Circle the set being added. Draw to show how many are in the set to start with. Write and trace to complete the addition sentence.

Problem Solving • Applications

WRITE
Math

7

_____ _ _ _ _ + _____ _ _ _ = _____ _ _ _

DIRECTIONS 7. Tell an addition word problem. Complete the addition sentence. Draw a picture of real objects to show the problem. Tell a friend about your drawing.

HOME ACTIVITY • Tell your child an addition word problem such as: There are some socks in the drawer. I added four more socks. Now there are ten socks in the drawer. How many socks were in the drawer to start with?

FOR MORE PRACTICE:
Standards Practice Book

Algebra • Number Pairs to 5

Essential Question How can you model and write addition sentences for number pairs for sums to 5?

Operations and Algebraic Thinking—K.OA.3
MATHEMATICAL PRACTICES
MP.2, MP.7

Listen and Draw

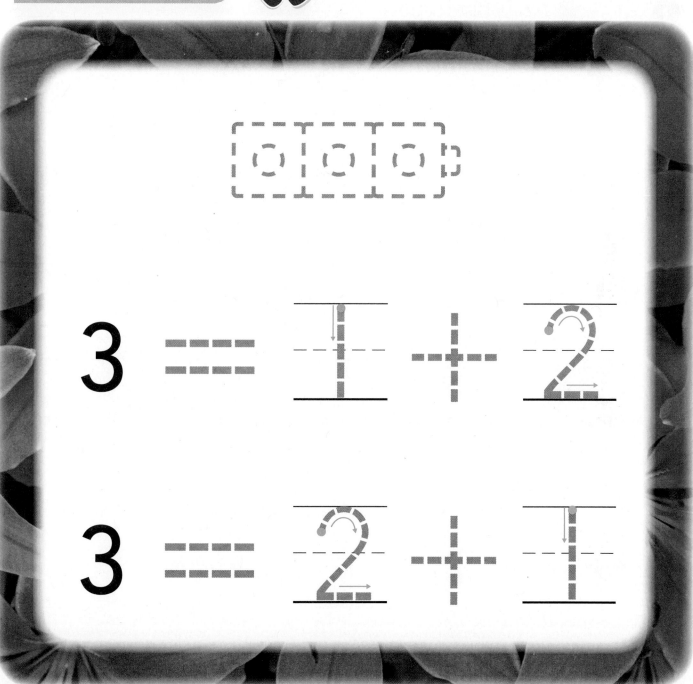

$$3 = 1 + 2$$

$$3 = 2 + 1$$

DIRECTIONS Place two colors of cubes on the cube train to show the number pairs that make 3. Trace the addition sentences to show some of the number pairs.

1 4 $=$ 3 $+$ 1

2 4 $=$ ___ $+$ ___

3 ✓ 4 $=$ ___ $+$ ___

DIRECTIONS Place two colors of cubes on the cube train to show the number pairs that make 4.   **1.** Trace the addition sentence to show one of the pairs.   **2–3.** Complete the addition sentence to show another number pair. Color the cube train to match the addition sentence in Exercise 3.

Name _____

❀ 4

5

_ _ _ _ _ _ _ _   ✚   _ _ _ _ _ _ _ _

5

5

_ _ _ _ _ _ _ _   ✚   _ _ _ _ _ _ _ _

6

5

_ _ _ _ _ _ _ _   ✚   _ _ _ _ _ _ _ _

7

5

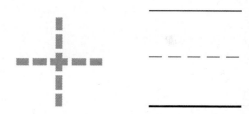

_ _ _ _ _ _ _ _   ✚   _ _ _ _ _ _ _ _

DIRECTIONS Place two colors of cubes on the cube train to show the number pairs that make 5. **4–7.** Complete the addition sentence to show a number pair. Color the cube train to match the addition sentence in Exercise 7.

© Houghton Mifflin Harcourt Publishing Company

Problem Solving • Applications

WRITE Math

8

$$5 = \underline{} + \underline{}$$

9

DIRECTIONS 8. Peyton and Ashley have five red apples. Peyton is holding five of the apples. How many is Ashley holding? Color the cube train to show the number pair. Complete the addition sentence. **9.** Draw to show what you know about a number pair to 5.

HOME ACTIVITY • Have your child tell you the number pairs for a set of objects up to five. Have him or her tell an addition sentence for one of the number pairs.

200 two hundred

FOR MORE PRACTICE:
Standards Practice Book

Name _____

Algebra • Number Pairs for 6 and 7

Essential Question How can you model and write addition sentences for number pairs for each sum of 6 and 7?

Operations and Algebraic Thinking—K.OA.3

MATHEMATICAL PRACTICES
MP.2, MP.7

 Listen and Draw

$$6 = 5 + 1$$

$$7 = 6 + 1$$

DIRECTIONS Place two colors of cubes on the cube trains to match the addition sentences. Color the cube trains. Trace the addition sentences.

Chapter 5 • Lesson 9

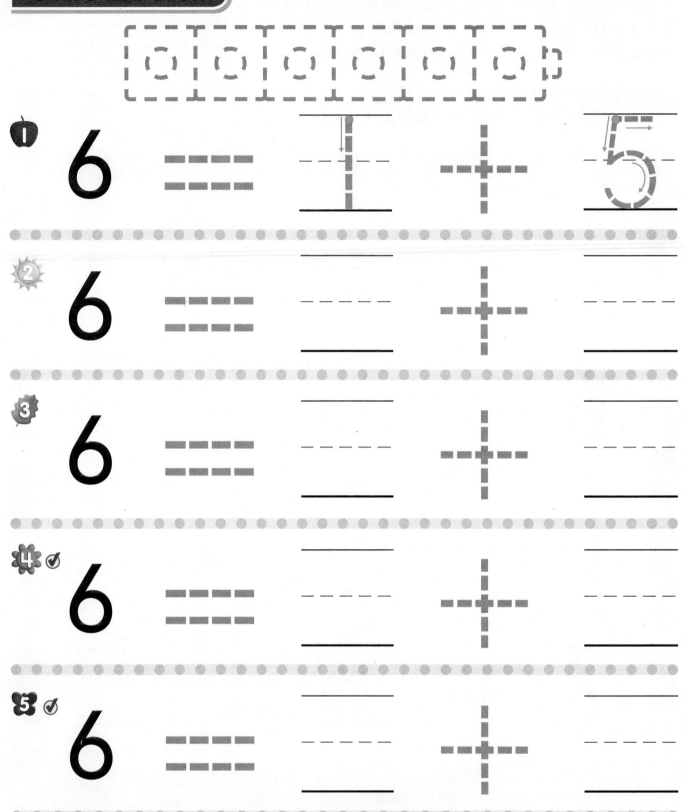

1. 6 ▪▪▪▪▪▪ = I + 5

2. 6 ▪▪▪▪▪▪ = ___ + ___

3. 6 ▪▪▪▪▪▪ = ___ + ___

4. 6 ▪▪▪▪▪▪ = ___ + ___

5. 6 ▪▪▪▪▪▪ = ___ + ___

DIRECTIONS Place two colors of cubes on the cube train to show the number pairs that make 6. **1.** Trace the addition sentence to show one of the pairs. **2–5.** Complete the addition sentence to show a number pair for 6. Color the cube train to match the addition sentence in Exercise 5.

6 7 = = = ___ ___ + ___ ___

7 7 = = ___ ___ + ___ ___

8 7 = = = ___ ___ + ___ ___

9 7 = = = ___ ___ + ___ ___

10 7 = = = ___ ___ + ___ ___

DIRECTIONS Place two colors of cubes on the cube train to show the number pairs that make 7. **6–10.** Complete the addition sentence to show a number pair for 7. Color the cube train to match the addition sentence in Exercise 10.

Problem Solving • Applications

 11.

$$6 = \underline{\quad} = \underline{\quad} + \underline{\quad}$$

12.

$$7 = \underline{\quad} = \underline{\quad} + \underline{\quad}$$

DIRECTIONS **11.** Peter and Grant have six toy cars. Peter has no cars. How many cars does Grant have? Color the cube train to show the number pair. Complete the addition sentence. **12.** Draw to show what you know about a number pair for 7 when one number is 0. Complete the addition sentence.

 **HOME ACTIVITY** • Have your child use his or her fingers on two hands to show a number pair for 6.

FOR MORE PRACTICE:
Standards Practice Book

Algebra • Number Pairs for 8

Essential Question How can you model and write addition sentences for number pairs for sums of 8?

Operations and Algebraic Thinking—K.OA.3
MATHEMATICAL PRACTICES
MP.2, MP.7

Listen and Draw Real World   Hands On

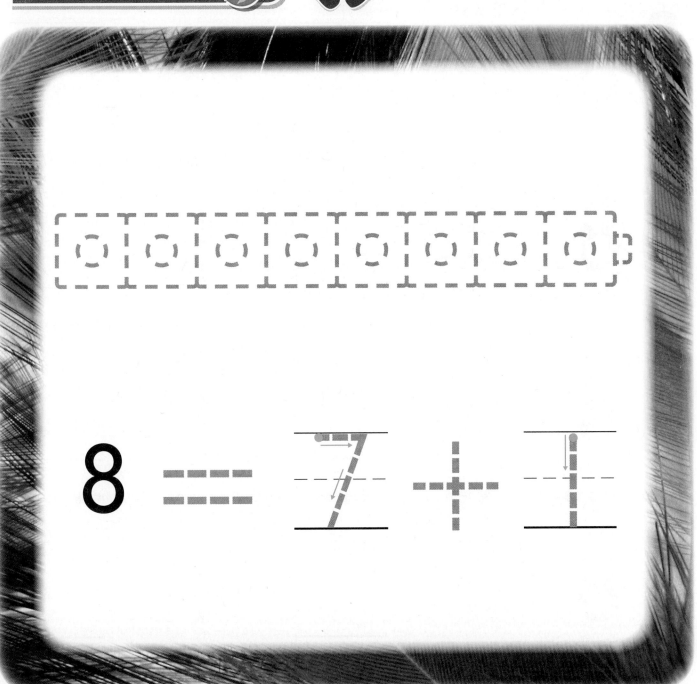

$$8 = 7 + 1$$

DIRECTIONS Use two colors of cubes to make a cube train to match the addition sentence. Color the cube train to show your work. Trace the addition sentence.

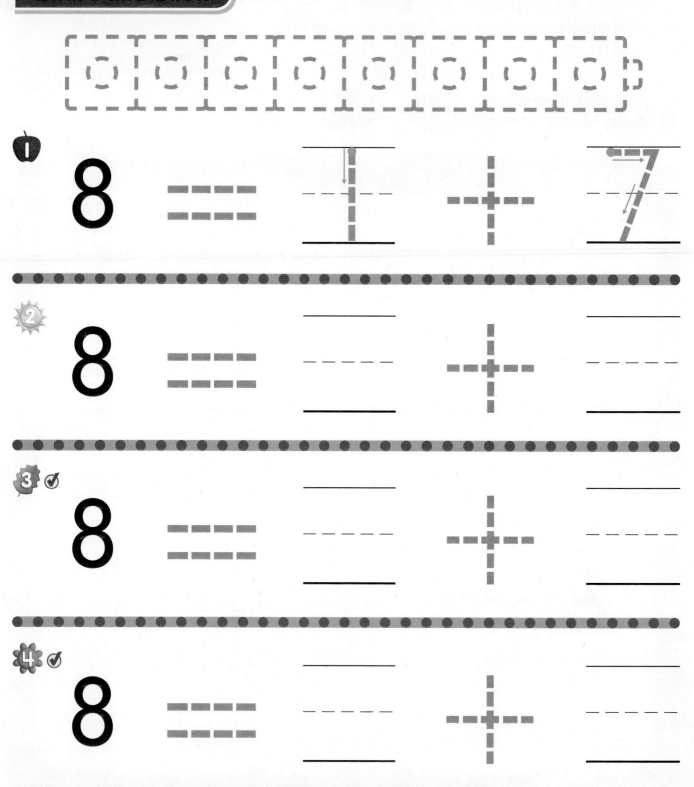

1. 8 === $1 + 7$

2. 8 === ___ + ___

3. 8 === ___ + ___

4. 8 === ___ + ___

DIRECTIONS Use two colors of cubes to make a cube train to show the number pairs that make 8. **1.** Trace the addition sentence to show one of the pairs. **2–4.** Complete the addition sentence to show a number pair for 8. Color the cube train to match the addition sentence in Exercise 4.

5

8 === ___ + ___

6

8 === ___ + ___

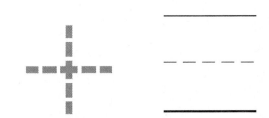

7

8 === ___ + ___

DIRECTIONS Use two colors of cubes to make a cube train to show the number pairs that make 8. **5–7.** Complete the addition sentence to show a number pair for 8. Color the cube train to match the addition sentence in Exercise 7.

Chapter 5 • Lesson 10

Problem Solving • Applications

 WRITE Math

8

8 = $\underline{\qquad}$ + $\underline{\qquad}$

9

8 = $\underline{\qquad}$ + $\underline{\qquad}$

DIRECTIONS 8. There are eight crayons in a packet. Eight of the crayons are red. How many are not red? Draw and color to show how you solved. Complete the addition sentence. **9.** Draw to show what you know about a different number pair for 8. Complete the addition sentence.

 **HOME ACTIVITY** • Have your child tell you the number pairs for a set of eight objects. Have him or her tell the addition sentence to match one of the number pairs.

FOR MORE PRACTICE: Standards Practice Book

Algebra • Number Pairs for 9

Essential Question How can you model and write addition sentences for number pairs for sums of 9?

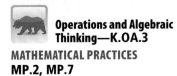

Operations and Algebraic Thinking—K.OA.3
MATHEMATICAL PRACTICES
MP.2, MP.7

Listen and Draw

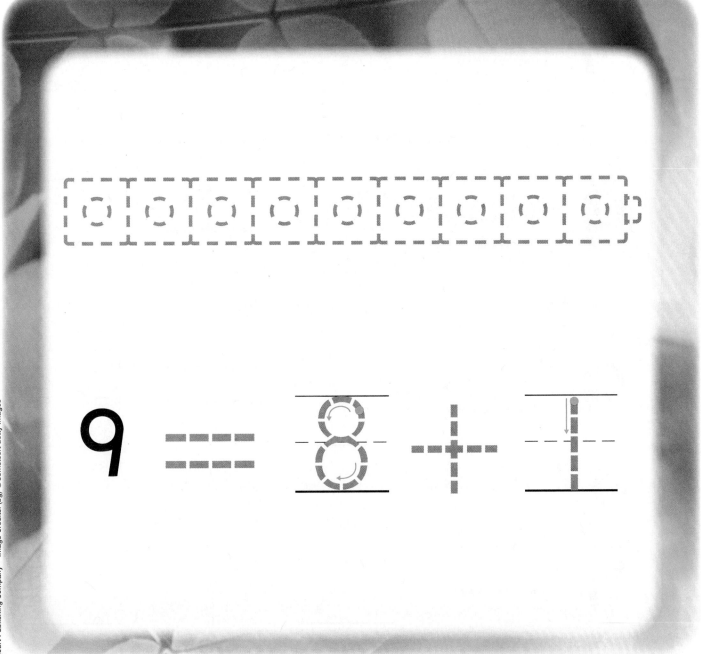

$$9 = 8 + 1$$

DIRECTIONS Use two colors of cubes to make a cube train to match the addition sentence. Color the cube train to show your work. Trace the addition sentence.

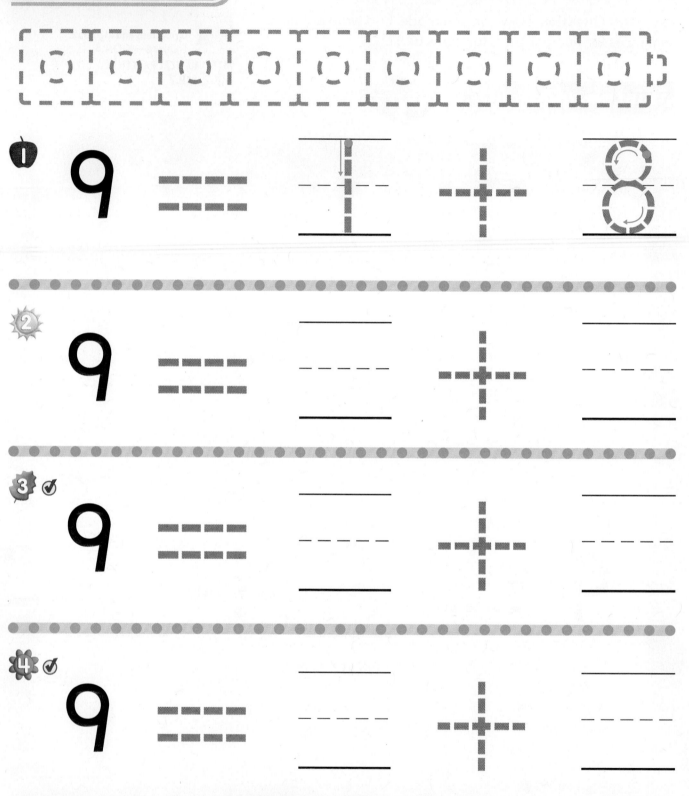

1 9 = 1 + 8

2 9 = ___ + ___

3 ✓ 9 = ___ + ___

4 ✓ 9 = ___ + ___

DIRECTIONS Use two colors of cubes to make a cube train to show the number pairs that make 9. **1.** Trace the addition sentence to show one of the pairs. **2–4.** Complete the addition sentence to show a number pair for 9. Color the cube train to match the addition sentence in Exercise 4.

Name _____

5 9 === ___   _ _ _   +   _ _ _

6 9 === ___   _ _ _   +   _ _ _

7 9 === ___   _ _ _   +   _ _ _

8 9 === ___   _ _ _   +   _ _ _

DIRECTIONS Use two colors of cubes to make a cube train to show the number pairs that make 9. **5–8.** Complete the addition sentence to show a number pair for 9. Color the cube train to match the addition sentence in Exercise 8.

Chapter 5 • Lesson 11

Problem Solving • Applications Real World

WRITE Math

9

9 ▦ = ____ ____ + ____ ____

10

9 ▦ = ____ ____ + ____ ____

DIRECTIONS 9. Shelby has nine friends. None of them are boys. How many are girls? Complete the addition sentence to show the number pair. **10.** Draw to show what you know about a different number pair for 9. Complete the addition sentence.

HOME ACTIVITY • Have your child use his or her fingers on two hands to show a number pair for 9.

212 two hundred twelve

FOR MORE PRACTICE:
Standards Practice Book

Name _____

Algebra • Number Pairs for 10

Essential Question How can you model and write addition sentences for number pairs for sums of 10?

Operations and Algebraic Thinking—K.OA.3
MATHEMATICAL PRACTICES
MP.2, MP.7

Listen and Draw

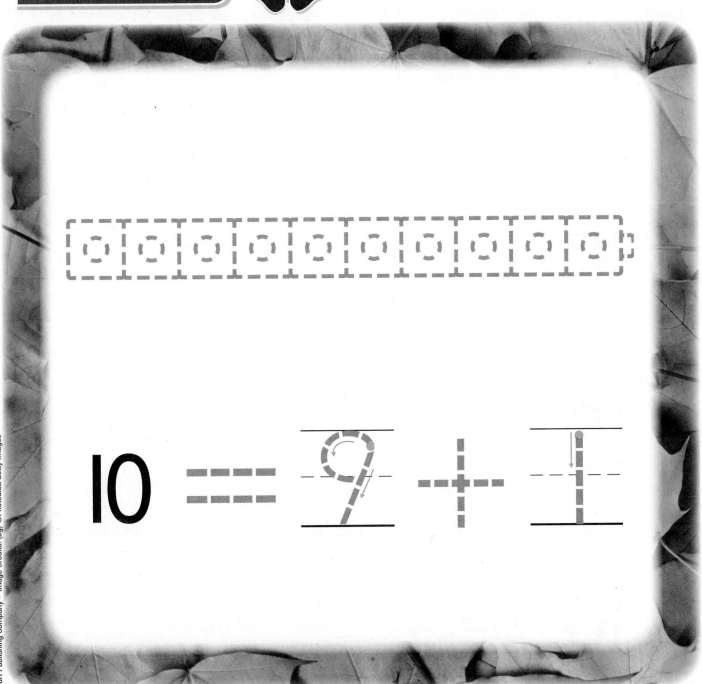

$$10 = 9 + 1$$

DIRECTIONS Use two colors of cubes to make a cube train to match the addition sentence. Color the cube train to show your work. Trace the addition sentence.

Chapter 5 • Lesson 12

1 10 == $\underline{\quad 1 \quad}$ + $\underline{\quad 9 \quad}$

2 10 == $\underline{\qquad}$ + $\underline{\qquad}$

3 ✓ 10 == $\underline{\qquad}$ + $\underline{\qquad}$

4 ✓ 10 == $\underline{\qquad}$ + $\underline{\qquad}$

DIRECTIONS Use two colors of cubes to build a cube train to show the number pairs that make 10. **1.** Trace the addition sentence to show one of the pairs. **2–4.** Complete the addition sentence to show a number pair for 10. Color the cube train to match the addition sentence in Exercise 4.

Name _____

5 10 = === ____ ____ + ____

6 10 = === ____ ____ + ____

7 10 = === ____ ____ + ____

8 10 = === ____ ____ + ____

DIRECTIONS Use two colors of cubes to build a cube train to show the number pairs that make 10. **5–8.** Complete the addition sentence to show a number pair for 10. Color the cube train to match the addition sentence in Exercise 8.

Problem Solving • Applications Real World

WRITE Math

9

10 = _____ _____ + _____
_____

10

10 = _____ _____ + _____
_____

DIRECTIONS 9. There are ten children in the cafeteria. Ten of them are drinking water. How many children are drinking milk? Complete the addition sentence to show the number pair. 10. Draw to show what you know about a different number pair for 10. Complete the addition sentence.

HOME ACTIVITY • Have your child tell you the number pairs for a set of ten objects. Have him or her tell the addition sentence to match one of the number pairs.

FOR MORE PRACTICE:
Standards Practice Book

✓ **Chapter 5 Review/Test**

 1.

____   **and**   ____

 2.

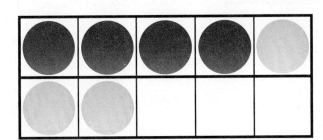

○ **4 plus 3**

○ **4 plus 1**

○ **4 + 1**

3.

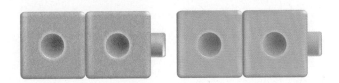

 +  =

DIRECTIONS   1. How many puppies are sitting? How many puppies are being added to the group? Write the numbers.   **2.** Sonja put 4 red counters in the ten frame. Then she put 3 yellow counters in the ten frame. Choose all the ways that show the counters being put together.   **3.** How many of each color cube is being added? Trace the numbers and symbols. Write the number that shows how many cubes in all.

4 THINK SMARTER ➕

$2 + 2 = \underline{\hspace{2cm}}$

5

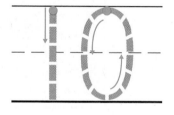

  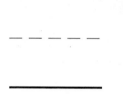

$7 + \underline{\hspace{1cm}} = 10$

6

$3 + \underline{\hspace{1cm}} = 5$

DIRECTIONS **4.** Annabelle has 2 red cubes. She has 2 yellow cubes. How many cubes does she have? Draw the cubes. Trace the numbers and symbols. Write how many in all. **5.** Look at the cube train. How many red cubes do you see? How many more cubes do you need to add to make 10? Draw the cubes. Color them blue. Write and trace to show this as an addition sentence. **6.** Write and trace the numbers to complete the addition sentence.

Name _____

$$4 + \underline{} = 6$$

 *THINK* SMARTER +

$$5 = \underline{} + \underline{}$$

$5 + 2$	○ Yes	○ No
$4 + 3$	○ Yes	○ No
$2 + 4$	○ Yes	○ No

DIRECTIONS **7.** Write the numbers and trace the symbols to complete the addition sentence. **8.** Nora has I green crayon. Gary has some red crayons. Together they have 5 crayons. Draw to show how many red crayons Gary has. Complete the number pair. **9.** Does this show a number pair for 7? Choose Yes or No.

$$4 + 5 \qquad 2 + 6 \qquad 1 + 7$$

9 ═ ─── + ───

10 ═ ─── + ───

DIRECTIONS 10. Circle all the number pairs for 8. 11. Larry counted out 9 cubes. The cubes were either red or blue. How many red and blue cubes could he have? Color the cubes to show the number of red and blue cubes. Write the numbers to complete the addition sentence. 12. Complete the addition sentence to show a number pair for 10.

Curious About Math with

Curious George

Penguins are birds with black and white feathers.

• There are 4 penguins on the ice. One penguin jumps in the water. How many penguins are on the ice now?

Name _____

Fewer

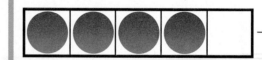

Compare Numbers to 10

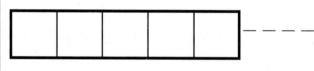

This page checks understanding of important skills needed for success in Chapter 6.

DIRECTIONS 1–2. Count and tell how many. Draw a set with one fewer counter. Write how many in each set.   3. Write the number of cubes in each set. Circle the number that is less than the other number.

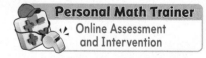
Personal Math Trainer
Online Assessment
and Intervention

Name _____

Vocabulary Builder

add

DIRECTIONS Add the set of bees and the set of butterflies. Write how many insects altogether.

• Interactive Student Edition
• Multimedia *eGlossary*

Game

Spin for More

Spin for More				

Player 1

Player 2

DIRECTIONS Play with a partner. Decide who goes first. Take turns spinning to get a number from each spinner. Use cubes to model a cube train with the number from the first spin. Say the number. Add the cubes from the second spin. Compare your number with your partner's. Mark an X on the table for the player who has the greater number. The first player to have five Xs wins the game.

MATERIALS two paper clips, connecting cubes

Name _____

Subtraction: Take From

Essential Question How can you show subtraction as taking from?

Operations and Algebraic Thinking—K.OA.1
MATHEMATICAL PRACTICES
MP.1, MP.2

Listen and Draw Real World

 take away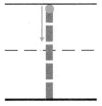

DIRECTIONS Listen to the subtraction word problem. Trace the number that shows how many children in all. Trace the number that shows how many children are leaving. Trace the number that shows how many children are left.

Chapter 6 • Lesson 1

two hundred twenty-five **225**

4 take away _____

_____

_____

_____

DIRECTIONS I. Listen to the subtraction word problem. Trace the number that shows how many children in all. Write the number that shows how many children are leaving. Write the number that shows how many children are left.

_____   _____

- - - - -   - - - - -

_____   **take away**   _____

_____

- - - - -

_____

DIRECTIONS 2. Listen to the subtraction word problem. Write the number that shows how many children in all. Write the number that shows how many children are leaving. Write the number that shows how many children are left.

Problem Solving • Applications Real World

WRITE Math

3

_____ _____

_ _ _ _ _ _ _ _ _ _ _ _

_____ take away _____

4

_____

_ _ _ _ _ _

_____

DIRECTIONS 3. Blair has two marbles. His friend takes one marble from him. Draw to show the subtraction. Write the numbers. 4. Write the number that shows how many marbles Blair has now.

HOME ACTIVITY • Show your child a set of four small objects. Have him or her tell how many objects there are. Take one of the objects from the set. Have him or her tell you how many objects there are now.

228 two hundred twenty-eight

FOR MORE PRACTICE: Standards Practice Book

Name _____

Subtraction: Take Apart

Essential Question How can you show subtraction as taking apart?

Operations and Algebraic Thinking—K.OA.1
MATHEMATICAL PRACTICES
MP.2, MP.4, MP.5

 Listen and Draw *Real World*

 Hands On

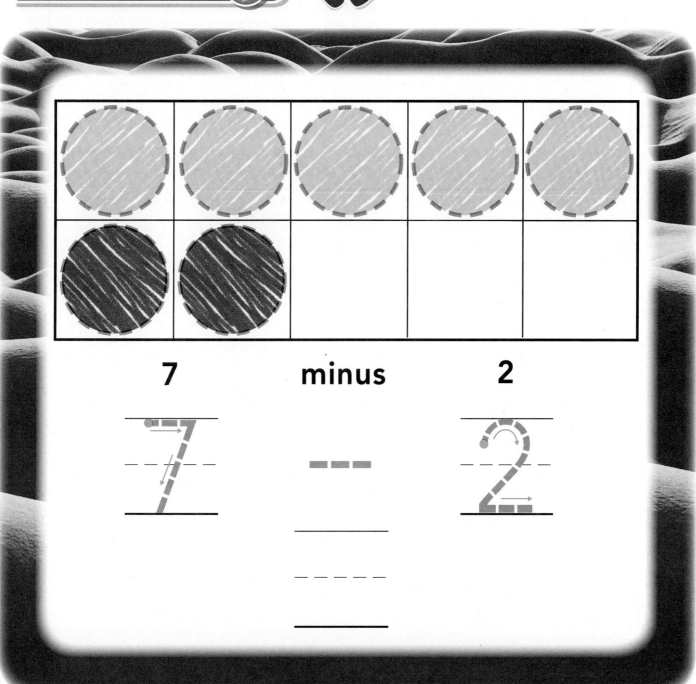

7   **minus**   **2**

DIRECTIONS Listen to the subtraction word problem. Place seven counters in the ten frame as shown. Trace the counters. Trace the number that shows how many in all. Trace the number that shows how many are red. Write the number that shows how many are yellow.

Chapter 6 • Lesson 2   two hundred twenty-nine **229**

<table>
<tr><td></td><td></td><td></td><td></td><td></td></tr>
<tr><td></td><td></td><td></td><td></td><td></td></tr>
</table>

8   minus   1

DIRECTIONS 1. Listen to the subtraction word problem. Place eight counters in the ten frame. Draw and color the counters. Trace the number that shows how many in all. Write the number that shows how many are yellow. Write the number that shows how many are red.

230 two hundred thirty

10   minus   4

_____   _____

– – – – – – –   ▬▬▬   – – – – – – –

_____   _____

_____

– – – – – –

_____

DIRECTIONS   2. Listen to the subtraction word problem. Place ten counters in the ten frame. Draw and color the counters. Write the number that shows how many in all. Write the number that shows how many are red. Write the number that shows how many are yellow.

Problem Solving • Applications

_____

- - - - -   ▬ ▬ ▬   - - - - -

_____   _____

_____

- - - - -

_____

DIRECTIONS 3. Juanita has nine apples. One apple is red. The rest of the apples are yellow. Draw the apples. Write the numbers and trace the symbol. 4. Write the number that shows how many apples are yellow.

HOME ACTIVITY • Show your child a set of seven small objects. Now take away four objects. Have him or her tell a subtraction word problem about the objects.

© Houghton Mifflin Harcourt Publishing Company

FOR MORE PRACTICE: Standards Practice Book

Name _____

Problem Solving • Act Out Subtraction Problems

Essential Question How can you solve problems using the strategy *act it out*?

Operations and Algebraic Thinking—K.OA.1
Also K.OA.2, K.OA.5
MATHEMATICAL PRACTICES
MP.1, MP.2, MP.4

Unlock the Problem Real World

 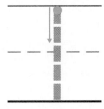  

DIRECTIONS Listen to and act out the subtraction word problem. Trace the subtraction sentence. How can you use subtraction to tell how many children are left?

Chapter 6 • Lesson 3

two hundred thirty-three **233**

Try Another Problem

 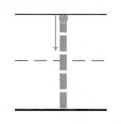 

DIRECTIONS I. Listen to and act out the subtraction word problem. Trace the numbers and the symbols. Write the number that shows how many children are left.

Name _____

....

DIRECTIONS 2. Listen to and act out the subtraction word problem. Trace the numbers and the symbols. Write the number that shows how many children are left.

On Your Own Real World

WRITE Math

3

$$4 - 1 = \underline{\hspace{2cm}}$$

4

$$4 - 3 = \underline{\hspace{2cm}}$$

DIRECTIONS 3. Tell a subtraction word problem about the kittens. Trace the numbers and the symbols. Write the number that shows how many kittens are left. 4. Draw to show what you know about the subtraction sentence. Write how many are left. Tell a friend a subtraction word problem to match.

HOME ACTIVITY • Tell your child a short subtraction word problem. Have him or her use objects to act out the word problem.

236 two hundred thirty-six

FOR MORE PRACTICE:
Standards Practice Book

Name _____

Algebra • Model and Draw Subtraction Problems

Essential Question How can you use objects and drawings to solve subtraction word problems?

Operations and Algebraic Thinking—K.OA.5
Also K.OA.1, K.OA.2
MATHEMATICAL PRACTICES
MP.1, MP.2, MP.4

Listen and Draw

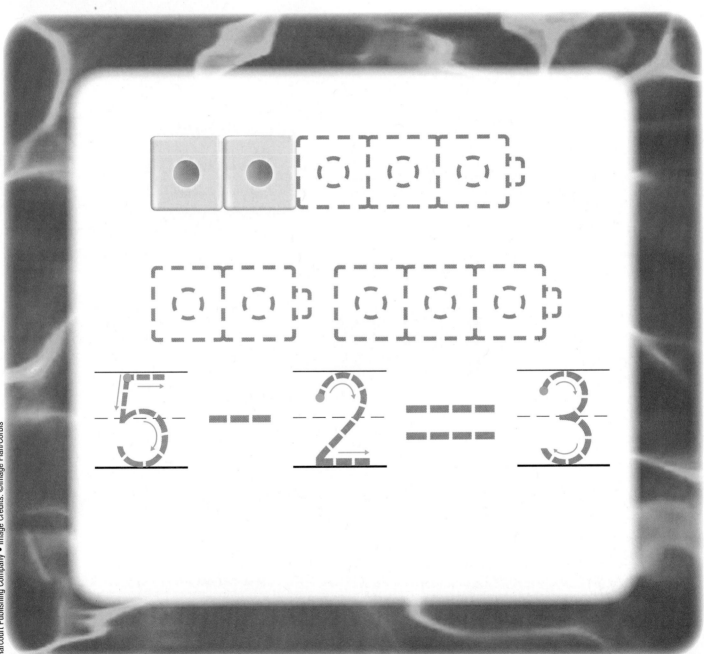

DIRECTIONS Model a five-cube train. Two cubes are yellow and the rest are red. Take apart the train to show how many cubes are red. Draw and color the cube trains. Trace the subtraction sentence.

Chapter 6 • Lesson 4

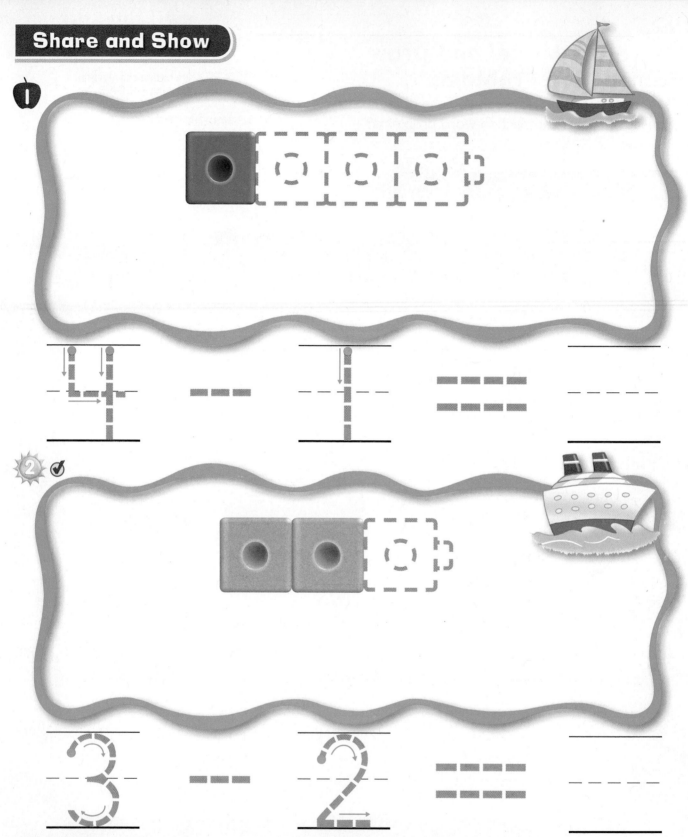

1

$$4 - 1 =$$

2 ✓

$$3 - 2 =$$

DIRECTIONS 1. Model a four-cube train. One cube is blue and the rest are green. Take apart the train to show how many cubes are green. Draw and color the cube trains. Trace and write to complete the subtraction sentence. 2. Model a three-cube train. Two cubes are orange and the rest are blue. Take apart the train to show how many cubes are blue. Draw and color the cube trains. Trace and write to complete the subtraction sentence.

238 two hundred thirty-eight

Name _____

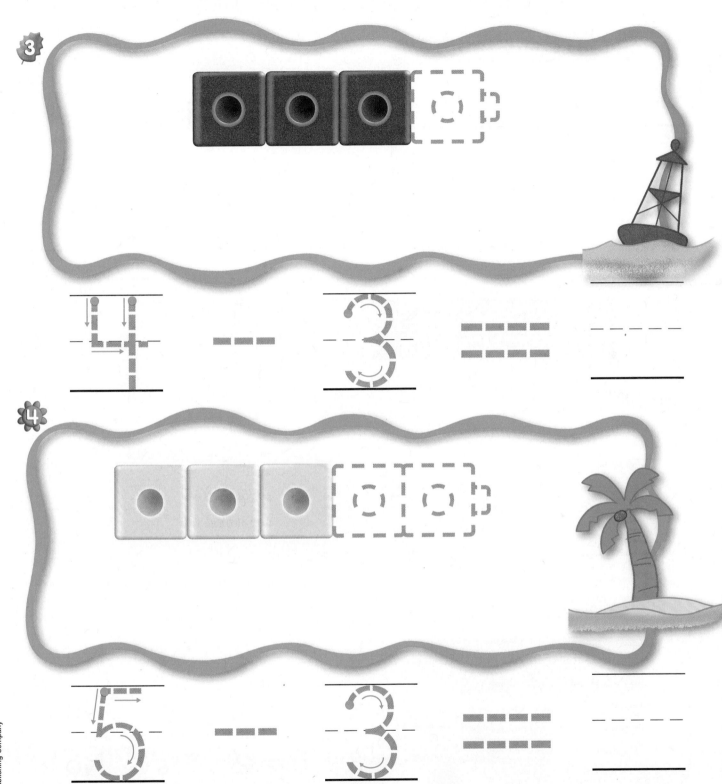

4 − 3 = ___

5 − 3 = ___

DIRECTIONS **3.** Model a four-cube train. Three cubes are red and the rest are blue. Take apart the train to show how many cubes are blue. Draw and color the cube trains. Trace and write to complete the subtraction sentence. **4.** Model a five-cube train. Three cubes are yellow and the rest are green. Take apart the train to show how many cubes are green. Draw and color the cube trains. Trace and write to complete the subtraction sentence.

HOME ACTIVITY • Show your child two small objects. Take apart the set of objects. Have him or her tell a word problem to match the subtraction.

Chapter 6 • Lesson 4

FOR MORE PRACTICE: Standards Practice Book

Concepts and Skills

 1

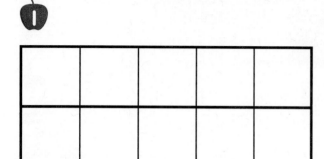

$$6 \qquad \text{minus} \qquad 1$$

_____   ___   _____

- - - - - - -   ▬▬▬   - - - - - -

_____   _____

2

 - - 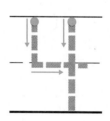 === - - - - - -

3 THINK SMARTER

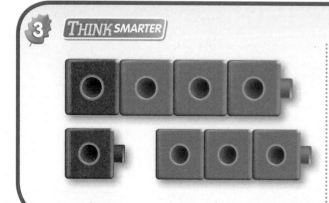

$4 - 2 = 2$	Yes ○ No ○
$4 - 3 = 1$	Yes ○ No ○
$3 - 1 = 2$	Yes ○ No ○

DIRECTIONS **1.** Listen to the subtraction word problem. Draw and color the six circles in the ten frame. Write the number that shows how many in all. Write the number that shows how many are yellow. (K.OA.1) **2.** Model a five-cube train. Four cubes are blue and the rest are orange. Take apart the cube train to show how many are orange. Draw and color the cube trains. Trace and write to complete the subtraction sentence. (K.OA.5) **3.** Circle Yes or No. Does the subtraction sentence match the model? (K.OA.5)

Name _____

Algebra • Write Subtraction Sentences

Operations and Algebraic Thinking—K.OA.5
Also K.OA.1, K.OA.2
MATHEMATICAL PRACTICES
MP.1, MP.2

Essential Question How can you solve subtraction word problems and complete the equation?

Listen and Draw Real World

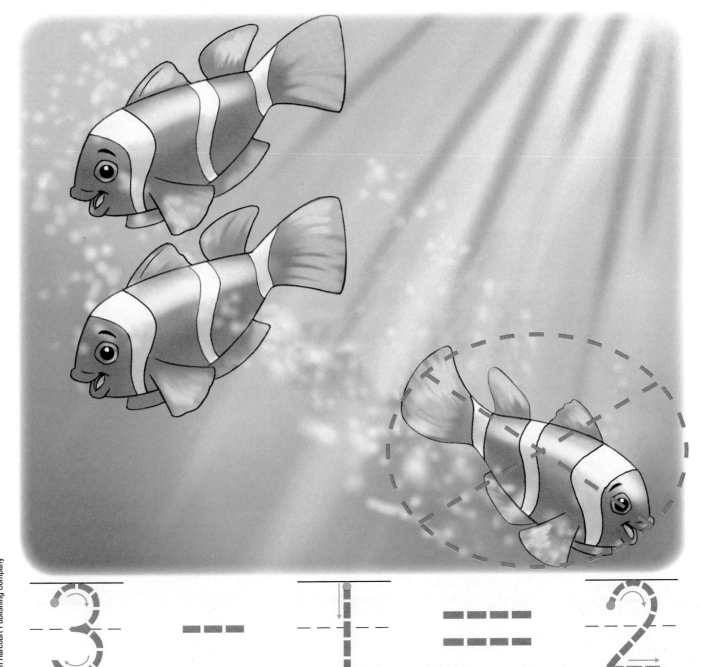

DIRECTIONS There are three fish. Some fish swim away. Now there are two fish. Trace the circle and X to show the fish swimming away. Trace the subtraction sentence.

Chapter 6 • Lesson 5

two hundred forty-one **241**

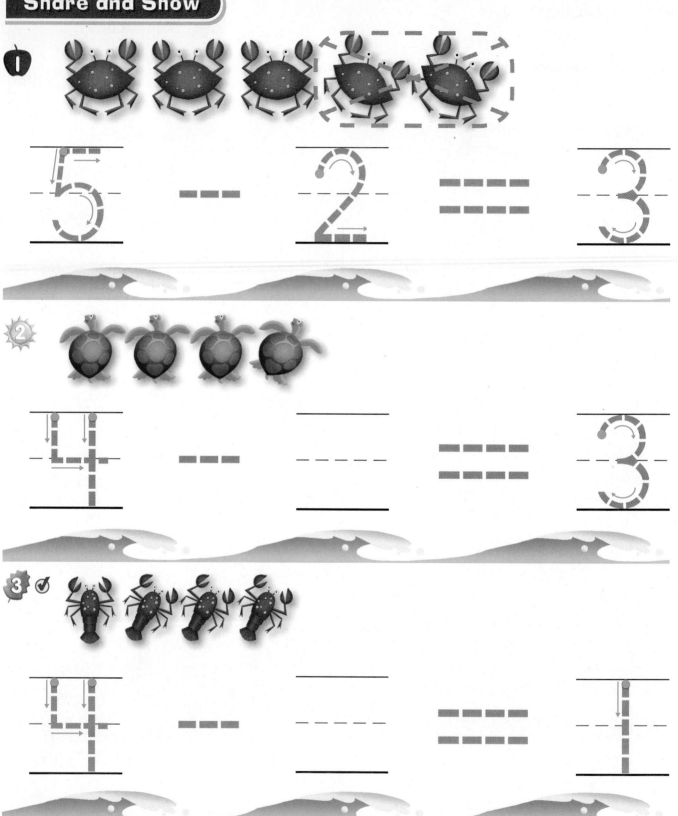

1 5 − 2 = 3

2 4 − ___ = 3

3 4 − ___ = 1

DIRECTIONS 1. Listen to the subtraction word problem. Trace the circle and X to show how many are being taken from the set. Trace to complete the subtraction sentence. 2–3. Listen to the subtraction word problem. Circle and mark an X to show how many are being taken from the set. Trace and write to complete the subtraction sentence.

Name _____

4

5 − ___ = 2

5

3 − ___ = 1

6

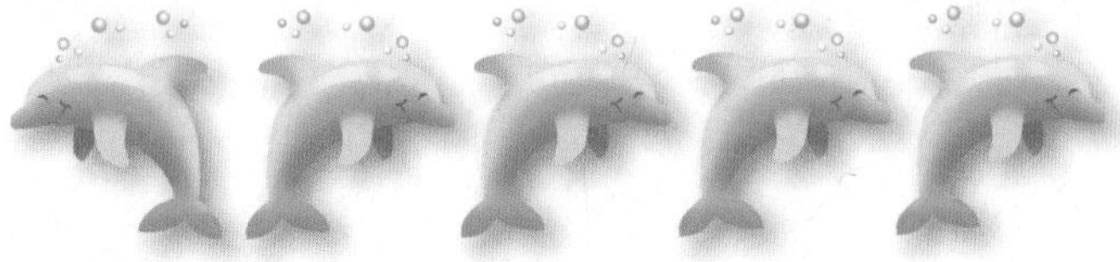

5 − ___ = 1

DIRECTIONS 4–6. Listen to the subtraction word problem. Circle and mark an X to show how many are being taken from the set. Trace and write to complete the subtraction sentence.

Problem Solving • Applications Real World

WRITE Math

7

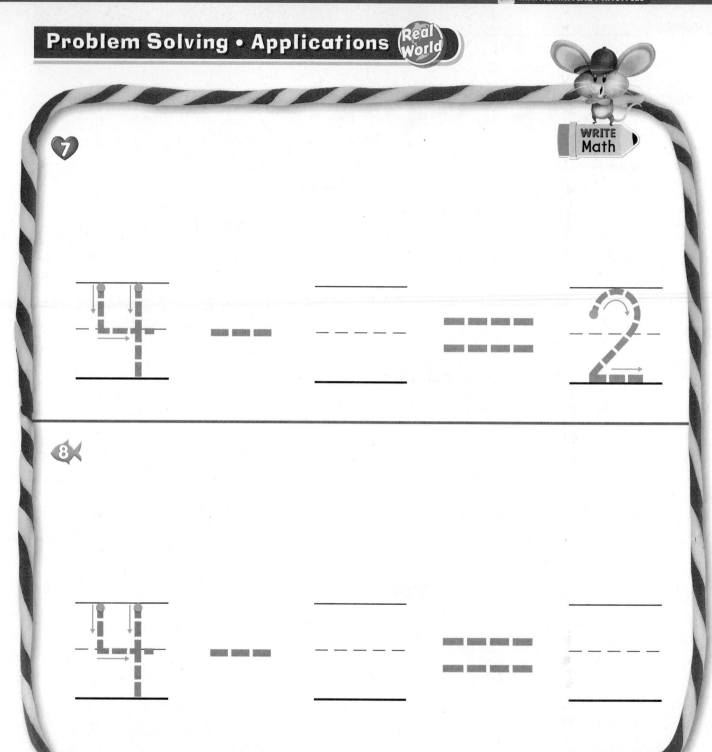

8

DIRECTIONS **7.** Kristen has four flowers. She gives her friend some flowers. Now Kristen has two flowers. How many did Kristen give her friend? Draw to solve the problem. Complete the subtraction sentence. **8.** Tell a different subtraction word problem about the flowers. Draw to solve the problem. Tell a friend about your drawing. Complete the subtraction sentence.

HOME ACTIVITY • Have your child draw a set of five or fewer balloons. Have him or her circle and mark an X on some balloons to show that they have popped. Then have your child tell a word problem to match the subtraction.

FOR MORE PRACTICE:
Standards Practice Book

Name _____

Algebra • Write More Subtraction Sentences

 Operations and Algebraic Thinking—K.OA.2
Also K.OA.1

MATHEMATICAL PRACTICES
MP.1, MP.2

Essential Question How can you solve subtraction word problems and complete the equation?

Listen and Draw *Real World*

DIRECTIONS There are some birds. One bird flies away. Trace the circle and X around that bird. How many birds are left? Trace the subtraction sentence. How many birds did you start with? Circle that number.

Chapter 6 • Lesson 6

two hundred forty-five **245**

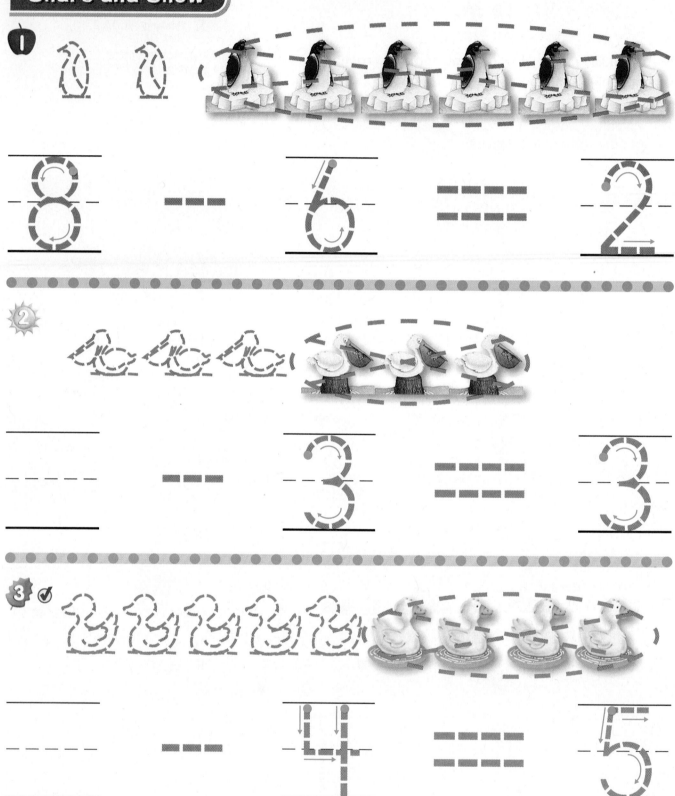

1 8 — 6 = 2

2 ___ — 3 = 3

3 ✓ ___ — 4 = 5

DIRECTIONS 1–3. Listen to the subtraction word problem. How many birds are taken from the set? Trace the circle and X. How many birds are left? How many birds were there in all to begin with? Write and trace to complete the subtraction sentence.

❀ 4

_ _ _ _ _   – –   5   = = =   1

● ● ● ● ● ● ● ● ● ● ● ● ● ● ● ●

5

_ _ _ _ _   – –   6   = = =   3

● ● ● ● ● ● ● ● ● ● ● ● ● ● ● ●

6

_ _ _ _ _   – –   3   = = =   5

● ● ● ● ● ● ● ● ● ● ● ● ● ● ● ●

DIRECTIONS 4–6. Listen to the subtraction word problem.
How many birds are taken from the set? Trace the circle and X.
How many birds are left? How many birds were there in all to
begin with? Write and trace to complete the subtraction sentence.

Chapter 6 • Lesson 6   two hundred forty-seven **247**

Problem Solving • Applications Real World

7

WRITE Math

_____ − 6 = 2

DIRECTIONS 7. Complete the subtraction sentence. Draw a picture of real objects to show what you know about this subtraction sentence. Tell a friend about your drawing.

HOME ACTIVITY • Tell your child you have some small objects in your hand. Tell him or her that you are taking two objects from the set and now there are five objects left. Ask him or her to tell you how many objects were in the set to start with.

© Houghton Mifflin Harcourt Publishing Company

FOR MORE PRACTICE: Standards Practice Book

Name _____

Algebra • Addition and Subtraction

Essential Question How can you solve word problems using addition and subtraction?

Operations and Algebraic Thinking—K.OA.2
Also K.OA.1
MATHEMATICAL PRACTICES
MP.2, MP.5, MP.8

 Listen and Draw *Real World* Hands On

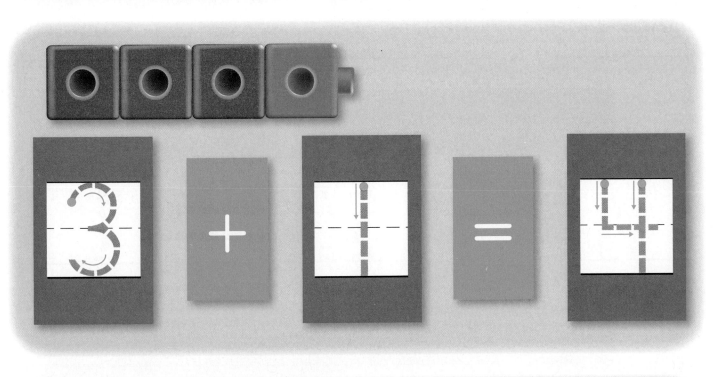

DIRECTIONS Listen to the addition and subtraction word problems. Use cubes and Number and Symbol Tiles as shown to match the word problems. Trace to complete the number sentences.

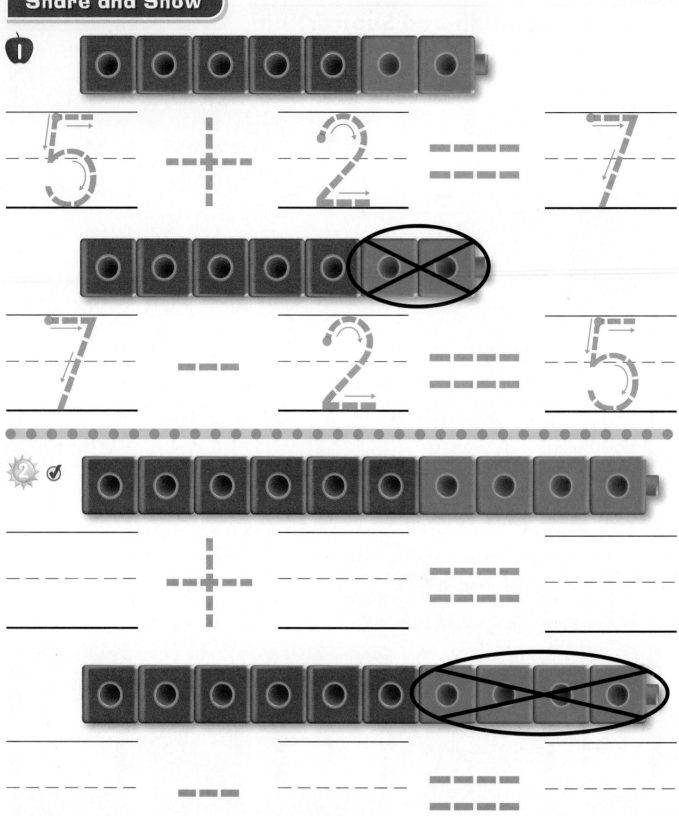

1. $5 + 2 = 7$

$7 - 2 = 5$

2. $\underline{\hspace{1cm}} + \underline{\hspace{1cm}} = \underline{\hspace{1cm}}$

$\underline{\hspace{1cm}} - \underline{\hspace{1cm}} = \underline{\hspace{1cm}}$

DIRECTIONS Tell addition and subtraction word problems. Use cubes to add and to subtract. **1.** Trace the number sentences. **2.** Complete the number sentences.

3

_____ + _____ = _____

_____ _____ = _____

_____ + _____ = _____

4

_____ + _____ = _____

_____ _____ = _____

_____ + _____ = _____

DIRECTIONS 3–4. Tell addition and subtraction word problems. Use cubes to add and subtract. Complete the number sentences.

Problem Solving • Applications Real World

WRITE Math

$$6 + 3 = 9$$

5

_____   _____   ═══ ═══ ═══   _____
- - - - - -   ═══ ═══   - - - - - -   ═══ ═══ ═══   - - - - - -
_____   _____   ═══ ═══ ═══   _____

6

_____   _____   ═══ ═══ ═══   _____
- - - - - -   ═══ ═══   - - - - - -   ═══ ═══ ═══   - - - - - -
_____   _____   ═══ ═══ ═══   _____

DIRECTIONS Look at the addition sentence at the top of the page. **5–6.** Tell a related subtraction word problem. Complete the subtraction sentence.

HOME ACTIVITY • Ask your child to use objects to model a simple addition problem. Then have him or her explain how to make it into a subtraction problem.

252 two hundred fifty-two

FOR MORE PRACTICE:
Standards Practice Book

Name _____

✓ Chapter 6 Review/Test

1

4
take away _____

_____
- - - - -

_____
- - - - -
_____

2

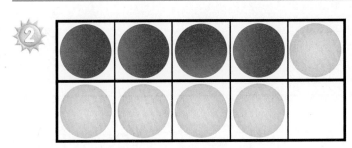

9 – 1   ○ Yes   ○ No

9 – 5   ○ Yes   ○ No

8 – 3   ○ Yes   ○ No

Personal Math Trainer

3 THINK SMARTER ➕

5 – 2 = _____

DIRECTIONS 1. Write how many owls are flying away. Write how many owls are left. 2. Which answers show how many counters are red? Choose Yes or No. 3. Model a five-cube train. Two cubes are yellow and the rest are blue. Take apart the cube train to show how many are blue. Draw the cube trains. Trace and write to complete the subtraction sentence.

GO DIGITAL Assessment Options Chapter Test

4

4 - 2 = ___

5

___ - 3 = 4

 6

5 − 4 = 1	Yes No
4 + 1 = 5	Yes No
5 − 2 = 3	Yes No

7

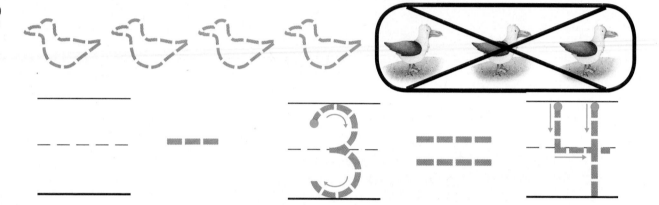

9 = 3 + 6   10 = 3 + 7   3 + 7 = 10

○   ○   ○

DIRECTIONS **4.** There are 4 penguins. Two penguins are taken from the set. How many penguins are left? Trace and write to complete the subtraction sentence. **5.** There are some birds. Three birds are taken from the set. How many birds are left? How many birds were there in all to start? Write and trace to complete the subtraction sentence. **6.** Does the number sentence match the picture? Circle Yes or No. **7.** Mark under all the number sentences that match the cubes.

Name _____

$4 - 3 = \underline{\hspace{2cm}}$

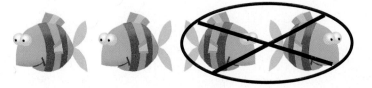

$8 - 1 = \underline{\hspace{2cm}}$

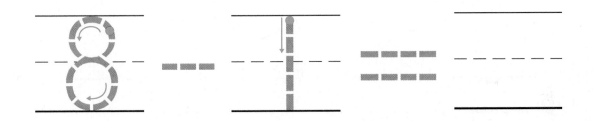

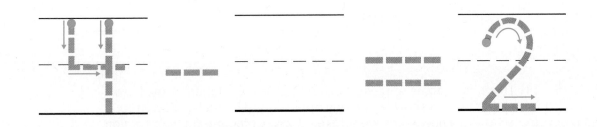

$4 - \underline{\hspace{1cm}} = 2$

DIRECTIONS **8.** Model a four-cube train. Three cubes are red and the rest are blue. Take apart the train to show how many cubes are blue. Draw the cube trains. Complete the subtraction sentence. **9–10.** Complete the subtraction sentence to match the picture.

© Houghton Mifflin Harcourt Publishing Company

Chapter 6

two hundred fifty-five 255

11. THINK SMARTER +

$$\text{------} \ - \ \text{------} \ = \ 0$$

12.

$$\text{------} \ - \ 2 \ = \ 3$$

13.

$$6 \ - \ \text{------} \ = \ 4$$

DIRECTIONS **11.** There were some apples on a tree. Some were taken away. Now there are zero apples left. Draw to show how many apples there could have been to start. Cross out apples to show how many were taken away. Complete the subtraction sentence. **12.** There are some birds. Two birds are taken from the set. How many birds are left? How many birds were there in all to begin with? Write the number to complete the subtraction sentence. **13.** Erica has 6 balloons. She gives some of her balloons to a friend. Now Erica has 4 balloons. How many did Erica give to her friend? Draw to solve the problem. Complete the subtraction sentence.

256 two hundred fifty-six

Represent, Count, and Write 11 to 19

Curious About Math with

Curious George

Shells come in many colors and patterns.

- Is the number of shells greater than or less than 10?

Name _____

Show What You Know ✓

Draw Objects to 10

 1

10

 2

9

Write Numbers to 10

 3

_____

 **4**

_____

5

_____

6

_____

This page checks understanding of important skills needed for success in Chapter 7.

DIRECTIONS 1. Draw 10 oranges. 2. Draw 9 apples. 3–6. Count and tell how many. Write the number.

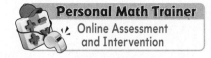
Personal Math Trainer
Online Assessment and Intervention

Vocabulary Builder

FINISH

one 1
two
three
four
5 five
8 eight
7 seven
six 6
9 nine
ten 10

CABBAGE PARK RUN

DIRECTIONS Circle the number word that is greater than nine.

GO DIGITAL
• Interactive Student Edition
• Multimedia eGlossary

© Houghton Mifflin Harcourt Publishing Company

Game Sweet and Sour Path

DIRECTIONS Play with a partner. Place game markers on START. Take turns. Toss the number cube. Move that number of spaces. If a player lands on a lemon, the player reads the number and moves back that many spaces. If a player lands on a strawberry, the player reads the number and moves forward that many spaces. The first player to reach END wins.

MATERIALS two game markers, number cube (1–6)

Name _____

Model and Count 11 and 12

Essential Question How can you use objects to show 11 and 12 as ten ones and some more ones?

Listen and Draw

DIRECTIONS Use counters to show the number 11. Add more to show the number 12. Draw the counters. Tell a friend what you know about these numbers.

Number and Operations in Base Ten—K.NBT.1
Also K.CC.4b, K.CC.4c, K.CC.5
MATHEMATICAL PRACTICES
MP.2, MP.3, MP.7

1 **11**
   eleven

2 ✓

3

____ ____

ones and _____ **one**

DIRECTIONS 1. Count and tell how many. Trace the number. 2. Use counters to show the number 11. Draw the counters. 3. Look at the counters you drew. How many ones are in the ten frame? Trace the number. How many more ones are there? Write the number.

262 two hundred sixty-two

12
twelve

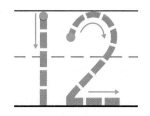

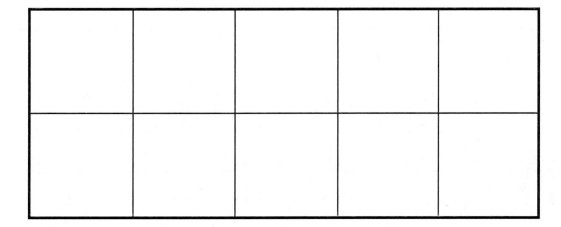

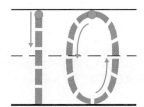

ones and _____ **ones**

DIRECTIONS **4.** Count and tell how many. Trace the number. **5.** Use counters to show the number 12. Draw the counters. **6.** Look at the counters you drew. How many ones are in the ten frame? Trace the number. How many more ones are there? Write the number.

Problem Solving • Applications Real World

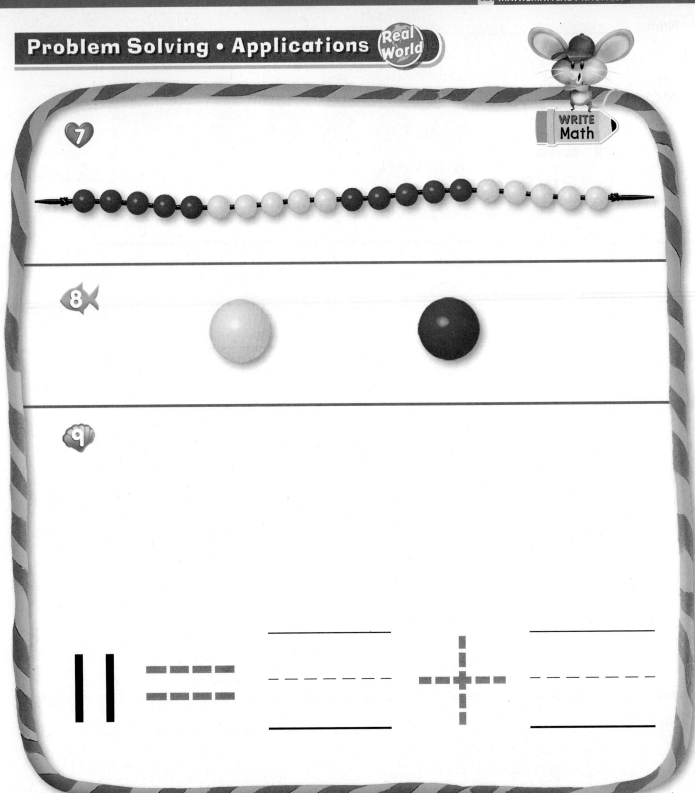

7

8

9

11 = ___	___	+ ___

DIRECTIONS **7.** Maria makes a bracelet with 11 beads. She starts with the blue bead on the left. Circle to show the beads Maria uses to make her bracelet. **8.** Are there more blue beads or more yellow beads in those 11 beads? Circle the color bead that has more. **9.** Draw a set of 11 objects. If you circle 10 of the objects, how many more objects are there? Complete the addition sentence to match.

HOME ACTIVITY • Draw a ten frame on a sheet of paper. Have your child use small objects, such as buttons, pennies, or dried beans, to show the numbers 11 and 12.

FOR MORE PRACTICE:
Standards Practice Book

Name _____

Count and Write 11 and 12

Essential Question How can you count and write 11 and 12 with words and numbers?

Number and Operations in Base Ten—K.NBT.1
Also K.CC.3, K.CC.4b
MATHEMATICAL PRACTICES
MP.2, MP.7, MP.8

Listen and Draw

DIRECTIONS Count and tell how many. Trace the numbers and the words.

Chapter 7 • Lesson 2

two hundred sixty-five **265**

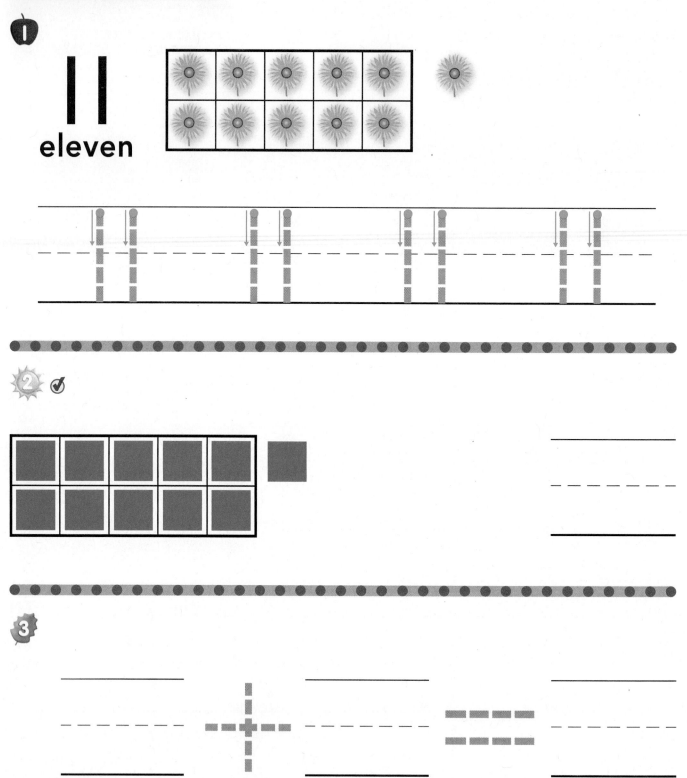

eleven

DIRECTIONS I. Count and tell how many. Trace the numbers. **2.** Count and tell how many. Write the number. **3.** Look at the ten ones and some more ones in Exercise 2. Complete the addition sentence to match.

4

12
twelve

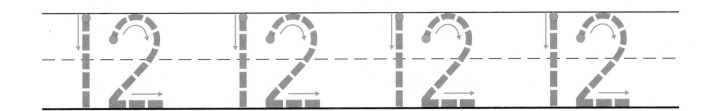

5

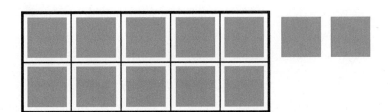

_____

- - - - - - - - - - -

_____

6

_____   +   _____   =   _____

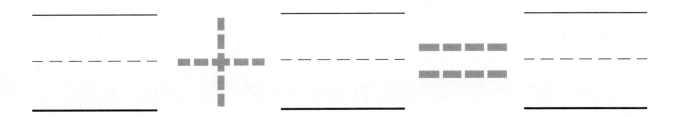

DIRECTIONS **4.** Count and tell how many. Trace the numbers. **5.** Count and tell how many. Write the number. **6.** Look at the ten ones and some more ones in Exercise 5. Complete the addition sentence to match.

Problem Solving • Applications

7

WRITE Math

11

12

13

8

$$ 12 = \underline{\quad\quad} + \underline{\quad\quad} $$

DIRECTIONS 7. Brooke picked a number of flowers. Circle the number of flowers Brooke picked. Draw more flowers to show that number. **8.** Draw a set of 12 objects. If you circle 10 of the objects, how many more objects are there? Complete the addition sentence to match.

 **HOME ACTIVITY** • Ask your child to count and write the number for a set of 11 or 12 objects, such as coins or buttons.

FOR MORE PRACTICE:
Standards Practice Book

Name _____

Model and Count 13 and 14

Essential Question How can you use objects to show 13 and 14 as ten ones and some more ones?

Number and Operations in Base Ten—K.NBT.1
Also K.CC.4b, K.CC.4c, K.CC.5

MATHEMATICAL PRACTICES
MP.2, MP.3, MP.7

Listen and Draw

DIRECTIONS Use counters to show the number 13. Add more to show the number 14. Draw the counters. Tell a friend what you know about these numbers.

1

13
thirteen

2 ✓

3

ones and _____ ones

DIRECTIONS 1. Count and tell how many. Trace the number. **2.** Use counters to show the number 13. Draw the counters. **3.** Look at the counters you drew. How many ones are in the ten frame? Trace the number. How many more ones are there? Write the number.

14
fourteen

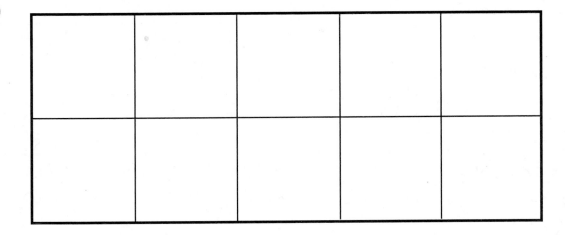

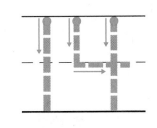

5

6

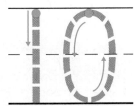 **ones and** _____ **ones**

DIRECTIONS **4.** Count and tell how many. Trace the number. **5.** Use counters to show the number 14. Draw the counters. **6.** Look at the counters you drew. How many ones are in the ten frame? Trace the number. How many more ones are there? Write the number.

Problem Solving • Applications Real World

WRITE Math

7

8

9

$$13 = \underline{\hspace{2cm}} + \underline{\hspace{2cm}}$$

DIRECTIONS **7.** Erika makes a bracelet with 13 beads. She starts with the blue bead on the left. Circle to show the beads Erika uses to make her bracelet. **8.** Are there more blue beads or more yellow beads in those 13 beads? Circle the color bead that has more. **9.** Draw a set of 13 objects. If you circle 10 of the objects, how many more objects are there? Complete the addition sentence to match.

HOME ACTIVITY • Draw a ten frame on a sheet of paper. Have your child use small objects, such as buttons, pennies, or dried beans, to show the numbers 13 and 14.

FOR MORE PRACTICE:
Standards Practice Book

Name _____

Count and Write 13 and 14

Essential Question How can you count and write 13 and 14 with words and numbers?

Number and Operations in Base Ten—K.NBT.1
Also K.CC.3, K.CC.4b

MATHEMATICAL PRACTICES
MP.2, MP.7, MP.8

Listen and Draw

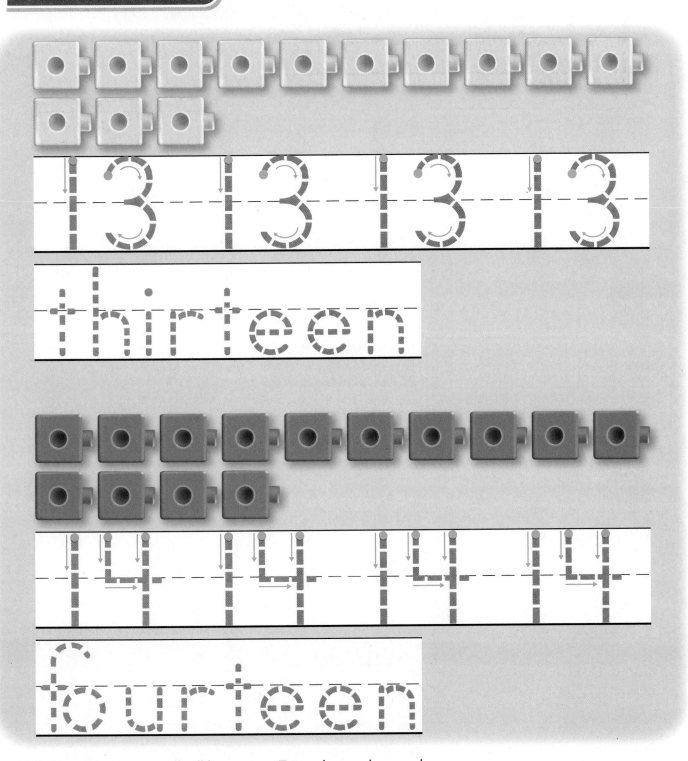

DIRECTIONS Count and tell how many. Trace the numbers and the words.

Chapter 7 • Lesson 4

© Houghton Mifflin Harcourt Publishing Company

1

13
thirteen

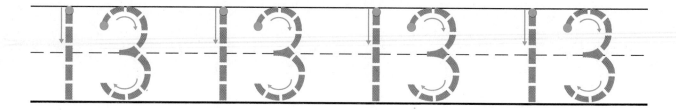

2

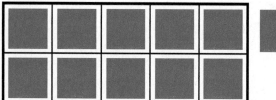

_____

- - - - - - -

_____

3

_ _ _ _ _   +   _ _ _ _ _   = = =   _ _ _ _ _
_____   +   _____   = = =   _____

DIRECTIONS 1. Count and tell how many. Trace the numbers. **2.** Count and tell how many. Write the number. **3.** Look at the ten ones and some more ones in Exercise 2. Complete the addition sentence to match.

274 two hundred seventy-four

4

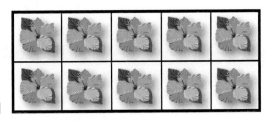

14
fourteen

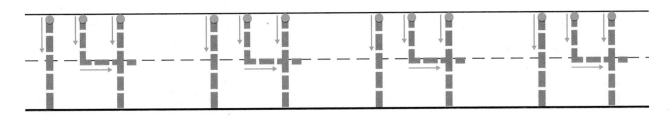

5

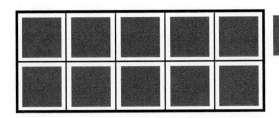

6

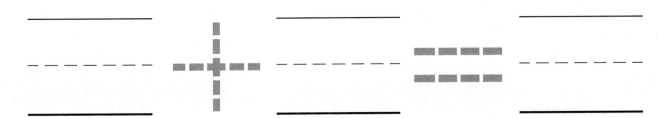

DIRECTIONS **4.** Count and tell how many. Trace the numbers. **5.** Count and tell how many. Write the number. **6.** Look at the ten ones and some more ones in Exercise 5. Complete the addition sentence to match.

Problem Solving • Applications Real World

7

12

13

14

8

$$14 = \underline{\hspace{2cm}} + \underline{\hspace{2cm}}$$

HOME ACTIVITY • Ask your child to count and write the number for a set of 13 or 14 objects, such as coins or buttons.

FOR MORE PRACTICE:
Standards Practice Book

Name _____

Model, Count, and Write 15

Essential Question How can you use objects to show 15 as ten ones and some more ones and show 15 as a number?

Number and Operations in Base Ten—K.NBT.1
Also K.CC.3, K.CC.4b, K.CC.5
MATHEMATICAL PRACTICES
MP.2, MP.5, MP.7

Listen and Draw

DIRECTIONS Use counters to show the number 15. Draw the counters. Tell a friend about the counters.

Chapter 7 • Lesson 5

two hundred seventy-seven **277**

15
fifteen

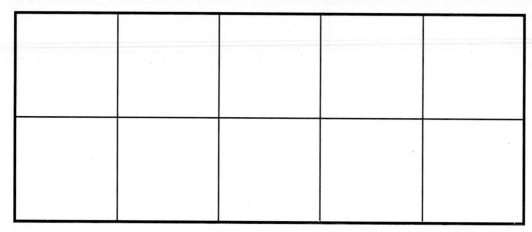

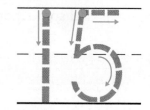

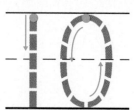 _____

- - - - - -

ones and _____ **ones**

DIRECTIONS 1. Count and tell how many. Trace the number. 2. Use counters to show the number 15. Draw the counters. 3. Look at the counters you drew. How many ones are in the ten frame? Trace the number. How many more ones? Write the number.

Name _____

4

15
fifteen

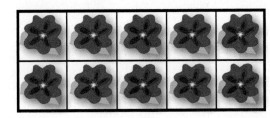

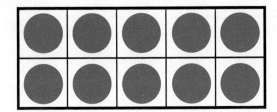

5

6

_____ + _____ = _____

DIRECTIONS **4.** Count and tell how many. Trace the numbers.
5. Count and tell how many. Write the number.   **6.** Look at the ten
ones and some more ones in Exercise 5. Complete the addition sentence
to match.

Problem Solving • Applications

 WRITE Math

7

8

9

15 === _____ + _____

DIRECTIONS **7.** Martha makes a necklace with 15 beads. She starts with the blue bead on the left. Circle to show the beads Martha uses to make her necklace. **8.** Are there more blue beads or more yellow beads in those 15 beads? Circle the color bead that has more. **9.** Draw a set of 15 objects. If you circle 10 of the objects, how many more objects are there? Complete the addition sentence to match.

 **HOME ACTIVITY •** Have your child use two different kinds of objects to show all the ways he or she can make 15, such as 8 coins and 7 buttons.

FOR MORE PRACTICE: Standards Practice Book

Problem Solving • Use Numbers to 15

Essential Question How can you solve problems using the strategy *draw a picture*?

 Counting and Cardinality—K.CC.3

MATHEMATICAL PRACTICES
MP.1, MP.2, MP.4

 Unlock the Problem Real World

_____

_ _ _ _ _

_____ chairs

DIRECTIONS There are 14 children sitting on chairs. There is one chair with no child on it. How many chairs are there? Draw to show how you solved the problem.

Chapter 7 • Lesson 6

1

_____

_ _ _ _ _

____ more bees

DIRECTIONS 1. There are 15 flowers. Ten flowers have 1 bee on them. How many more bees would you need to have one bee on each flower? Draw to solve the problem. Write how many more bees.

Share and Show

_____ boys

DIRECTIONS 2. There are 15 children in Miss Sully's class. There are 5 children in each row. There are 3 boys and 2 girls in each row. How many boys are in the class? Draw to solve the problem.

HOME ACTIVITY • Draw a ten frame on a sheet of paper. Have your child use small objects, such as buttons, pennies, or dried beans, to show the number 15.

Chapter 7 • Lesson 6

FOR MORE PRACTICE: Standards Practice Book

Concepts and Skills

1

_____

- - - - - - - - - - -

_____

2

14 ═══ _____ **+** _____

3

_____

- - - - - - - - - -

_____

4

_____

- - - - - - - - - -

_____

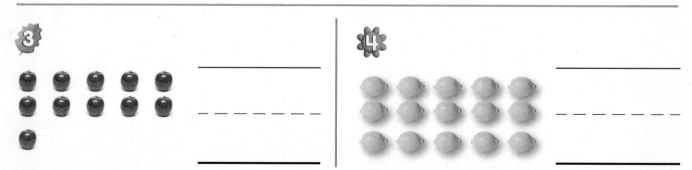

5 THINK SMARTER

_____

- - - - - - - - - -

_____

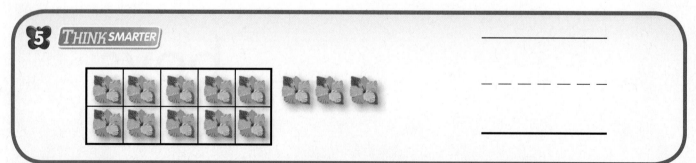

DIRECTIONS 1. Count and tell how many. Write the number.
(K.CC.3) **2.** Draw a set of 14 objects. If you circle 10 of the objects, how many more objects are there? Complete the addition sentence to match.
(K.CC.3) **3–4.** Count and tell how many. Write the number. (K.NBT.1)
5. Write the number that shows how many flowers. (K.CC.3)

Name _____

Model and Count 16 and 17

Essential Question How can you use objects to show 16 and 17 as ten ones and some more ones?

Listen and Draw

Number and Operations in Base Ten—K.NBT.1
Also K.CC.4b, K.CC.4c, K.CC.5
MATHEMATICAL PRACTICES
MP.2, MP.3, MP.7

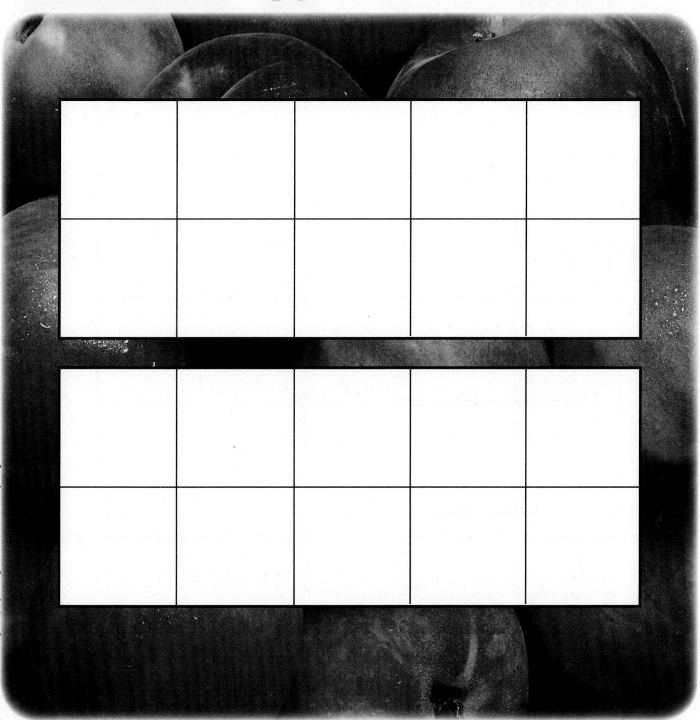

DIRECTIONS Use counters to show the number 16. Add more to show the number 17. Draw the counters. Tell a friend what you know about these numbers.

Chapter 7 • Lesson 7

two hundred eighty-five **285**

1

16
sixteen

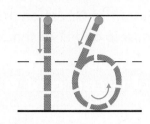

3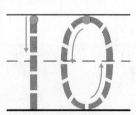

_____

------ ------

ones and _____ ones

DIRECTIONS 1. Count and tell how many. Trace the number. 2. Place counters in the ten frames to show the number 16. Draw the counters. 3. Look at the counters you drew in the ten frames. How many ones are in the top ten frame? Trace the number. How many ones are in the bottom ten frame? Write the number.

Name _____

17
seventeen

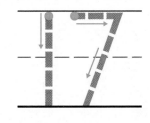

5

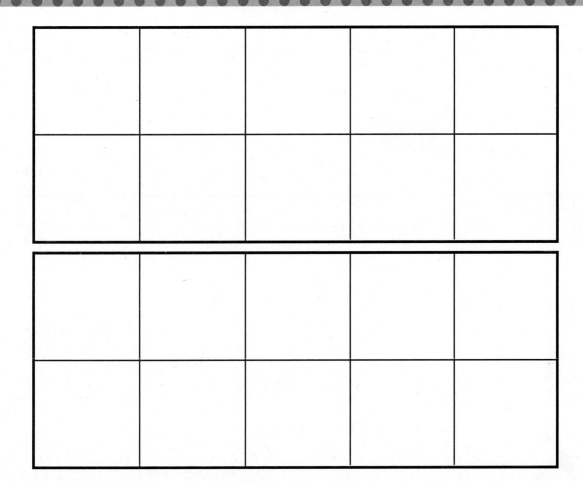

6

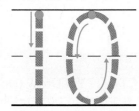

_____

- - - - - - - - - - -

ones and _____ **ones**

DIRECTIONS **4.** Count and tell how many. Trace the number. **5.** Place counters in the ten frames to show the number 17. Draw the counters. **6.** Look at the counters you drew in the ten frames. How many ones are in the top ten frame? Trace the number. How many ones are in the bottom ten frame? Write the number.

Problem Solving • Applications Real World

7

WRITE Math

8

9

$$16 = \text{\underline{\hspace{2cm}}} + \text{\underline{\hspace{2cm}}}$$

DIRECTIONS **7.** Chloe makes a necklace with 16 beads. She starts with the blue bead on the left. Circle to show the beads Chloe uses to make her necklace. **8.** Are there more blue beads or more yellow beads in those 16 beads? Circle the color bead that has more. **9.** Draw a set of 16 objects. If you circle 10 of the objects, how many more objects are there? Complete the addition sentence to match.

HOME ACTIVITY • Draw two ten frames on a sheet of paper. Have your child use small objects, such as buttons, pennies, or dried beans, to show the numbers 16 and 17.

FOR MORE PRACTICE:
Standards Practice Book

Name _____

Count and Write 16 and 17

Essential Question How can you count and write 16 and 17 with words and numbers?

Number and Operations in Base Ten—K.NBT.1
Also K.CC.3, K.CC.4b
MATHEMATICAL PRACTICES
MP.2, MP.7, MP.8

Listen and Draw

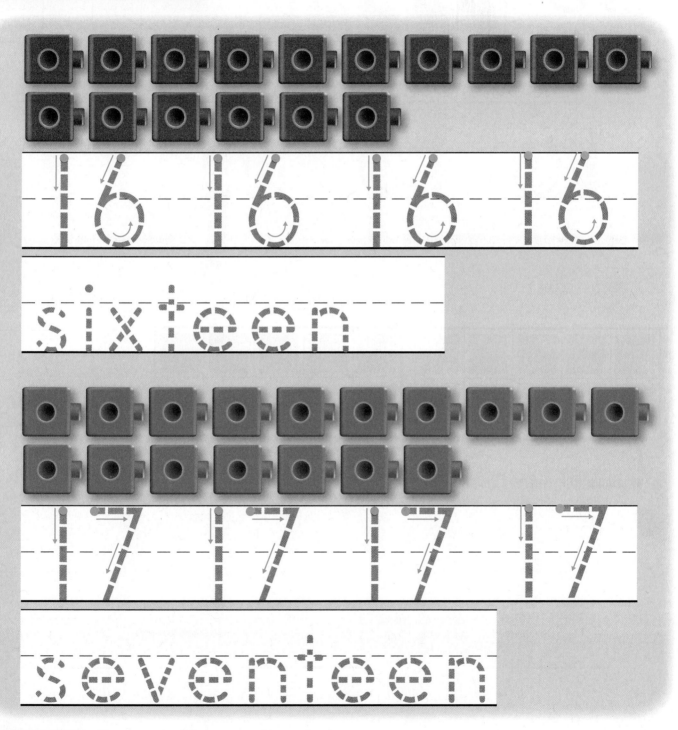

DIRECTIONS Count and tell how many. Trace the numbers and the words.

1

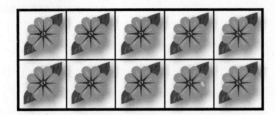

16
sixteen

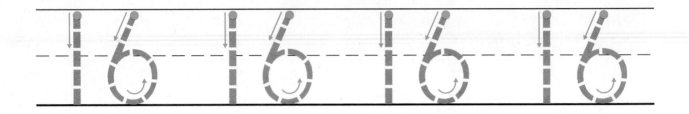

2 ✓

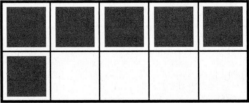

3

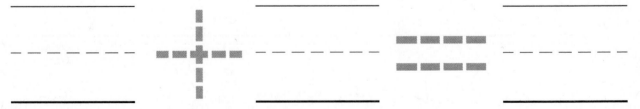

DIRECTIONS **1.** Count and tell how many. Trace the numbers. **2.** Count and tell how many. Write the number. **3.** Look at the ten frames in Exercise 2. Complete the addition sentence to match.

Name _____

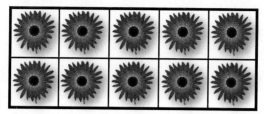

17

seventeen

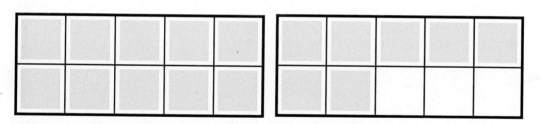

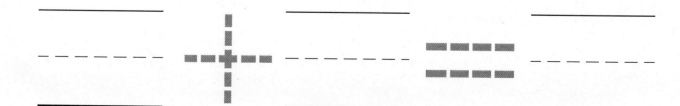

DIRECTIONS **4.** Count and tell how many. Trace the numbers. **5.** Count
and tell how many. Write the number. **6.** Look at the ten frames in Exercise
5. Complete the addition sentence to match.

Chapter 7 • Lesson 8   two hundred ninety-one **291**

Problem Solving • Applications

WRITE Math

7

17

18

19

8

17 === _____ _____ + _____
       _____   _____

DIRECTIONS **7.** Emily picked 10 flowers. Then she picked 7 more flowers. Circle the number of flowers Emily picked. Draw more flowers to show that number. Explain how you know. **8.** Draw a set of 17 objects. If you circle 10 of the objects, how many more objects are there? Complete the addition sentence to match.

 **HOME ACTIVITY** • Ask your child to count and write the number for a set of 16 or 17 objects, such as coins or buttons.

FOR MORE PRACTICE: Standards Practice Book

Model and Count 18 and 19

Essential Question How can you use objects to show 18 and 19 as ten ones and some more ones?

Number and Operations in Base Ten—K.NBT.1
Also K.CC.4b, K.CC.4c, K.CC.5
MATHEMATICAL PRACTICES
MP.2, MP.3, MP.7

Listen and Draw

DIRECTIONS Use counters to show the number 18. Add more to show the number 19. Draw the counters. Tell a friend what you know about these numbers.

Chapter 7 • Lesson 9

1 **18**
eighteen

2 ✓

3

_____ ones and _____ ones

DIRECTIONS 1. Count and tell how many. Trace the number. **2.** Place counters in the ten frames to show the number 18. Draw the counters. **3.** Look at the counters you drew in the ten frames. How many ones are in the top ten frame? Trace the number. How many ones are in the bottom ten frame? Write the number.

Name _____

19
nineteen

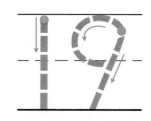

5

6

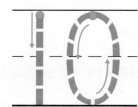

ones and _____ ones

DIRECTIONS 4. Count and tell how many. Trace the number. **5.** Place counters in the ten frames to show the number 19. Draw the counters. **6.** Look at the counters you drew in the ten frames. How many ones are in the top ten frame? Trace the number. How many ones are in the bottom ten frame? Write the number.

Problem Solving • Applications Real World

 7

 WRITE Math

 8

 9

18 === ___ + ___
___ ___

DIRECTIONS **7.** Kaylyn makes a necklace with 18 beads. She starts with the blue bead on the left. Circle to show the beads Kaylyn uses to make her necklace. **8.** Are there more blue beads or more yellow beads in those 18 beads? Circle the color bead that has more. **9.** Draw a set of 18 objects. If you circle 10 of the objects, how many more objects are there? Complete the addition sentence to match.

 HOME ACTIVITY • Draw two ten frames on a sheet of paper. Have your child use small objects, such as buttons, pennies, or dried beans, to model the numbers 18 and 19.

FOR MORE PRACTICE:
Standards Practice Book

Name _____

Count and Write 18 and 19

Essential Question How can you count and write 18 and 19 with words and numbers?

Number and Operations in Base Ten—K.NBT.1
Also K.CC.3, K.CC.4b
MATHEMATICAL PRACTICES
MP.2, MP.7, MP.8

Listen and Draw

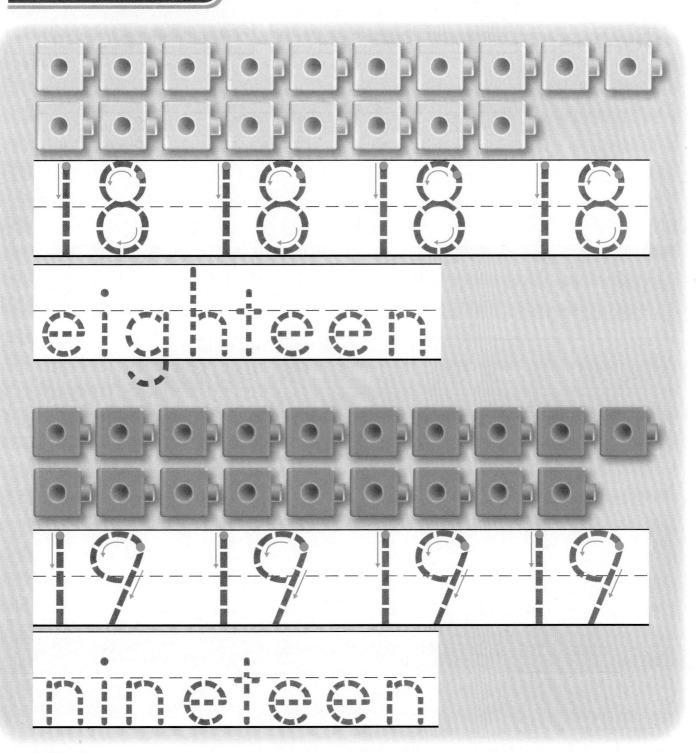

DIRECTIONS Count and tell how many. Trace the numbers and the words.

1

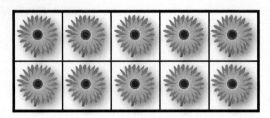
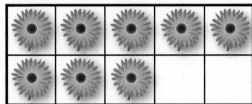

18
eighteen

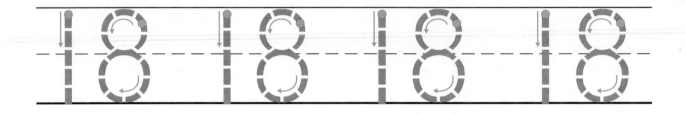

2

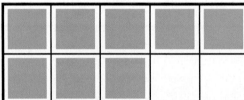

3

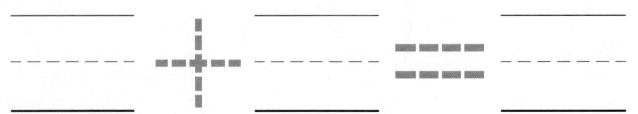

DIRECTIONS 1. Count and tell how many. Trace the numbers. 2. Count and tell how many. Write the number. 3. Look at the ten frames in Exercise 2. Complete the addition sentence to match.

Name _____

4

19
nineteen

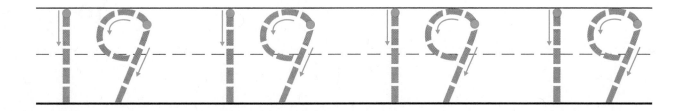

5

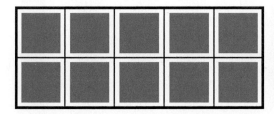

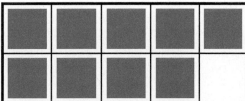

_____

- - - - - - - - - - -

6

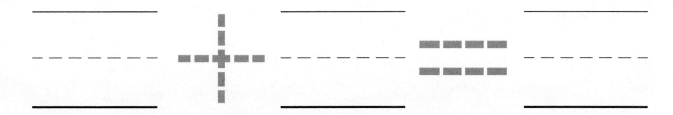

DIRECTIONS **4.** Count and tell how many. Trace the numbers. **5.** Count and tell how many. Write the number. **6.** Look at the ten frames in Exercise 5. Complete the addition sentence to match.

Chapter 7 • Lesson 10

Problem Solving • Applications

7

17

18

19

8

$19 = \underline{\hspace{2cm}} + \underline{\hspace{2cm}}$

DIRECTIONS **7.** Grace picked a number of flowers 1 more than 17. Circle the number of flowers Grace picked. Draw more flowers to show that number. **8.** Draw a set of 19 objects. If you circle 10 of the objects, how many more objects are there? Complete the addition sentence to match.

HOME ACTIVITY • Ask your child to count and write the number for a set of 18 or 19 objects, such as coins or buttons.

FOR MORE PRACTICE: Standards Practice Book

✓ Chapter 7 Review/Test

1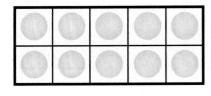

_____

– – – – – – – – – – –

_____

2

_____

– – – – – – – – – – –

_____

3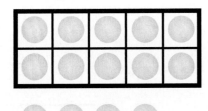

12 | 10 + 2

4

13	○ Yes	○ No
14	○ Yes	○ No
10 + 3	○ Yes	○ No

DIRECTIONS 1–2. How many counters are there? Write the number.
3. Choose all the ways that show 12. **4.** Is this a way to write the number of flowers in the set? Choose Yes or No.

Assessment Options
Chapter Test

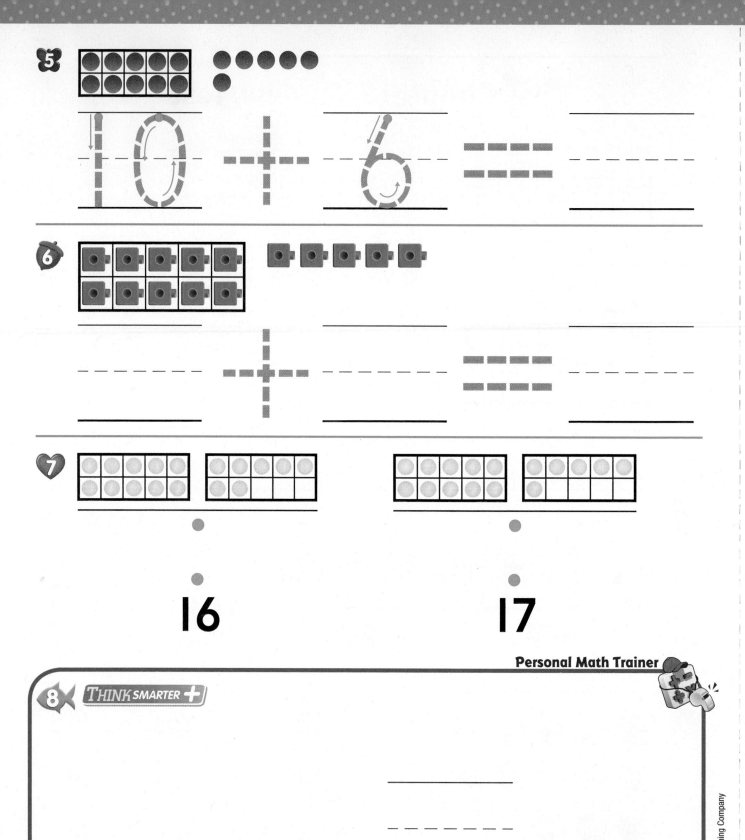

5 10 + 6 = _____

6 _____ + _____ = _____

7 • 16   • 17

8 THINK SMARTER +

_____

_____

_____ flowers

DIRECTIONS 5–6. Count how many. Write the number. Complete the addition sentence. **7.** Draw lines to match the ten frames to the numbers they show. **8.** Draw 8 yellow flowers and 7 red flowers. Circle a group of 10. How many flowers are there in all?

9

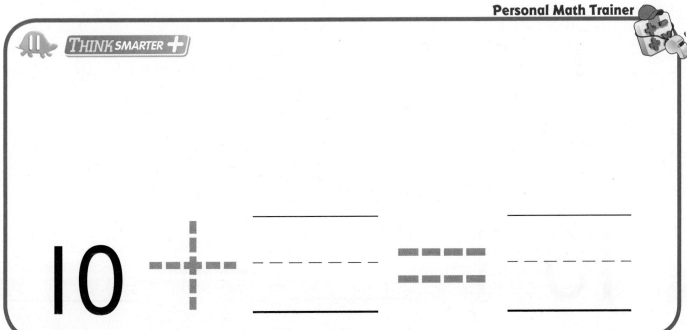

10 ones and

┌─────────┐
│ **8** │
│   │
│ **9** │
└─────────┘

ones

10

[ten frames with squares]

_____ + _____ **=** _____

_____

© Houghton Mifflin Harcourt Publishing Company • Image Credits: ©Stockbyte/Getty Images

Personal Math Trainer

11 THINK SMARTER +

10 + _____ **=** _____

DIRECTIONS   **9.** How many more ones are needed to show the number of peaches? Circle the number.   **10.** Look at the ten frames. Complete the addition sentence.   **11.** Ten people are sitting at one table. There are two extra people. How many people are there in all? Draw the table and the people. Complete the addition sentence.

Chapter 7

three hundred three **303**

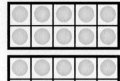

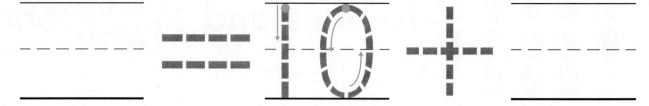

_____ = 10 + _____

11 = _____ + _____

10 + _____ = _____

DIRECTIONS **12.** What number do the ten frames show? Complete the addition sentence to show the number. **13.** Draw a set of 11 objects. Circle 10 of the objects. How many more objects are there? Complete the addition sentence to match. **14.** Carrie picked 14 apples. Draw the apples. Circle a group of 10 apples. Count the remaining apples. Complete the addition sentence.

Represent, Count, and Write 20 and Beyond

Curious About Math with

Curious George

Watermelon is actually a vegetable and not a fruit.

- How many seeds can you count on this watermelon?

Name _____

Explore Numbers to 10

Compare Numbers to 10

    _____      _____

___

Write Numbers to 10

    _____ _____   _____

3   6   8

This page checks understanding of important skills needed for success in Chapter 8.

DIRECTIONS 1. Circle all of the sets that show 9. 2. Circle all of the sets that show 8. 3. Count and tell how many. Write the number. Circle the number that is less. 4. Write the numbers in order as you count forward.

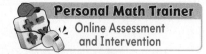

Personal Math Trainer
Online Assessment and Intervention

Vocabulary Builder

eighteen

fifteen

DIRECTIONS Point to each otter as you count. Point to the
number word that shows how many otters in all. How many are
wearing glasses? Write the number.

 • **Interactive Student Edition**
• **Multimedia eGlossary**

Chapter 8

Game

Who Has More?

Player 1

Player 2

DIRECTIONS Play with a partner. Each player shuffles a set of numeral cards and places them facedown in a stack. Each player turns over the top card on his or her stack and models that number by placing cube trains on the work space. Partners compare the cube trains. The player with the greater number keeps both of the numeral cards. If both numbers are the same, each player returns the card to the bottom of his or her stack. The player with the most cards at the end of the game wins.

MATERIALS 2 sets of numeral cards 11–20, cubes

Name _____

Model and Count 20

Essential Question How can you show and count 20 objects?

Counting and Cardinality—K.CC.5
Also K.CC.4a, K.CC.4b, K.CC.4c
MATHEMATICAL PRACTICES
MP.2, MP.5, MP.6

Listen and Draw

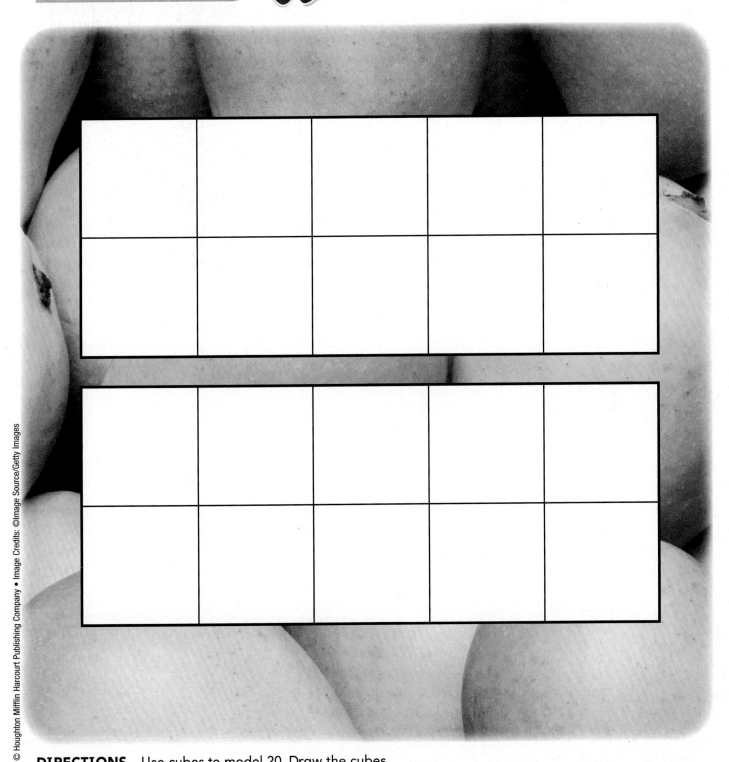

DIRECTIONS Use cubes to model 20. Draw the cubes.

Chapter 8 • Lesson 1

three hundred nine **309**

20
twenty

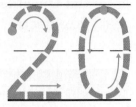

②

③

DIRECTIONS 1. Count and tell how many. Trace the number.
2. Use cubes to model the number 20. Draw the cubes. **3.** Use the
cubes from Exercise 2 to model ten-cube trains. Draw the cube trains.

4

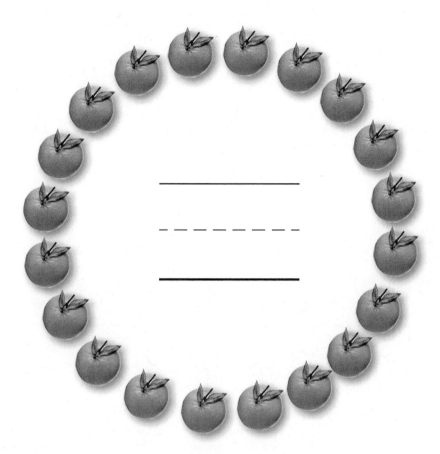

_____

- - - - - - - - - -

_____

5

_____

- - - - - - - - -

_____

DIRECTIONS **4–5.** Count and tell how many pieces of fruit.
Write the number. Tell a friend how you counted the oranges.

Problem Solving • Applications Real World

WRITE Math

6

7 _____   _____

_____   _____

8

_____

_____

_____

DIRECTIONS **6.** Lily makes a necklace with 20 beads. Circle to show the beads Lily uses to make her necklace. **7.** How many of each color bead did you circle? Write the numbers. Tell a friend about the number of each color beads. **8.** Draw and write to show what you know about 20. Tell a friend about your drawing.

HOME ACTIVITY • Draw two ten frames on a sheet of paper. Have your child show the number 20 by placing small objects, such as buttons or dried beans, in the ten frames.

312 three hundred twelve

FOR MORE PRACTICE:
Standards Practice Book

Name _____

Count and Write to 20

Essential Question How can you count and write up to 20 with words and numbers?

Counting and Cardinality—K.CC.3
Also K.CC.4b, K.CC.5
MATHEMATICAL PRACTICES
MP.2

Listen and Draw

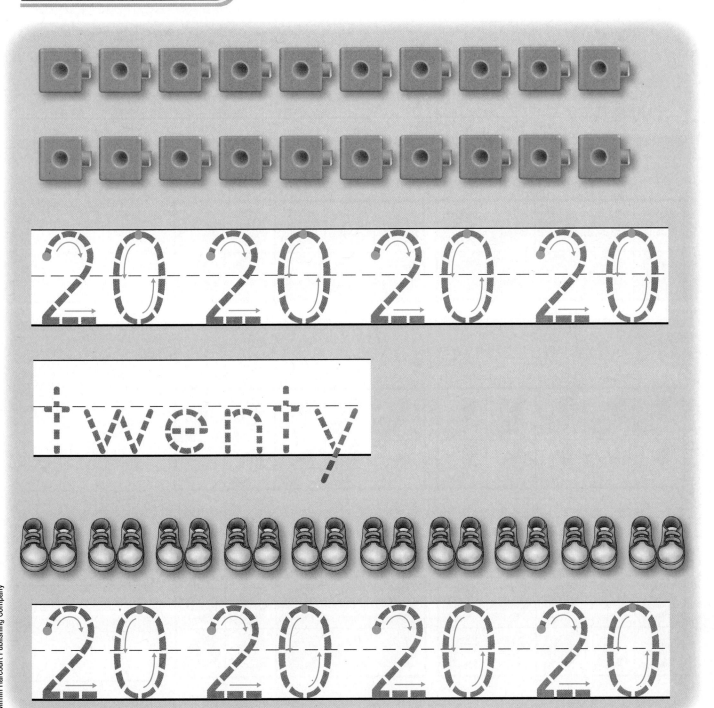

DIRECTIONS Count and tell how many cubes. Trace the numbers and the word. Count and tell how many shoes. Trace the numbers.

Chapter 8 • Lesson 2

three hundred thirteen **313**

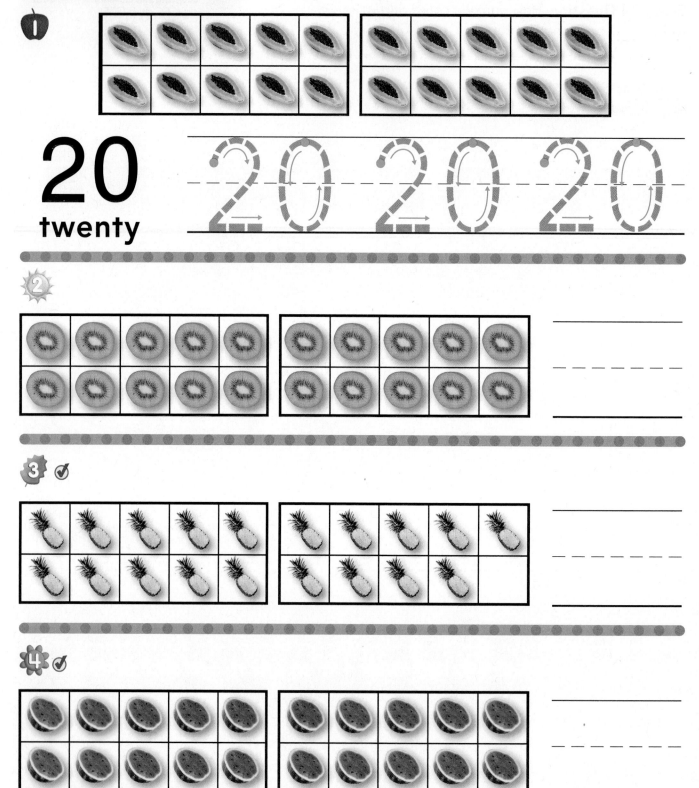

❶

20
twenty

20 20 20

❷

❸ ✓

❹ ✓

DIRECTIONS **1.** Count and tell how many pieces of fruit. Trace the numbers as you say them. **2–4.** Count and tell how many pieces of fruit. Write the number.

Name _____

5

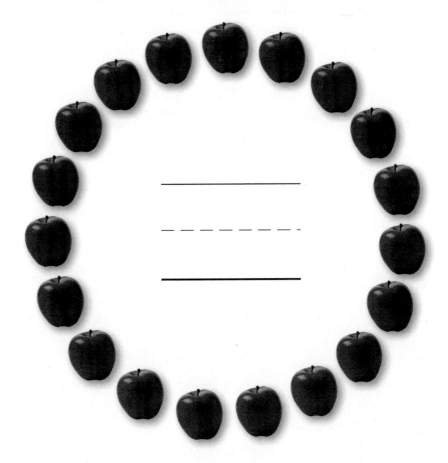

_____

- - - - - - -

_____

6

_____

- - - - - - -

_____

DIRECTIONS 5–6. Count and tell how many pieces of fruit. Write the number.

Problem Solving • Applications

WRITE Math

7

18

19

20

8

_____

_ _ _ _ _ _ _ _

_____

DIRECTIONS **7.** David served fruit at his party. Circle a number to show how many pieces of fruit he served. Draw more fruit to show that number. **8.** Draw a set of objects that has a number of objects one greater than 19. Write how many objects are in the set. Tell a friend about your drawing.

316 three hundred sixteen

HOME ACTIVITY • Have your child use small objects, such as pebbles or pasta pieces, to show the number 20. Then have him or her write the number on a piece of paper.

© Houghton Mifflin Harcourt Publishing Company • Image Credits: (kiwi) ©Digital Vision/Getty Images

FOR MORE PRACTICE:
Standards Practice Book

Name _____

Count and Order to 20

Essential Question How can you count forward to 20 from a given number?

**Counting and Cardinality—
K.CC.2**
MATHEMATICAL PRACTICES
MP.2

Listen and Draw

1 2 3 4 5 6 7 8 9 10 11 12 13 14 15 16 17 18 19 20

DIRECTIONS Draw a line under a number. Count forward to 20 from that number. Use the terms ***greater than*** and ***less than*** to compare and describe the order of numbers. Circle the number that is one greater than the number you underlined. Build cube trains to model the numbers you marked. Draw the cube trains. Circle the larger cube train.

Chapter 8 • Lesson 3

three hundred seventeen **317**

1 2 3 4 5 6 7 8 9 10 11 12 13 14 15 16 17 18 19 20

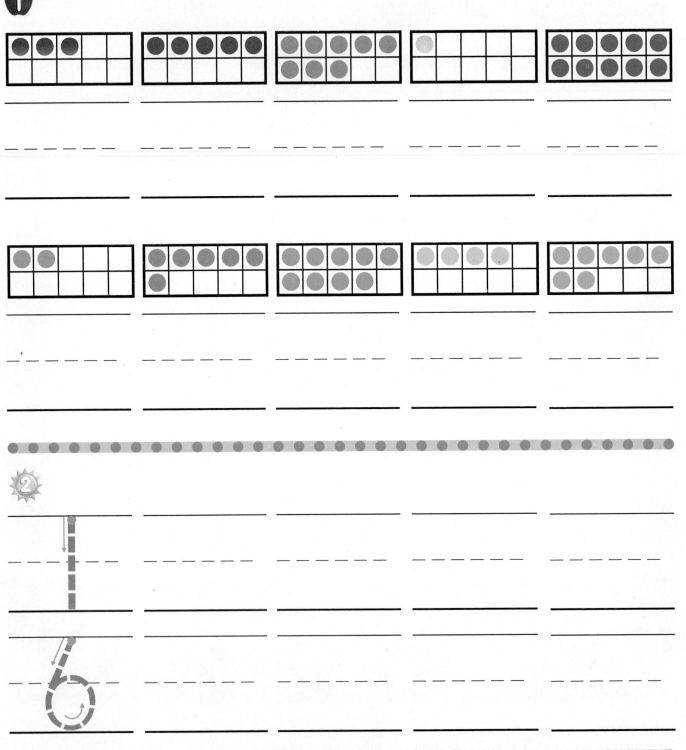

DIRECTIONS 1. Count the dots of each color in the ten frames. Write the numbers.   2. Trace and write those numbers in order.

318 three hundred eighteen

_____ _____ _____ _____ _____

_ _ _ _ _ _ _ _   _ _ _ _ _ _ _ _   _ _ _ _ _ _ _ _   _ _ _ _ _ _ _ _   _ _ _ _ _ _ _ _

_____ _____ _____ _____ _____

_____ _____ _____ _____ _____

_ _ _ _ _ _ _ _   _ _ _ _ _ _ _ _   _ _ _ _ _ _ _ _   _ _ _ _ _ _ _ _   _ _ _ _ _ _ _ _

_____ _____ _____ _____ _____

DIRECTIONS **3.** Count the dots of each color in the ten frames.
Write the numbers. **4.** Trace and write those numbers in order.

Chapter 8 • Lesson 3   three hundred nineteen **319**

Problem Solving • Applications Real World

WRITE
Math

5

1	2	———	4	5
6	7	8	9	———
11	———	13	14	15
16	17	———	19	20

DIRECTIONS 5. Write to show the numbers in order. Count forward to 20 from one of the numbers you wrote.

HOME ACTIVITY • Give your child a set of 11 objects, a set of 12 objects, and a set of 13 objects. Have him or her count the objects in each set and place the sets in order from smallest to largest.

FOR MORE PRACTICE:
Standards Practice Book

Name _____

Problem Solving • Compare Numbers to 20

Essential Question How can you solve problems using the strategy *make a model*?

Counting and Cardinality—K.CC.6
Also K.CC.7
MATHEMATICAL PRACTICES
MP.2, MP.4, MP.5

Unlock the Problem

DIRECTIONS Alma has a number of yellow cubes one greater than 15. Juan has a number of green cubes one less than 17. Show the cubes. Compare the sets of cubes. Draw the cubes. Tell a friend about your drawing.

Chapter 8 • Lesson 4

DIRECTIONS 1. Kiara has 18 apples. She has a number of apples two greater than Cristobal. Use cubes to model the sets of apples. Compare the sets. Which set is larger? Draw the cubes. Write how many in each set. Circle the greater number. Tell a friend how you compared the numbers.

Name _____

DIRECTIONS 2. Salome has 19 oranges. Zion has a number of oranges two less than Salome. Use cubes to model the sets of oranges. Compare the sets. Which set is smaller? Draw the cubes. Write how many in each set. Circle the number that is less. Tell a friend how you compared the numbers.

HOME ACTIVITY • Have your child count two sets of objects in your home, and write how many are in each set. Then have him or her circle the greater number. Repeat with sets of different numbers.

FOR MORE PRACTICE:
Standards Practice Book

Chapter 8 • Lesson 4

three hundred twenty-three **323**

Concepts and Skills

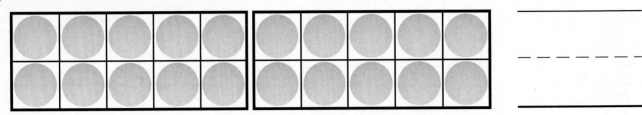

_____

- - - - - - - - - - - -

_____

_____

   - - - - - - - - - - - -      _____

_____   _____

③

_____   _____

   - - - - - - - - - - - -      - - - - - - - - - - - -

_____   _____

④ **THINK SMARTER**

15   16   17   18   19
**   20**

DIRECTIONS 1. Count and tell how many. Write the number. (K.CC.3)
2. Write how many pieces of fruit are in each picture. Circle the number
that is less. (K.CC.6)   **3.** Write how many pieces of fruit are in each picture.
Circle the number that is greater. (K.CC.6)   **4.** What number comes next in
counting order? Circle the number. (K.CC.3)

324 three hundred twenty-four

Name _____

Count to 50 by Ones

Essential Question How does the order of numbers help you count to 50 by ones?

Counting and Cardinality—K.CC.1
Also K.CC.2
MATHEMATICAL PRACTICES
MP.7, MP.8

Listen and Draw

1	2	3	4	5	6	7	8	9	10
11	12	13	14	15	16	17	18	19	20
21	22	23	24	25	26	27	28	29	30
31	32	33	34	35	36	37	38	39	40
41	42	43	44	45	46	47	48	49	50

DIRECTIONS Point to each number as you count to 50. Trace the circle around the number 50.

Chapter 8 • Lesson 5

three hundred twenty-five **325**

1	2	3	4	5	6	7	8	9	10
11	12	13	14	15	16	17	18	19	20
21	22	23	24	25	26	27	28	29	30
31	32	33	34	35	36	37	38	39	40
41	42	43	44	45	46	47	48	49	50

DIRECTIONS 1. Point to each number as you count to 50. Circle the number 15. Begin with 15 and count forward to 50. Draw a line under the number 50.

Name _____

1	2	3	4	5	6	7	8	9	10
11	12	13	14	15	16	17	18	19	20
21	22	23	24	25	26	27	28	29	30
31	32	33	34	35	36	37	38	39	40
41	42	43	44	45	46	47	48	49	50

DIRECTIONS **2.** Look away and point to any number. Circle that number. Count forward from that number. Draw a line under the number 50.

Problem Solving • Applications Real World

③ WRITE Math

1	2	3	4	5	6	7	8	9	10
11	12	13	14	15	16	17	18	19	20
21	22	23	24	25	26	27	28	29	30
31	32	33	34	35	36	37	38	39	40
41	42	43	44	45	46	47	48	49	50

DIRECTIONS 3. I am greater than 17 and less than 19. What number am I? Use blue to color that number. I am greater than 24 and less than 26. What number am I? Use red to color that number.

HOME ACTIVITY • Think of a number between 1 and 50. Say *greater than* and *less than* to describe your number. Have your child say the number.

328 three hundred twenty-eight

FOR MORE PRACTICE: Standards Practice Book

Name _____

Count to 100 by Ones

Essential Question How does the order of numbers help you count to 100 by ones?

Counting and Cardinality—K.CC.1
Also K.CC.2

MATHEMATICAL PRACTICES
MP.7, MP.8

Listen and Draw

1	2	3	4	5	6	7	8	9	10
11	12	13	14	15	16	17	18	19	20
21	22	23	24	25	26	27	28	29	30
31	32	33	34	35	36	37	38	39	40
41	42	43	44	45	46	47	48	49	50
51	52	53	54	55	56	57	58	59	60
61	62	63	64	65	66	67	68	69	70
71	72	73	74	75	76	77	78	79	80
81	82	83	84	85	86	87	88	89	90
91	92	93	94	95	96	97	98	99	100

DIRECTIONS Point to each number as you count to 100. Trace the circle around the number 100.

Chapter 8 • Lesson 6

three hundred twenty-nine **329**

1

1	2	3	4	5	6	7	8	9	10
11	12	13	14	15	16	17	18	19	20
21	22	23	24	25	26	27	28	29	30
31	32	33	34	35	36	37	38	39	40
41	42	43	44	45	46	47	48	49	50
51	52	53	54	55	56	57	58	59	60
61	62	63	64	65	66	67	68	69	70
71	72	73	74	75	76	77	78	79	80
81	82	83	84	85	86	87	88	89	90
91	92	93	94	95	96	97	98	99	100

DIRECTIONS 1. Point to each number as you count to 100. Circle the number 11. Begin with 11 and count forward to 100. Draw a line under the number 100.

1	2	3	4	5	6	7	8	9	10
11	12	13	14	15	16	17	18	19	20
21	22	23	24	25	26	27	28	29	30
31	32	33	34	35	36	37	38	39	40
41	42	43	44	45	46	47	48	49	50
51	52	53	54	55	56	57	58	59	60
61	62	63	64	65	66	67	68	69	70
71	72	73	74	75	76	77	78	79	80
81	82	83	84	85	86	87	88	89	90
91	92	93	94	95	96	97	98	99	100

DIRECTIONS **2.** Point to each number as you count to 100. Look away and point to any number. Circle that number. Count forward to 100 from that number. Draw a line under the number 100.

Problem Solving • Applications

③

1	2	3	4	------	6	7	8	9	10
11	12	13	------	**15**	------	17	18	19	20
21	22	23	24	25	26	27	28	29	30

DIRECTIONS 3. Place your finger on the number 15. Write or trace to show the numbers that are "neighbors" to the number 15. Say *greater than* and *less than* to describe the numbers. **4.** Draw to show what you know about some other "neighbor" numbers in the chart.

HOME ACTIVITY • Show your child a calendar. Point to a number on the calendar. Have him or her tell you all the numbers that are "neighbors" to that number.

332 three hundred thirty-two

FOR MORE PRACTICE: Standards Practice Book

Name _____

Count to 100 by Tens

Essential Question How can you count to 100 by tens on a hundred chart?

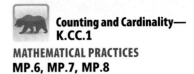

Counting and Cardinality—K.CC.1

MATHEMATICAL PRACTICES
MP.6, MP.7, MP.8

Listen and Draw

1	2	3	4	5	6	7	8	9	10
11	12	13	14	15	16	17	18	19	20
21	22	23	24	25	26	27	28	29	30
31	32	33	34	35	36	37	38	39	40
41	42	43	44	45	46	47	48	49	50
51	52	53	54	55	56	57	58	59	60
61	62	63	64	65	66	67	68	69	70
71	72	73	74	75	76	77	78	79	80
81	82	83	84	85	86	87	88	89	90
91	92	93	94	95	96	97	98	99	100

DIRECTIONS Trace the circles around the numbers that end in a 0. Beginning with 10, count those numbers in order. Tell a friend how you are counting.

1	2	3	4	5	6	7	8	9	
11	12	13	14	15	16	17	18	19	
21	22	23	24	25	26	27	28	29	30
31	32	33	34	35	36	37	38	39	40
41	42	43	44	45	46	47	48	49	50

DIRECTIONS I. Write the numbers to complete the counting order to 20. Trace the numbers to complete the counting order to 50. Count by tens as you point to the numbers you wrote and traced.

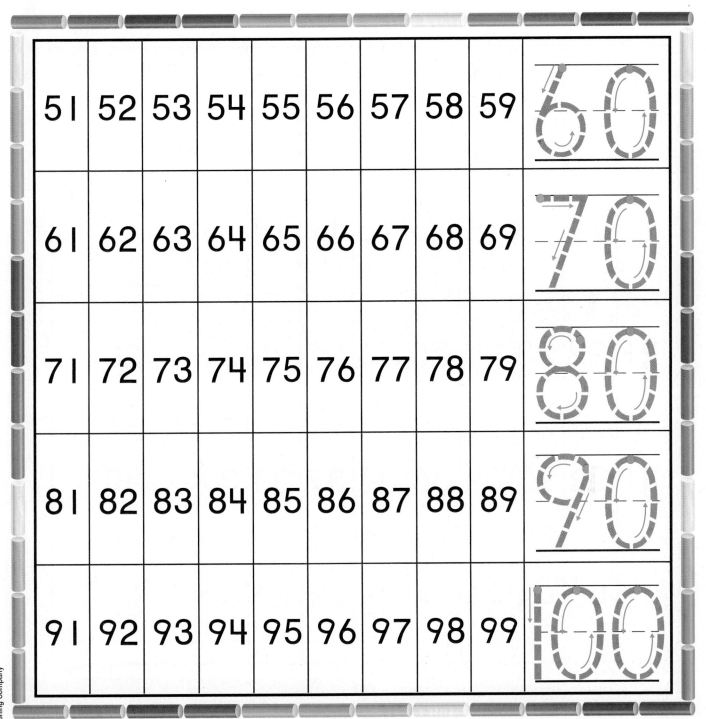

51	52	53	54	55	56	57	58	59	60
61	62	63	64	65	66	67	68	69	70
71	72	73	74	75	76	77	78	79	80
81	82	83	84	85	86	87	88	89	90
91	92	93	94	95	96	97	98	99	100

DIRECTIONS 2. Trace the numbers to complete the counting order to 100. Count by tens as you point to the numbers you traced.

Problem Solving • Applications

WRITE
Math

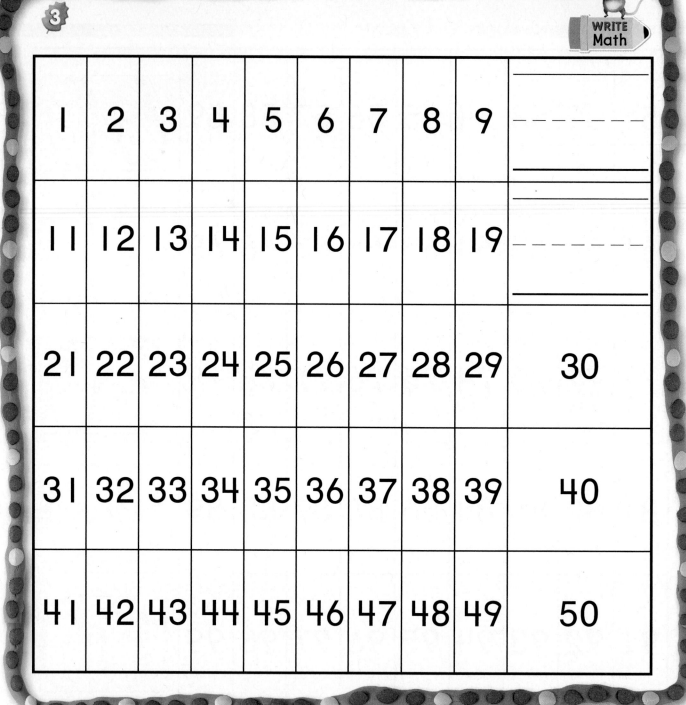

1	2	3	4	5	6	7	8	9	
11	12	13	14	15	16	17	18	19	
21	22	23	24	25	26	27	28	29	30
31	32	33	34	35	36	37	38	39	40
41	42	43	44	45	46	47	48	49	50

DIRECTIONS **3.** Antonio has 10 marbles. Write the number in order. Jasmine has ten more marbles than Antonio. Write that number in order. Lin has ten more marbles than Jasmine. Draw a line under the number that shows how many marbles Lin has. When counting by tens, what number comes right after 40? Circle the number.

HOME ACTIVITY • Show your child a calendar. Use pieces of paper to cover the numbers that end in 0. Ask your child to say the numbers that are covered. Then have him or her remove the pieces of paper to check.

336 three hundred thirty-six

FOR MORE PRACTICE:
Standards Practice Book

Name _____

Count by Tens

Essential Question How can you use sets of tens to count to 100?

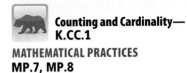

Listen and Draw Real World

DIRECTIONS Point to each set of cube towers as you count by tens. Trace the numbers as you count by tens.

Chapter 8 • Lesson 8

© Houghton Mifflin Harcourt Publishing Company • Image Credits: ©Artville/Getty Images

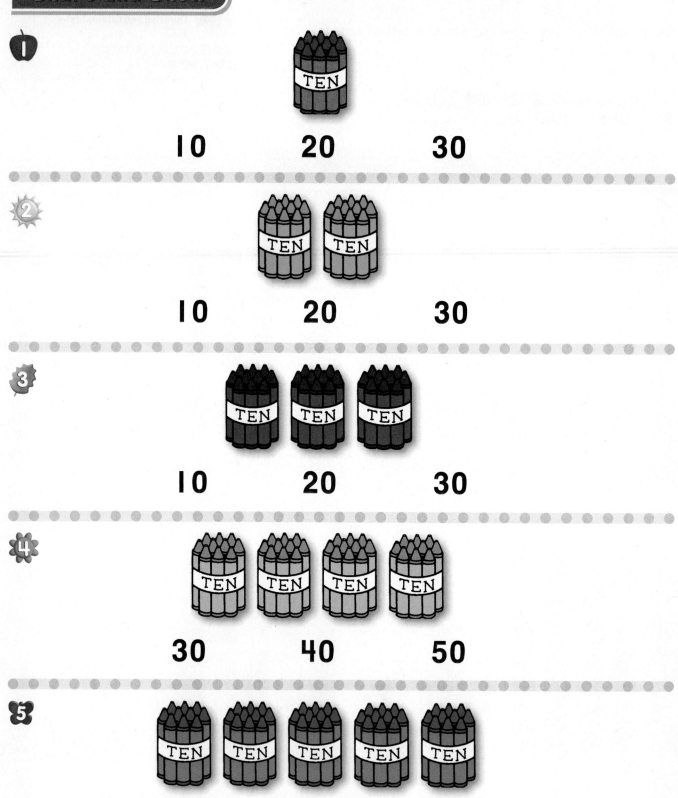

1 10 20 30

2 10 20 30

3 10 20 30

4 30 40 50

5 30 40 50

DIRECTIONS 1–5. Point to each set of 10 as you count by tens.
Circle the number that shows how many.

Name _____

6 ✓

60　　　　**70**　　　　**80**

7 ✓

60　　　　**70**　　　　**80**

8

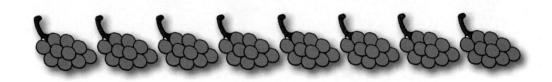

80　　　　**90**　　　　**100**

9

80　　　　**90**　　　　**100**

10

80　　　　**90**　　　　**100**

DIRECTIONS 6–10. Point to each set of 10 as you count by tens.
Circle the number that shows how many.

Problem Solving • Applications

WRITE Math

DIRECTIONS 11. Circle sets of 10 stars. Count the sets of stars by tens.

HOME ACTIVITY • Give your child some coins or buttons and ten cups. Ask him or her to place ten coins into each cup. Then have him or her point to each cup as he or she counts by tens to 100.

340 three hundred forty

FOR MORE PRACTICE: Standards Practice Book

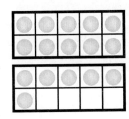 **Chapter 8 Review/Test**

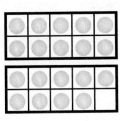 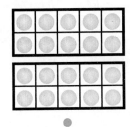

1

20   19   16

2

_____

- - - - - - - - - -

_____

3   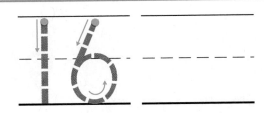 ____ 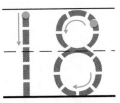 ____

DIRECTIONS   1. Match the ten frames to the numbers that tell how many
counters.   **2.** Sandy has 20 beads. Circle how many beads she has. Write the number
of beads.   **3.** Start with 16. Count forward. Trace and write the numbers in order.

18

○   ○   ○   ○

5

31	32	33	34	35	36	37	38	39	40
41	42	43	44	45	46	47	48	49	50

6

94   95   96   97   98   99 | 90 |
                               | 100 |

DIRECTIONS   4. Choose all the sets with a number of watermelons less than 18.   **5.** Begin with 31. Point to each number as you count. Draw a line under the last number counted.   **6.** Point to each number as you count. Circle the number that comes next in counting order.

| 81 | 82 | 83 | 84 | 85 | 86 | 87 | 88 | 89 | 90 |
| 91 | 92 | 93 | 94 | 95 | 96 | 97 | 98 | 99 | 100 |

8

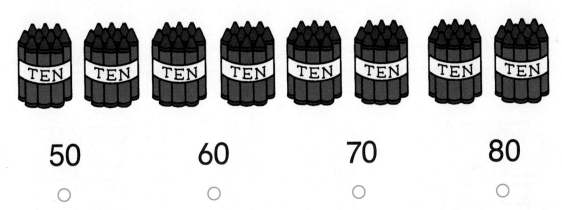

50   60   70   80

○   ○   ○   ○

Personal Math Trainer

9 THINK SMARTER ➕

_____

_ _ _ _ _ _ _ _

_____

DIRECTIONS **7.** Circle the numbers that end in a zero. **8.** Count the crayons by tens. Mark under the number that shows how many. **9.** Dexter has 20 pencils. He has a number of pencils 1 greater than Jane. Draw the number of pencils Jane has. Write the number.

13	14	15	Yes	No
11	15	12	Yes	No
16	17	18	Yes	No

10 ___ 30 40 50

Personal Math Trainer

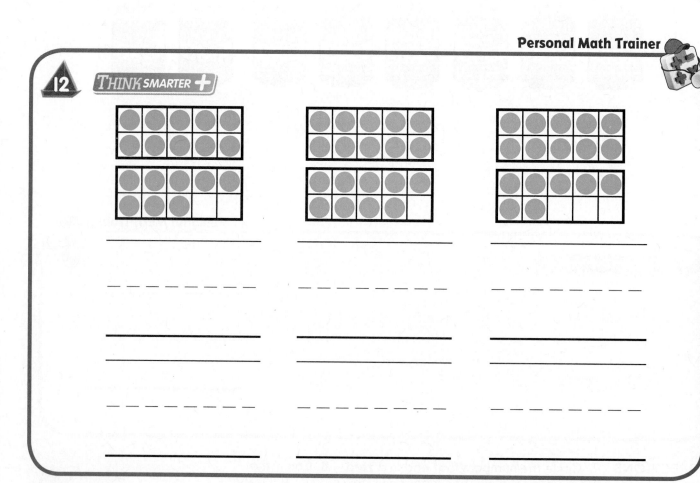

DIRECTIONS 10. Are the numbers in counting order? Circle Yes or No. 11. Count by tens. Trace and write to complete the counting order. 12. What number does each set of counters show? Write the numbers. Then write the numbers in counting order.

344 three hundred forty-four

School Fun

written by Ann Dickson

 **CRITICAL AREA** Describing shapes and space

1. Sign in.

2. Put your book bag away.

3. Choose a center.

Here is my classroom. Come on in.

Learning time is about to begin.

Social Studies

Why do we have rules?

These are the book bags

we hang by our names.

Circle the ones that look the same.

Social Studies

Why do we need to take turns?

Here are the books. We read them all!

Which books are big?

Which books are small?

Social Studies

Why do we help others?

Here are markers of every kind.

Name all of the colors that you can find.

Social Studies

Why do we put things away?

Our blocks and toys are over there.

Which shapes are round?

Which shapes are square?

Social Studies

Why do we share?

Write About the Story

Vocabulary Review
alike
different

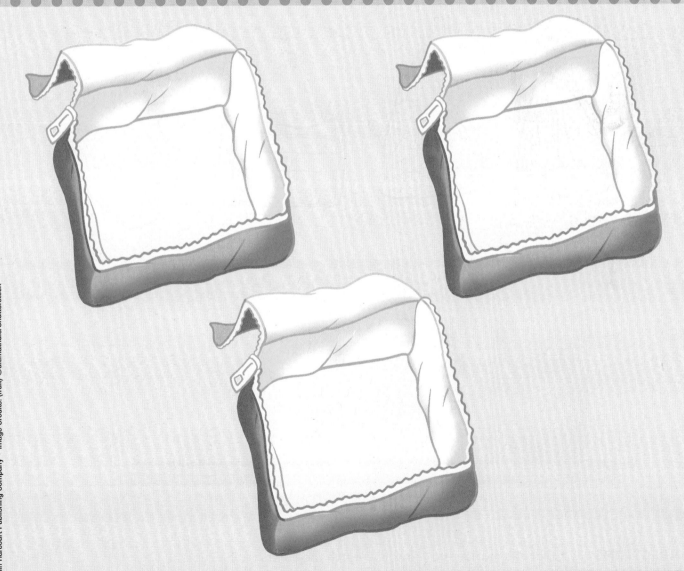

DIRECTIONS These lunch boxes are alike. In one lunch box draw something that you like to eat. Now circle the lunch box that is different.

Alike and Different

1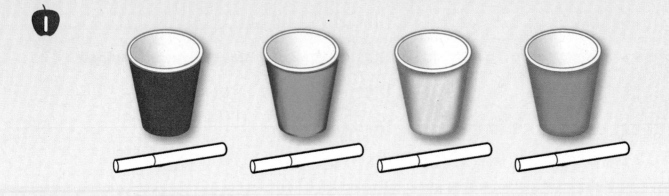

2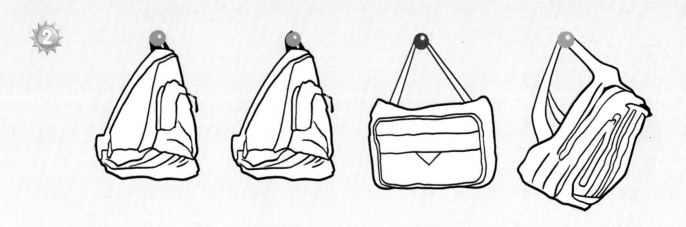

3

DIRECTIONS I. Color the markers so that they match the colors of the cups. 2. Color the book bags that are alike by shape. 3. This classroom needs some books. Draw a book that is a different size.

Identify and Describe Two-Dimensional Shapes

Curious About Math with

Curious George

The sails on these boats are shaped like a triangle.

- How many stripes can you count on the first sail?

96728

Name _____

 Show What You Know ✓

Shape

 1

 |

 2

 |

 3

 |

Count Objects

 4

_____

- - - - - - -

_____

 5

_____

- - - - - - -

_____

 6

_____

- - - - - - -

_____

This page checks understanding of important skills needed for success in Chapter 9.

DIRECTIONS 1–3. Look at the shape at the beginning of the row. Mark an X on the shape that is alike. 4–6. Count and tell how many. Write the number.

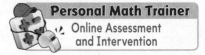 **Personal Math Trainer**
Online Assessment
and Intervention

Name _____

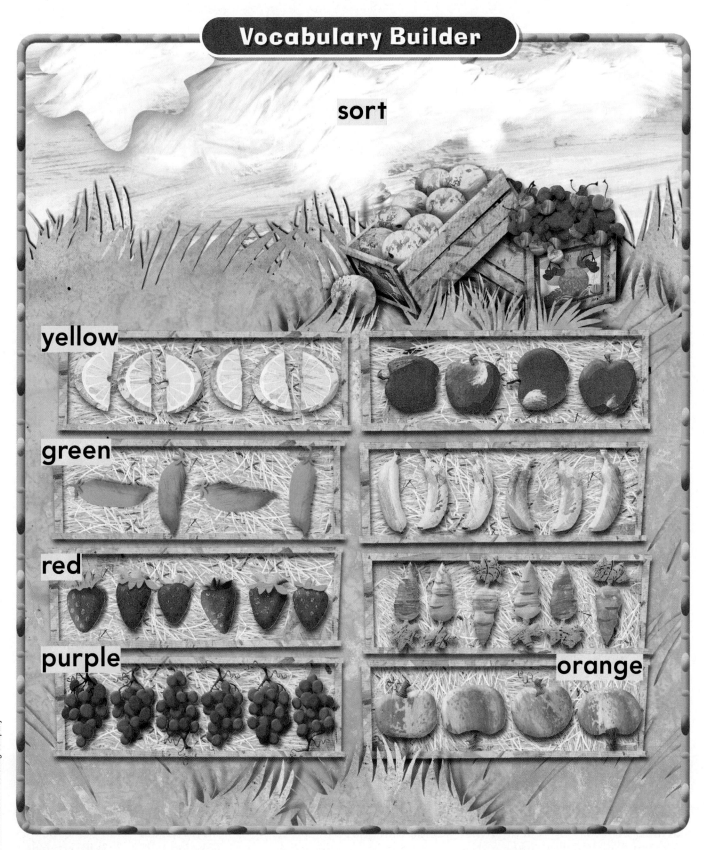

Vocabulary Builder

sort

yellow

green

red

purple

orange

DIRECTIONS Circle the box that is sorted by green vegetables. Mark an X on the box that is sorted by purple fruit.

 • **Interactive Student Edition**
• **Multimedia** *eGlossary*

Number Picture

DIRECTIONS Play with a partner. Decide who goes first. Toss the number cube. Color a shape in the picture that matches the number rolled. A player misses a turn if a number is rolled and all shapes with that number are colored. Continue until all shapes in the picture are colored.

MATERIALS number cube (labeled 1, 2, 2, 3, 3, 4), crayons

356 three hundred fifty-six

Name _____

Identify and Name Circles

Essential Question How can you identify and name circles?

 Geometry—K.G.2

MATHEMATICAL PRACTICES
MP.5, MP.6, MP.7

Listen and Draw Real World Hands On

circles	not circles

DIRECTIONS Place two-dimensional shapes on the page. Identify and name the circles. Sort the shapes by circles and not circles. Trace and color the shapes on the sorting mat.

Chapter 9 • Lesson 1 three hundred fifty-seven **357**

1

DIRECTIONS 1. Mark an X on all of the circles.

Name _____

DIRECTIONS 2. Color the circles in the picture.

Chapter 9 • Lesson 1   three hundred fifty-nine **359**

Problem Solving • Applications

3

4

© Houghton Mifflin Harcourt Publishing Company

DIRECTIONS **3.** Neville puts his shapes in a row. Which shape is a circle? Mark an X on that shape. **4.** Draw to show what you know about circles. Tell a friend about your drawing.

HOME ACTIVITY • Have your child show you an object that is shaped like a circle.

360 three hundred sixty

FOR MORE PRACTICE:
Standards Practice Book

Name _____

Describe Circles

Essential Question How can you describe circles?

Geometry—K.G.4

MATHEMATICAL PRACTICES
MP.5, MP.7

Listen and Draw Real World

curve

DIRECTIONS Use your finger to trace around the circle.
Talk about the curve. Trace around the curve.

Chapter 9 • Lesson 2

1

circle

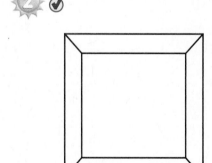

DIRECTIONS 1. Use your finger to trace around the circle. Trace the curve around the circle. 2. Color the object that is shaped like a circle.

3

DIRECTIONS 3. Use a pencil to hold one end of a large paper clip on one of the dots in the center of the page. Place another pencil in the other end of the paper clip. Move the pencil around to draw a circle.

Problem Solving • Applications

4

DIRECTIONS 4. I have a curve. What shape am I? Draw the shape. Tell a friend the name of the shape.

HOME ACTIVITY • Have your child describe a circle.

FOR MORE PRACTICE: Standards Practice Book

Name _____

Identify and Name Squares

Essential Question How can you identify and name squares?

Geometry—K.G.2

MATHEMATICAL PRACTICES
MP.5, MP.6, MP.7

squares	not squares

DIRECTIONS Place two-dimensional shapes on the page. Identify and name the squares. Sort the shapes by squares and not squares. Trace and color the shapes on the sorting mat.

Chapter 9 • Lesson 3

DIRECTIONS 1. Mark an X on all of the squares.

DIRECTIONS 2. Color the squares in the picture.

Problem Solving • Applications

WRITE Math

3

4

DIRECTIONS **3.** Dennis drew these shapes. Which shapes are squares? Mark an X on those shapes. **4.** Draw to show what you know about squares. Tell a friend about your drawing.

HOME ACTIVITY • Have your child show you an object that is shaped like a square.

368 three hundred sixty-eight

FOR MORE PRACTICE:
Standards Practice Book

Name _____

Describe Squares

Essential Question How can you describe squares?

Geometry—K.G.4

MATHEMATICAL PRACTICES
MP.2, MP.7, MP.8

Listen and Draw

vertex

side

DIRECTIONS Use your finger to trace around the square. Talk about the number of sides and the number of vertices. Draw an arrow pointing to another vertex. Trace around the sides.

Chapter 9 • Lesson 4

three hundred sixty-nine **369**

square

1. ☑ _____

   ___ vertices

2. ☀ ☑ _____

   ___ sides

DIRECTIONS 1. Place a counter on each corner, or vertex. Write how many corners, or vertices. 2. Trace around the sides. Write how many sides.

DIRECTIONS 3. Draw and color a square.

Problem Solving • Applications

WRITE Math

4

DIRECTIONS 4. I have 4 sides of equal length and 4 vertices. What shape am I? Draw the shape. Tell a friend the name of the shape.

HOME ACTIVITY • Have your child describe a square.

FOR MORE PRACTICE: Standards Practice Book

Name _____

Identify and Name Triangles

Essential Question How can you identify and name triangles?

Geometry—K.G.2

MATHEMATICAL PRACTICES
MP.5, MP.6, MP.7

Listen and Draw

triangles	not triangles

DIRECTIONS Place two-dimensional shapes on the page. Identify and name the triangles. Sort the shapes by triangles and not triangles. Trace and color the shapes on the sorting mat.

three hundred seventy-three **373**

1

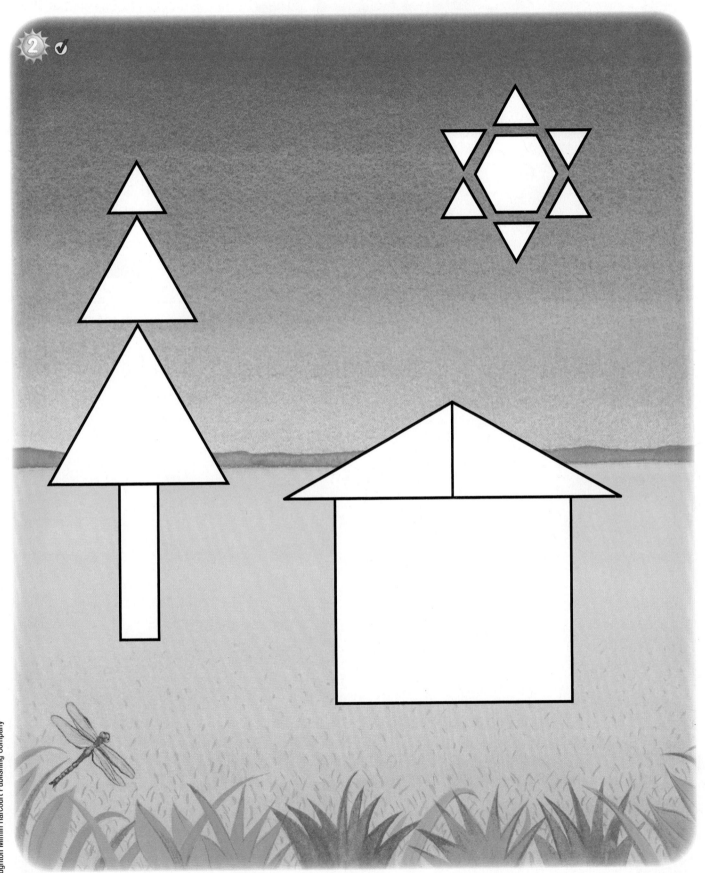

DIRECTIONS 2. Color the triangles in the picture.

Problem Solving • Applications

WRITE Math

3

4

DIRECTIONS 3. Anita put her shapes in a row. Which shapes are triangles? Mark an X on those shapes. 4. Draw to show what you know about triangles. Tell a friend about your drawing.

HOME ACTIVITY • Have your child show you an object that is shaped like a triangle.

376 three hundred seventy-six

FOR MORE PRACTICE:
Standards Practice Book

Name _____

Describe Triangles

Essential Question How can you describe triangles?

Geometry—K.G.4

MATHEMATICAL PRACTICES
MP.2, MP.7, MP.8

Listen and Draw

vertex

side

DIRECTIONS Use your finger to trace around the triangle. Talk about the number of sides and the number of vertices. Draw an arrow pointing to another vertex. Trace around the sides.

Chapter 9 • Lesson 6

three hundred seventy-seven **377**

triangle

 _____ **vertices**

_____ **sides**

DIRECTIONS 1. Place a counter on each corner, or vertex. Write how many corners, or vertices. 2. Trace around the sides. Write how many sides.

Name _____

DIRECTIONS 3. Draw and color a triangle.

HOME ACTIVITY • Have your child describe a triangle.

FOR MORE PRACTICE:
Standards Practice Book

Concepts and Skills

1

_ _ _ _ _ _ _
——————— sides

———————
_ _ _ _ _ _ _

_ _ _ _ _ _ _
——————— vertices

2

_ _ _ _ _ _ _
——————— sides

———————
_ _ _ _ _ _ _

_ _ _ _ _ _ _
——————— vertices

3

circle   square   triangle

DIRECTIONS **1–2.** Trace around each side. Write how many sides. Place a counter on each corner or vertex. Write how many vertices. **(K.G.4)** **3.** Draw lines to match the shape to its name. **(K.G.2)**

380 three hundred eighty

Identify and Name Rectangles

Essential Question How can you
identify and name rectangles?

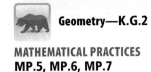

Geometry—K.G.2

MATHEMATICAL PRACTICES
MP.5, MP.6, MP.7

rectangles	not rectangles

DIRECTIONS Place two-dimensional shapes on the page. Identify
and name the rectangles. Sort the shapes by rectangles and not
rectangles. Trace and color the shapes on the sorting mat.

Chapter 9 • Lesson 7

1

DIRECTIONS I. Mark an X on all of the rectangles.

Name _____

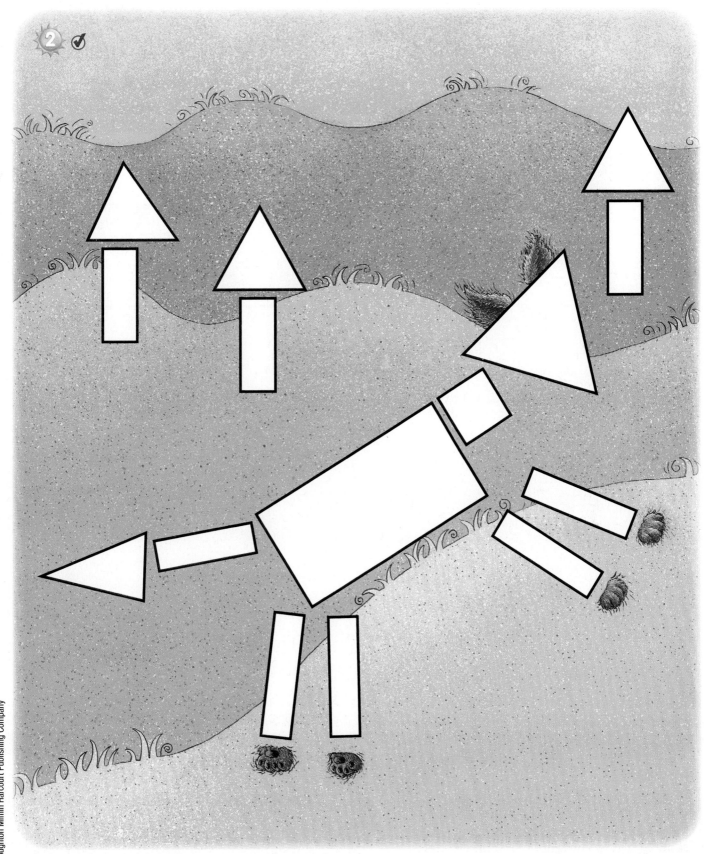

DIRECTIONS 2. Color the rectangles in the picture.

© Houghton Mifflin Harcourt Publishing Company

Problem Solving • Applications Real World

3

WRITE Math

4

DIRECTIONS **3.** Max looked at his shapes. Which of his shapes are rectangles? Mark an X on those shapes. **4.** Draw to show what you know about rectangles. Tell a friend about your drawing.

HOME ACTIVITY • Have your child show you an object that is shaped like a rectangle.

FOR MORE PRACTICE:
Standards Practice Book

Name _____

Describe Rectangles

Essential Question How can you describe rectangles?

Geometry—K.G.4

MATHEMATICAL PRACTICES
MP.2, MP.7, MP.8

Listen and Draw

side

vertex

DIRECTIONS Use your finger to trace around the rectangle. Talk about the number of sides and the number of vertices. Draw an arrow pointing to another vertex. Trace around the sides.

three hundred eighty-five **385**

rectangle

 ____

____ **vertices**

2 ____

____ **sides**

DIRECTIONS 1. Place a counter on each corner, or vertex.
Write how many corners, or vertices. 2. Trace around the sides.
Write how many sides.

DIRECTIONS 3. Draw and color a rectangle.

Problem Solving • Applications

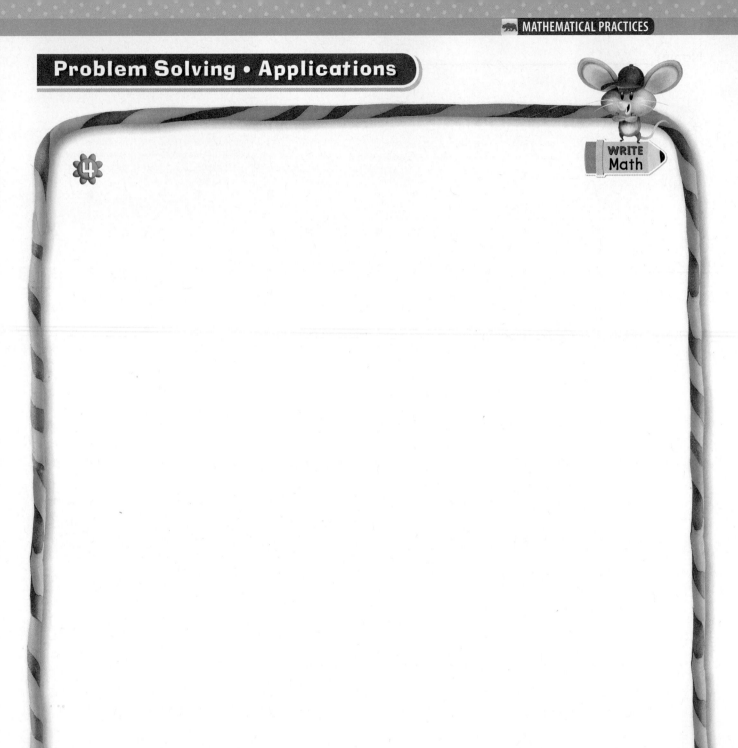

4

DIRECTIONS 4. I have 4 sides and 4 vertices. What shape am I? Draw the shape. Tell a friend the name of the shape.

HOME ACTIVITY • Have your child describe a rectangle.

FOR MORE PRACTICE:
Standards Practice Book

Name _____

Identify and Name Hexagons

Essential Question How can you identify and name hexagons?

 Geometry—K.G.2

MATHEMATICAL PRACTICES
MP.5, MP.6, MP.7

Listen and Draw Real World   Hands On

hexagons	not hexagons

DIRECTIONS Place two-dimensional shapes on the page. Identify and name the hexagons. Sort the shapes by hexagons and not hexagons. Trace and color the shapes on the sorting mat.

Chapter 9 • Lesson 9

three hundred eighty-nine **389**

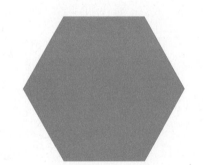

DIRECTIONS 1. Mark an X on all of the hexagons.

Name _____

DIRECTIONS 2. Color the hexagons in the picture.

Problem Solving • Applications Real World

WRITE Math

3

4

© Houghton Mifflin Harcourt Publishing Company

DIRECTIONS 3. Ryan is looking at his shapes. Which of his shapes are hexagons? Mark an X on those shapes. **4.** Draw to show what you know about hexagons. Tell a friend about your drawing.

HOME ACTIVITY • Draw some shapes on a page. Include several hexagons. Have your child circle the hexagons.

FOR MORE PRACTICE: Standards Practice Book

Name _____

Describe Hexagons

Essential Question How can you describe hexagons?

Geometry—K.G.4

MATHEMATICAL PRACTICES
MP.2, MP.7, MP.8

Listen and Draw

vertex

side

DIRECTIONS Use your finger to trace around the hexagon.
Talk about the number of sides and the number of vertices. Draw
an arrow pointing to another vertex. Trace around the sides.

Chapter 9 • Lesson 10

three hundred ninety-three **393**

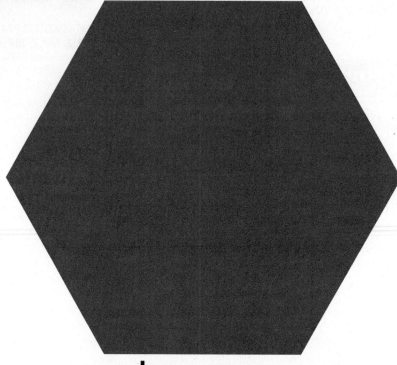

hexagon

_____ vertices

_____ sides

DIRECTIONS 1. Place a counter on each corner, or vertex. Write how many corners, or vertices. 2. Trace around the sides. Write how many sides.

DIRECTIONS 3. Draw and color a hexagon.

Problem Solving • Applications

WRITE
Math

4

DIRECTIONS 4. I have 6 sides and 6 vertices. What shape am I? Draw the shape. Tell a friend the name of the shape.

HOME ACTIVITY • Have your child describe a hexagon.

FOR MORE PRACTICE:
Standards Practice Book

Name _____

Algebra • Compare Two-Dimensional Shapes

Essential Question How can you use the words *alike* and *different* to compare two-dimensional shapes?

 Geometry—K.G.4

MATHEMATICAL PRACTICES
MP.5, MP.7, MP.8

Listen and Draw

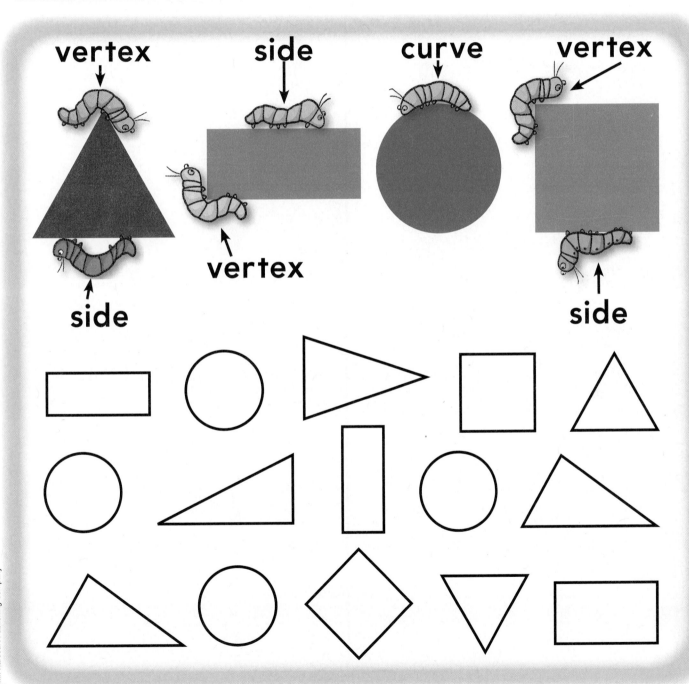

DIRECTIONS Look at the worms and the shapes. Use the words *alike* and *different* to compare the shapes. Use green to color the shapes with four vertices and four sides. Use blue to color the shapes with curves. Use red to color the shapes with three vertices and three sides.

1

alike	different

DIRECTIONS 1. Place two-dimensional shapes on the page. Sort the shapes by the number of vertices. Draw the shapes on the sorting mat. Use the words *alike* and *different* to tell how you sorted the shapes.

Name _____

alike	different

DIRECTIONS **2.** Place two-dimensional shapes on the page. Sort the shapes by the number of sides. Draw the shapes on the sorting mat. Use the words *alike* and *different* to tell how you sorted the shapes.

Problem Solving • Applications

WRITE
Math

3

4

curve	no curve

© Houghton Mifflin Harcourt Publishing Company

DIRECTIONS 3. I have a curve. What shape am I? Draw the shape. **4.** Draw to show shapes sorted by curves and no curves.

HOME ACTIVITY • Describe a shape and ask your child to name the shape that you are describing.

FOR MORE PRACTICE:
Standards Practice Book

Name _____

Problem Solving • Draw to Join Shapes

Essential Question How can you solve problems using the strategy *draw a picture*?

 Geometry—K.G.6

MATHEMATICAL PRACTICES
MP.5, MP.7, MP.8

 Unlock the Problem

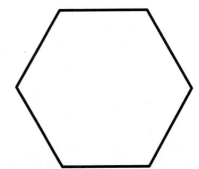

DIRECTIONS How can you join triangles to make the shapes? Draw and color the triangles.

Chapter 9 • Lesson 12

four hundred one **401**

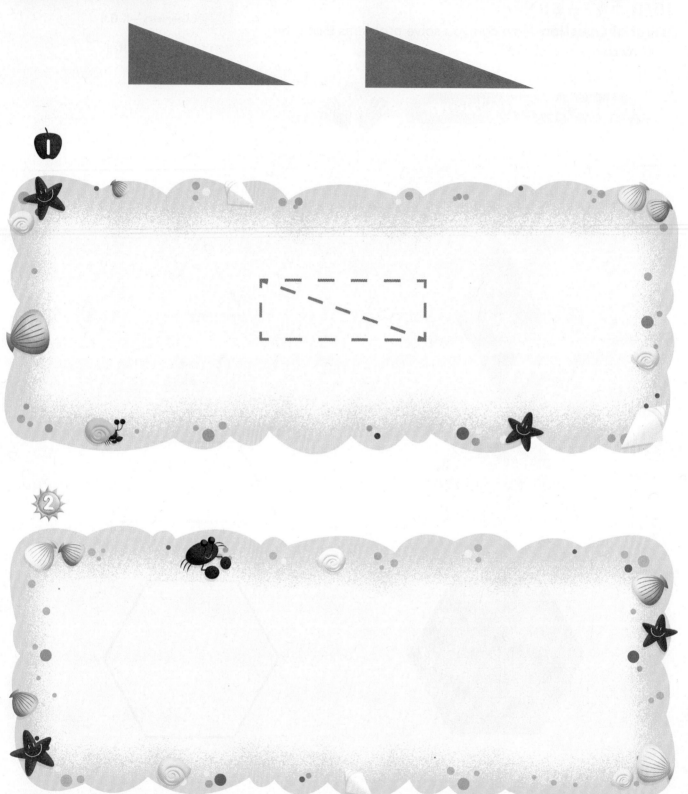

1

2

DIRECTIONS **1.** How can you join the two triangles to make a rectangle? Trace around the triangles to draw the rectangle. **2.** How can you join the two triangles to make a larger triangle? Use the triangle shapes to draw a larger triangle.

Name _____

3

4 ✓

DIRECTIONS **3.** How can you join some of the squares to make a larger square? Use the square shapes to draw a larger square. **4.** How can you join some or all of the squares to make a rectangle? Use the square shapes to draw a rectangle.

On Your Own

WRITE Math

DIRECTIONS **5.** Can you join these shapes to make a hexagon? Use the shapes to draw a hexagon. **6.** Which shapes could you join to make the larger shape? Draw and color to show the shapes you used.

HOME ACTIVITY • Have your child join shapes to form a larger shape, and then tell you about the shape.

404 four hundred four

FOR MORE PRACTICE:
Standards Practice Book

Chapter 9 Review/Test

1

        ○ Yes   ○ No

        ○ Yes   ○ No

        ○ Yes   ○ No

2

    ○   ○   ○   ○

3

_____
- - - - - -
_____ **squares**

DIRECTIONS 1. Is the shape a circle? Choose Yes or No. **2.** Mark under all the shapes that have curves. **3.** How many squares are in the picture? Write the number.

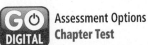

_____

\- \- \- \- \-

_____ **sides**

5

○   ○   ○   ○

Personal Math Trainer

6 THINK SMARTER ✚

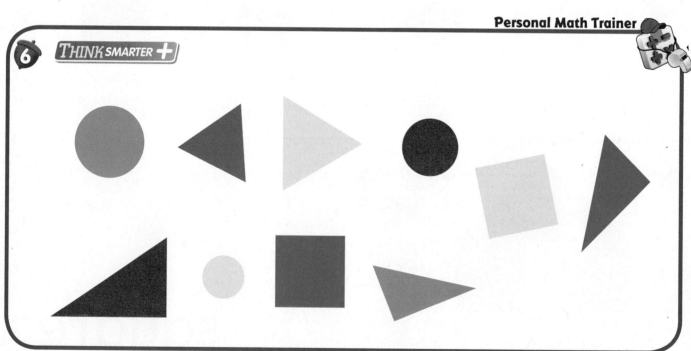

DIRECTIONS **4.** Look at the square. Write the number of sides on a square. **5.** Mark under all of the shapes that are triangles. **6.** Mark an X on each shape that has 3 sides and 3 vertices.

406 four hundred six

Name _____

7

8 THINK SMARTER +   Personal Math Trainer

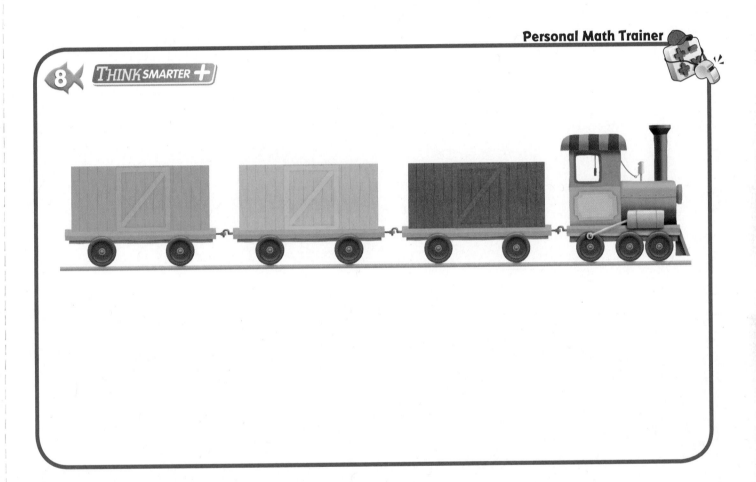

9

DIRECTIONS 7. Mark an X on the shape that is not a rectangle. **8.** Draw a shape that is the same as the boxcars on the train. **9.** Mark an X on all of the hexagons.

4 sides   **3 sides**   **6 sides**

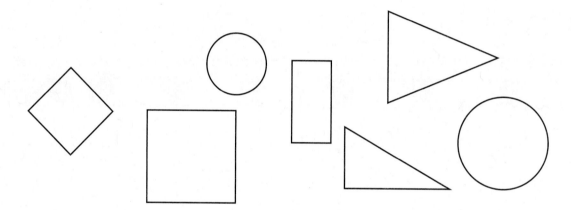

Personal Math Trainer

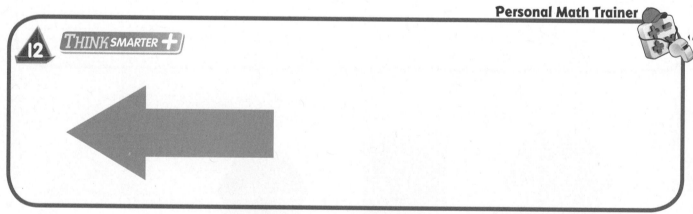

$\boxed{12}$ **THINK** SMARTER +

DIRECTIONS **10.** Match the shape to the number with that many sides. **11.** Look at the shapes. Compare them to see how they are alike and how they are different. Use red to color the shapes with four sides. Use green to color the shapes with curves. Use blue to color the shapes with three vertices. **12.** Draw the two shapes used to make the arrow.

Identify and Describe Three-Dimensional Shapes

Curious About Math with Curious George

Many of the shapes in our environment are three-dimensional shapes.

Name some of the shapes you see in this picture.

Show What You Know ✓

Identify Shapes

 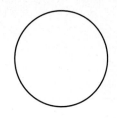 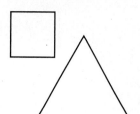   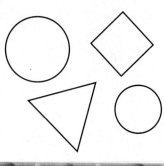

Describe Shapes

_____
- - - - -
_____ sides
- - - - -
_____ vertices

_____
- - - - -
_____ sides
- - - - -
_____ vertices

Sort Shapes

  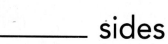 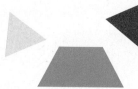 

This page checks understanding of important skills needed for success in Chapter 10.

DIRECTIONS 1. Use red to color the squares. Use blue to color the triangles. **2–3.** Look at the shape. Write how many sides. Write how many vertices. **4.** Mark an X on the shapes with three sides.

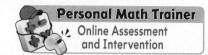

Personal Math Trainer
Online Assessment
and Intervention

© Houghton Mifflin Harcourt Publishing Company

Name _____

Vocabulary Builder

rectangle

circle

square

triangle

DIRECTIONS Mark an X on the food shaped like a circle.
Draw a line under the food shaped like a square. Circle the
food shaped like a triangle.

• **Interactive Student Edition**
• **Multimedia eGlossary**

Game

Follow the Shapes

DIRECTIONS Choose a shape from START. Follow the path that has the same shapes. Draw a line to show the path to the END with the same shape.

Name _____

Three-Dimensional Shapes

Essential Question How can you show which shapes stack, roll, or slide?

Geometry—K.G.4

MATHEMATICAL PRACTICES
MP.5, MP.6, MP.7

does stack	does not stack

DIRECTIONS Place three-dimensional shapes on the page. Sort the shapes by whether they stack or do not stack. Describe the shapes. Match a picture of each shape to the shapes on the sorting mat. Glue the shape pictures on the sorting mat.

Chapter 10 • Lesson 1

four hundred thirteen **413**

roll

roll and stack

stack

DIRECTIONS 1. Place three-dimensional shapes on the page. Sort the shapes by whether they roll or stack. Describe the shapes. Match a picture of each shape to the shapes. Glue the shape pictures on the page.

Name _____

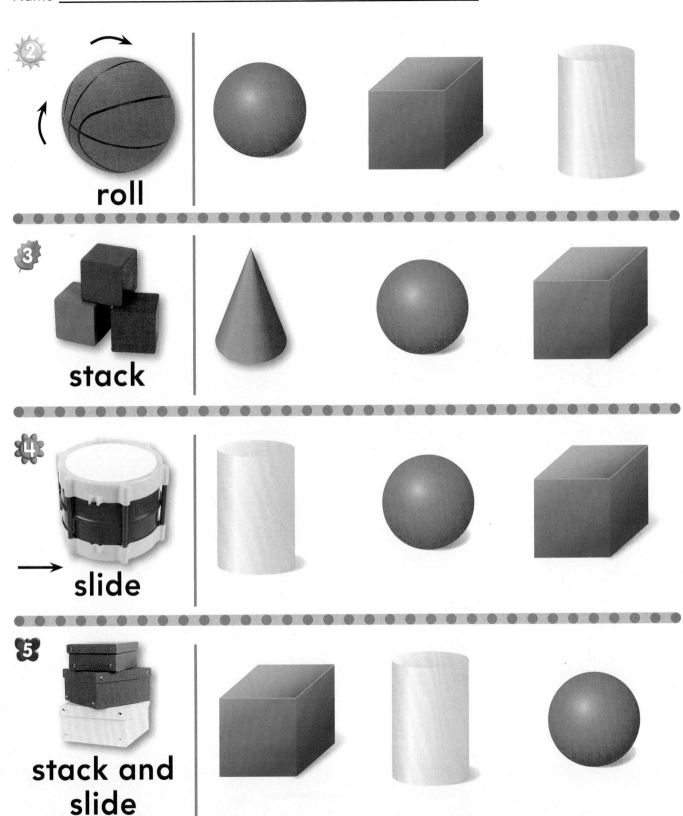

roll

stack

slide

stack and
slide

DIRECTIONS **2.** Which shape does not roll? Mark an X on that shape.
3. Which shapes do not stack? Mark an X on those shapes. **4.** Which shape
does not slide? Mark an X on that shape. **5.** Which shape does not stack
and slide? Mark an X on that shape.

Problem Solving • Applications Real World

WRITE Math

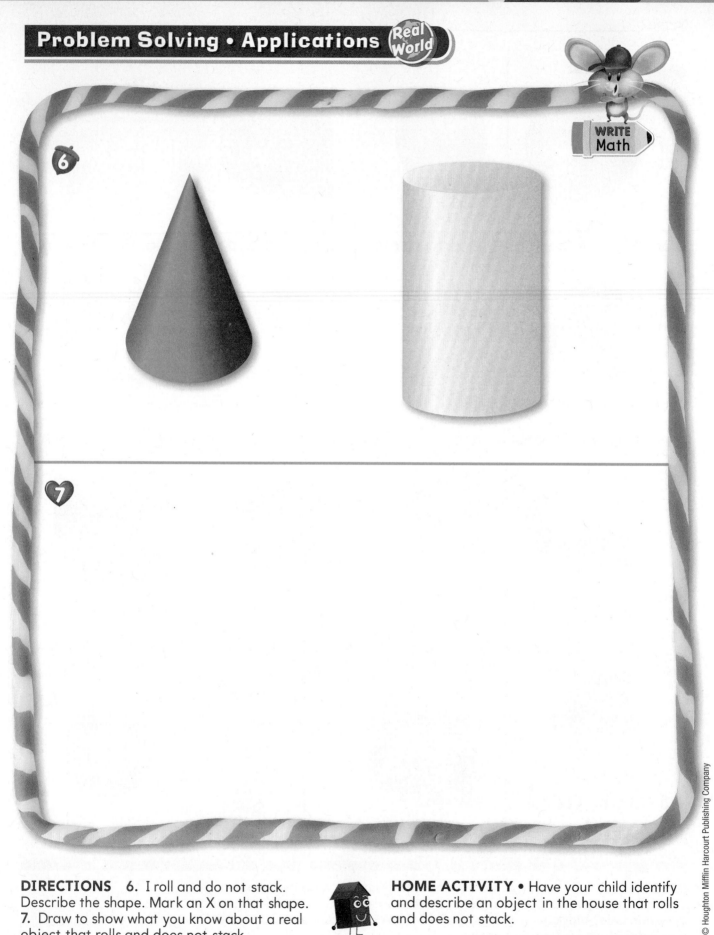

6

7

DIRECTIONS 6. I roll and do not stack. Describe the shape. Mark an X on that shape. 7. Draw to show what you know about a real object that rolls and does not stack.

HOME ACTIVITY • Have your child identify and describe an object in the house that rolls and does not stack.

FOR MORE PRACTICE:
Standards Practice Book

Name _____

Identify, Name, and Describe Spheres

Essential Question How can you identify, name, and describe spheres?

Geometry—K.G.2

MATHEMATICAL PRACTICES
MP.5, MP.6, MP.7

sphere	not a sphere

DIRECTIONS Place three-dimensional shapes on the page. Identify and name the sphere. Sort the shapes on the sorting mat. Describe the sphere. Match a picture of each shape to the shapes on the sorting mat. Glue the shape pictures on the sorting mat.

Chapter 10 • Lesson 2

sphere

flat surface

curved surface

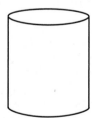   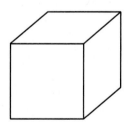

 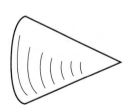 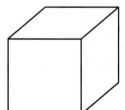 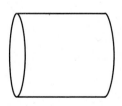

DIRECTIONS **1.** Look at the sphere. Circle the words that describe a sphere. **2.** Color the spheres.

Name _____

DIRECTIONS **3.** Identify the objects that are shaped like a sphere. Mark an X on those objects.

Chapter 10 • Lesson 2

four hundred nineteen **419**

Problem Solving • Applications

4

5

WRITE Math

DIRECTIONS **4.** I have a curved surface. Which shape am I? Mark an X on that shape. **5.** Draw to show what you know about a real object that is shaped like a sphere.

HOME ACTIVITY • Have your child identify and describe an object in the house that is shaped like a sphere.

FOR MORE PRACTICE:
Standards Practice Book

Name _____

Identify, Name, and Describe Cubes

Essential Question How can you identify, name, and describe cubes?

Geometry—K.G.2

MATHEMATICAL PRACTICES
MP.2, MP.5, MP.6

Listen and Draw *Real World*   Hands On

cube	not a cube

DIRECTIONS Place three-dimensional shapes on the page. Identify and name the cube. Sort the shapes on the sorting mat. Describe the cube. Match a picture of each shape to the shapes on the sorting mat. Glue the shape pictures on the sorting mat.

Chapter 10 • Lesson 3

cube

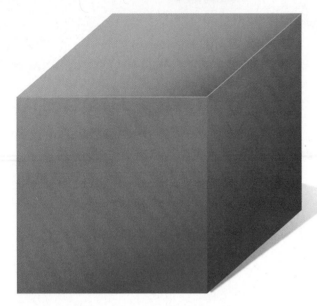

flat surface

curved surface

_____

_ _ _ _ _

_____ flat surfaces

DIRECTIONS 1. Look at the cube. Circle the words that describe a cube. 2. Use a cube to count how many flat surfaces. Write the number.

Name _____

DIRECTIONS **3.** Identify the objects that are shaped like a cube. Mark an X on those objects.

Chapter 10 • Lesson 3

Problem Solving • Applications Real World

4

5

DIRECTIONS 4. I have 6 flat surfaces. Which shape am I? Mark an X on that shape. 5. Draw to show what you know about a real object that is shaped like a cube.

HOME ACTIVITY • Have your child identify and describe an object in the house that is shaped like a cube.

FOR MORE PRACTICE:
Standards Practice Book

Name _____

Identify, Name, and Describe Cylinders

Essential Question How can you identify, name, and describe cylinders?

 Geometry—K.G.2

MATHEMATICAL PRACTICES
MP.2, MP.5, MP.6

Listen and Draw *Real World*

cylinder	not a cylinder

DIRECTIONS Place three-dimensional shapes on the page. Identify and name the cylinder. Sort the shapes on the sorting mat. Describe the cylinder. Match a picture of each shape to the shapes on the sorting mat. Glue the shape pictures on the sorting mat.

Chapter 10 • Lesson 4

four hundred twenty-five **425**

cylinder

flat surface

curved surface

_____

_ _ _ _ _ _

_____ **flat surfaces**

DIRECTIONS 1. Look at the cylinder. Circle the words that describe a cylinder.
2. Use a cylinder to count how many flat surfaces. Write the number.

426 four hundred twenty-six

Name _____

3

DIRECTIONS 3. Identify the objects that are shaped like a cylinder. Mark an X on those objects.

Chapter 10 • Lesson 4

four hundred twenty-seven **427**

Problem Solving • Applications

4

5

DIRECTIONS 4. I have 2 flat surfaces. Which shape am I? Mark an X on that shape. 5. Draw to show what you know about a real object that is shaped like a cylinder.

HOME ACTIVITY • Have your child identify and describe an object in the house that is shaped like a cylinder.

FOR MORE PRACTICE:
Standards Practice Book

Identify, Name, and Describe Cones

Essential Question How can you identify, name, and describe cones?

Geometry—K.G.2

MATHEMATICAL PRACTICES
MP.2, MP.5, MP.6

Listen and Draw Real World

cone	not a cone

DIRECTIONS Place three-dimensional shapes on the page. Identify and name the cone. Sort the shapes on the sorting mat. Describe the cone. Match a picture of each shape to the shapes on the sorting mat. Glue the shape pictures on the sorting mat.

Chapter 10 • Lesson 5

cone

flat surface

curved surface

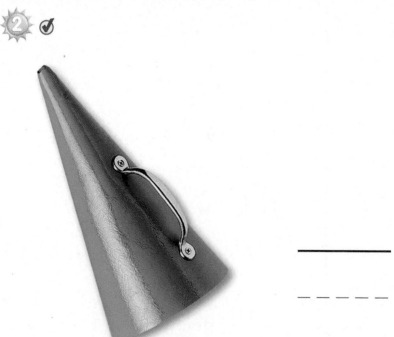

_____

- - - - - -

_____ flat surface

DIRECTIONS 1. Look at the cone. Circle the words that describe a cone. 2. Use a cone to count how many flat surfaces. Write the number.

DIRECTIONS 3. Identify the objects that are shaped like a cone. Mark an X on those objects.

HOME ACTIVITY • Have your child identify and describe an object in the house that is shaped like a cone.

Chapter 10 • Lesson 5

FOR MORE PRACTICE:
Standards Practice Book

four hundred thirty-one **431**

Concepts and Skills

1.

2. 3.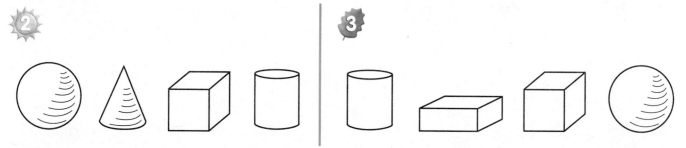

4. THINK SMARTER

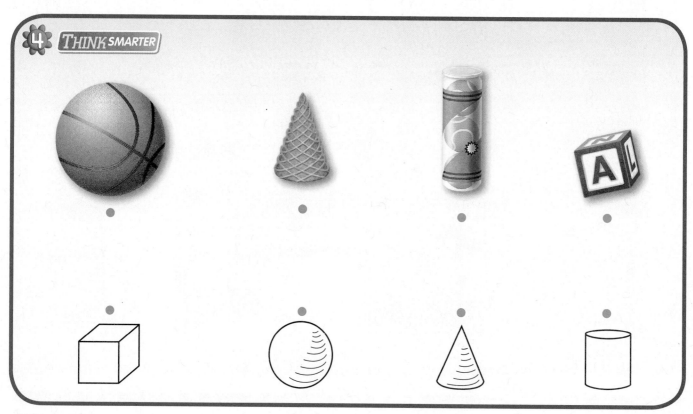

DIRECTIONS 1. Mark an X on the object that is shaped like a cylinder. (K.G.2)
2. Color the sphere. (K.G.2) 3. Color the cube. (K.G.2) 4. Draw lines to match the
objects to their shapes. (K.G.2)

Name _____

Problem Solving • Two- and Three-Dimensional Shapes

Essential Question How can you solve problems using the strategy *use logical reasoning*?

Geometry—K.G.3

MATHEMATICAL PRACTICES
MP.4, MP.5, MP.7

 Unlock the Problem *Real World* Hands On

two-dimensional shapes	three-dimensional shapes

DIRECTIONS Place shapes on the page. Sort the shapes on the sorting mat into sets of two-dimensional and three-dimensional shapes. Match a picture of each shape to a shape on the sorting mat. Glue the shape pictures on the sorting mat.

DIRECTIONS I. Identify the two-dimensional or flat shapes. Trace the circle around the square. Circle the other flat shapes. Identify the three-dimensional or solid shapes. Trace the X on the sphere. Mark an X on the other solid shapes.

Share and Show

  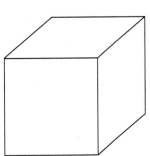

 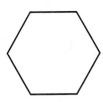 

 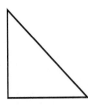 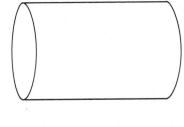

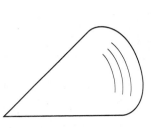 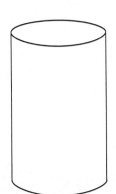 

DIRECTIONS   2. Identify the two-dimensional or flat shapes.
Use red to color the flat shapes. Identify the three-dimensional
or solid shapes. Use blue to color the solid shapes.

On Your Own **Real World**

WRITE Math

3

4

DIRECTIONS **3.** Draw to show what you know about a flat shape. Name the shape. **4.** Draw to show what you know about a real object that has a solid shape. Name the object and the shape.

HOME ACTIVITY • Have your child identify a household object that is shaped like a three-dimensional shape. Have him or her name the three-dimensional shape.

FOR MORE PRACTICE: Standards Practice Book

Name _____

Model Shapes

Essential Question How can you model shapes in the real world?

Geometry—K.G.5
Also K.G.2, K.G.3
MATHEMATICAL PRACTICES
MP.3, MP.8

 Listen and Draw (Real World)

 Hands On

DIRECTIONS Use your finger to trace around the shape. Name the shape. Tell a friend whether this shape is flat or solid. Talk about the number of sides and the number of vertices.

Chapter 10 • Lesson 7

four hundred thirty-seven **437**

1

2 ✓

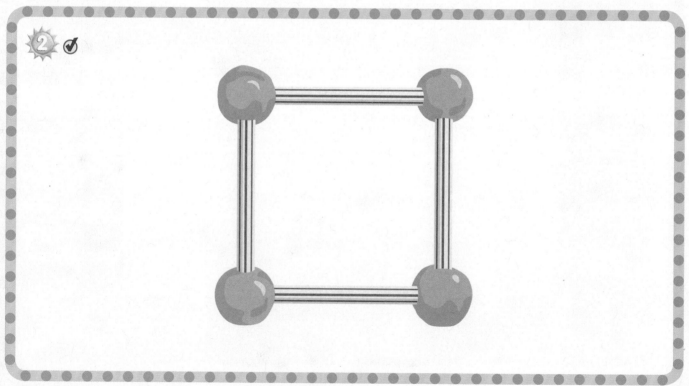

DIRECTIONS **1.** Use clay to model 4 spheres as shown. **2.** Place straws into the spheres as shown.

Name _____

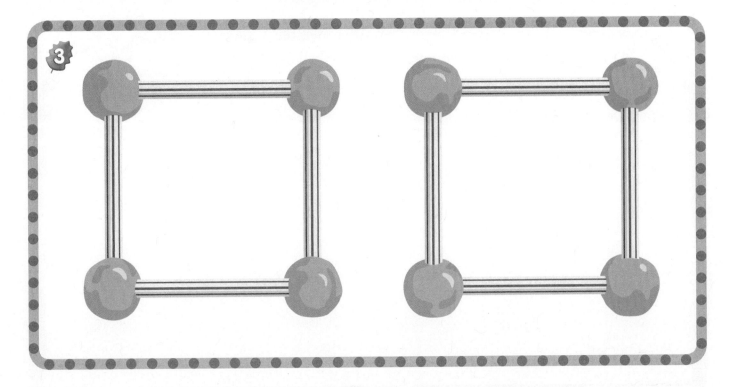

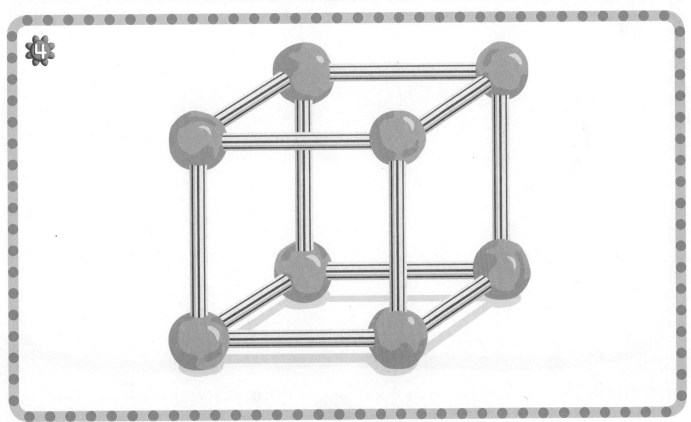

DIRECTIONS **3.** Use clay and straws to model another shape. Match the shape that you modeled in Exercise 2. **4.** Stand a straw into each corner of one of the shapes. Carefully lift the other shape and place it onto the straws as shown. Name the solid shape you modeled.

Chapter 10 • Lesson 7

four hundred thirty-nine **439**

Problem Solving • Applications

⑤

WRITE Math

⑥

DIRECTIONS 5. Maria's window has the shape of a square. Draw a picture of the shape. Tell a friend whether this shape is flat or solid. Talk about the number of sides and the number of vertices. **6.** Use objects such as clay, straws, and circles to model a solid shape. Draw a picture of the solid shape. Tell a friend about the shape.

HOME ACTIVITY • Have your child identify a household object that has a flat shape. Have your child model the shape with a drawing. Repeat the activity with a solid object, and have your child model the shape with materials such as clay and toothpicks.

FOR MORE PRACTICE:
Standards Practice Book

Name _____

Above and Below

Essential Question How can you use the terms *above* and *below* to describe shapes in the environment?

Geometry—K.G.1

MATHEMATICAL PRACTICES
MP.4

Listen and Draw *Real World*

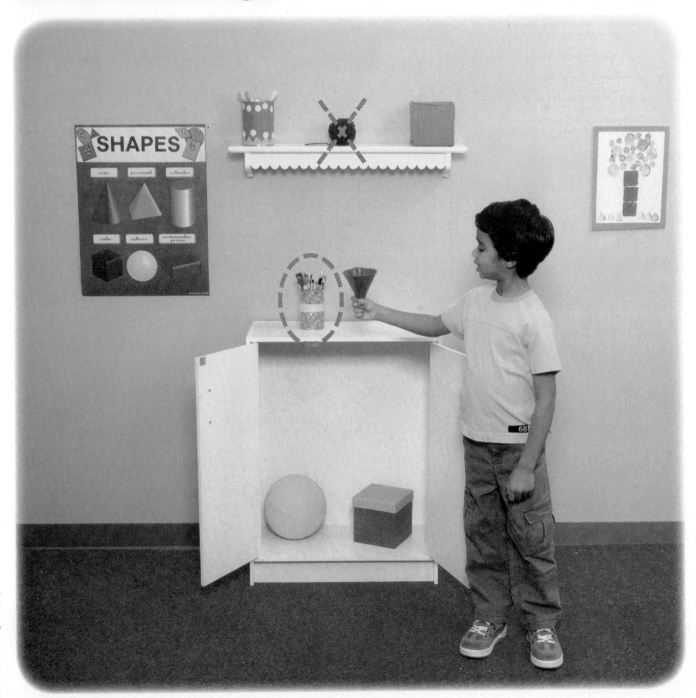

© Houghton Mifflin Harcourt Publishing Company

DIRECTIONS Trace the circle around the object shaped like a cylinder that is below the shelf. Trace the X on the object shaped like a sphere that is above the cabinet.

Chapter 10 • Lesson 8

four hundred forty-one **441**

1

DIRECTIONS I. Circle the object that is shaped like a cone below the play set. Mark an X on the object that is shaped like a cube above the play set. Color the object that is shaped like a cylinder above the play set.

DIRECTIONS 2. Circle the ball that is above the net. Mark an X on the box that is directly below the net.

Problem Solving • Applications Real World

③

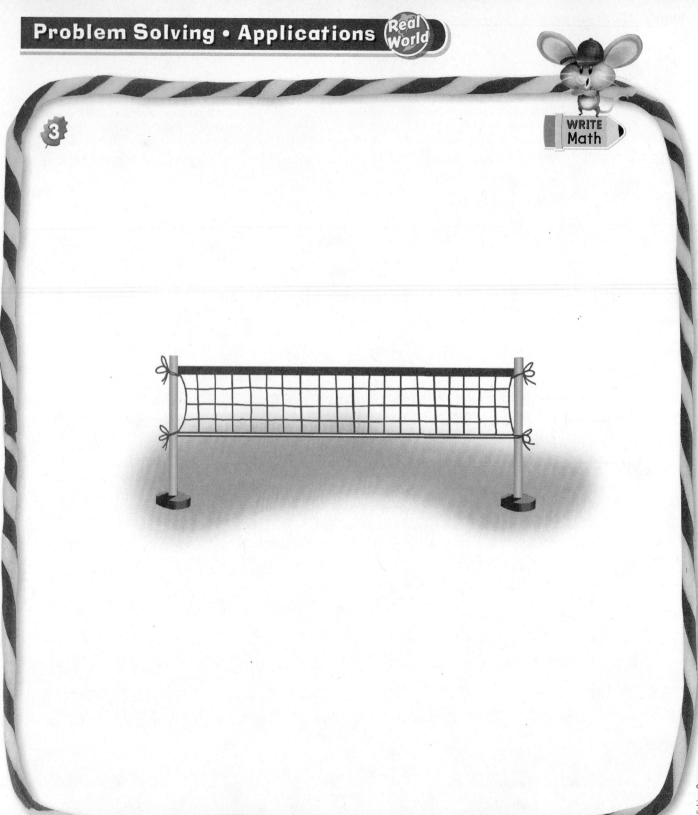

DIRECTIONS 3. Draw to show what you know about real world three-dimensional objects that might be above or below the net. Tell a friend about your drawing as you name the shape of the objects.

HOME ACTIVITY • Tell your child you are thinking of something in the room that is above or below another object. Have your child tell you what the object might be.

444 four hundred forty-four

FOR MORE PRACTICE:
Standards Practice Book

Beside and Next To

Essential Question How can you use the terms *beside* and *next to* to describe shapes in the environment?

Geometry—K.G.1

MATHEMATICAL PRACTICES
MP.3, MP.4, MP.6

Listen and Draw Real World

DIRECTIONS Trace the X on the object shaped like a cone that is beside the object shaped like a sphere. Trace the circle on the object shaped like a sphere that is next to the object shaped like a cube.

Chapter 10 • Lesson 9

four hundred forty-five **445**

Share and Show

DIRECTIONS I. Mark an X on the bead shaped like a cube that is beside the bead shaped like a cone. Draw a circle around the bead shaped like a cone that is next to the bead shaped like a cylinder. Use the words *next to* and *beside* to name the position of other bead shapes.

DIRECTIONS **2.** Mark an X on the object shaped like a cylinder that is next to the object shaped like a sphere. Draw a circle around the object shaped like a cone that is beside the object shaped like a cube. Use the words *next to* and *beside* to describe the position of other package shapes.

Chapter 10 • Lesson 9

four hundred forty-seven **447**

Problem Solving • Applications

3

DIRECTIONS 3. Draw or use pictures to show what you know about real world three-dimensional objects beside and next to other objects.

HOME ACTIVITY • Tell your child you are thinking of something in the room that is beside or next to another object. Have your child tell you the shape of the object.

FOR MORE PRACTICE:
Standards Practice Book

Name _____

In Front Of and Behind

Essential Question How can you use the terms *in front of* and *behind* to describe shapes in the environment?

 Geometry—K.G.1

MATHEMATICAL PRACTICES
MP.3, MP.4, MP.6

Listen and Draw *Real World*

DIRECTIONS Trace the X on the object shaped like a sphere that is in front of the object shaped like a cube. Trace the circle around the object shaped like a cylinder that is behind the object shaped like a cube.

Chapter 10 • Lesson 10

four hundred forty-nine **449**

1

DIRECTIONS 1. Mark an X on the object shaped like a cylinder that is behind the object shaped like a cube. Draw a circle around the object shaped like a sphere that is directly in front of the object shaped like a cone. Use the words *in front of* and *behind* to name the position of other shapes.

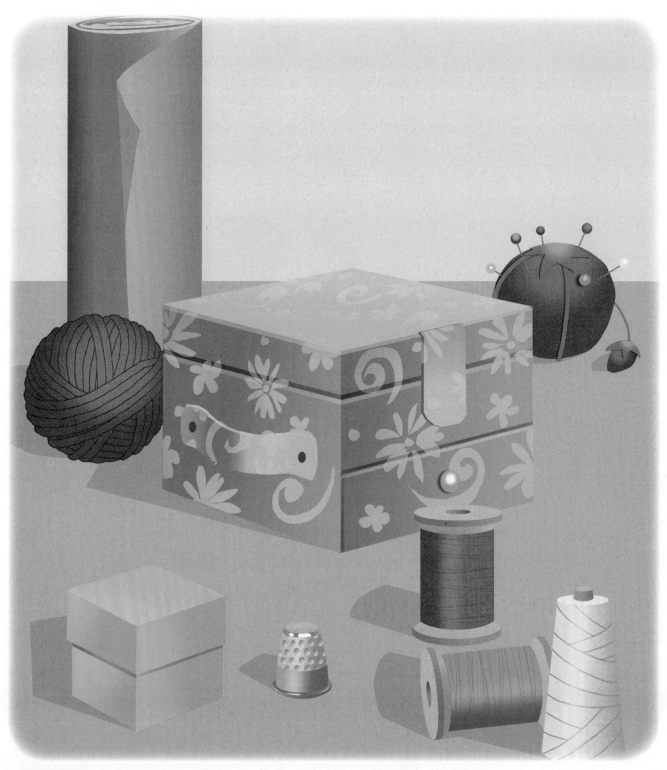

DIRECTIONS 2. Mark an X on the object shaped like a cube that is in front of the object shaped like a cylinder. Draw a circle around the object shaped like a cylinder that is behind the object shaped like a sphere. Use the words *in front of* and *behind* to name the position of other shaped objects.

Chapter 10 • Lesson 10   four hundred fifty-one **451**

Problem Solving • Applications

③

WRITE Math

DIRECTIONS **3.** Draw or use pictures to show what you know about real world three-dimensional objects in front of and behind other objects.

HOME ACTIVITY • Tell your child you are thinking of something in the room that is in front of or behind another object. Have your child tell you the shape of the object.

452 four hundred fifty-two

FOR MORE PRACTICE:
Standards Practice Book

✓ **Chapter 10 Review/Test**

1

○   ○   ○   ○

2

Personal Math Trainer

3 THINK SMARTER ✚

| 6 sides | Yes | No |
| curved surface | Yes | No |

DIRECTIONS 1. Mark under all the shapes that stack. 2. Which objects are shaped like a sphere? Mark an X on each of those objects. 3. Do the words describe a cube? Circle Yes or No.

 Assessment Options
Chapter Test

4

5

6 THINK SMARTER +

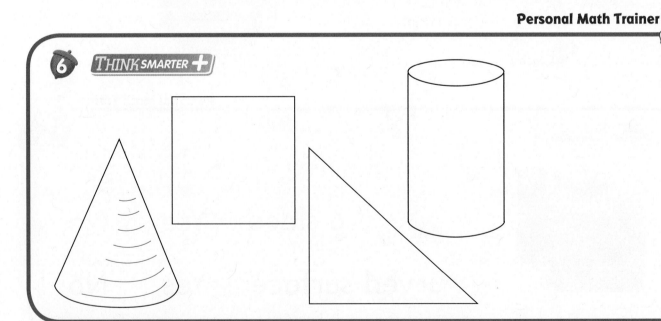

DIRECTIONS **4.** Draw lines to match the objects to their shapes.
5. Which objects are shaped like a cone? Mark an X on each of those
objects. **6.** Color the solid shapes blue. Color the flat shapes red. Draw a
another flat shape that is different.

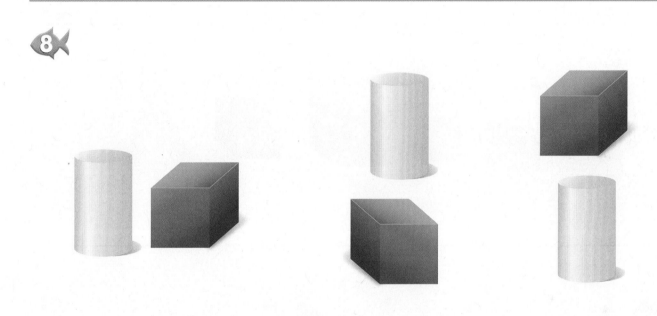

DIRECTIONS **7.** Draw an object that has the shape of a cylinder. **8.** Circle the shapes that show the cylinder above the cube. **9.** Mark an X on the object shaped like a cylinder next to the object shaped like a cone.

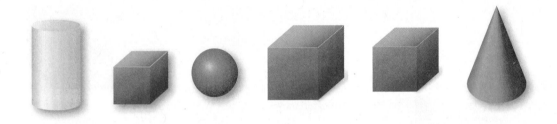

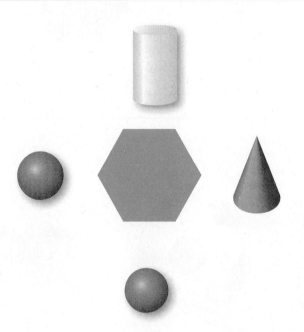

DIRECTIONS **10.** Mark an X on the cone in front of the cube. **11.** Mark an X on the cube that is beside the cone. **12.** Mark an X on the sphere that is below the hexagon.

Plants all Around

written by Tami Morton

CRITICAL AREA Representing, relating, and operating on whole numbers, initially with sets of objects

Two leaves fall from a tree.

Circle the leaf that is longer.

Science

Why do plants have leaves?

Two flowers grow near a wall.

Circle the flower that is shorter.

Science

Why do plants have flowers?

These carrots grow under the ground.

Circle the carrot that is longer.

© Houghton Mifflin Harcourt Publishing Company • Image Credits: (bkgd) Ferro Sims/Alamy

Science

Why do plants have roots?

Cattails can be short or tall.

Circle the two cattails that are about the same height.

Why do plants have stems?

One leaf is shorter than the other leaf.

Draw a leaf that is about the same length as

the shorter leaf.

© Houghton Mifflin Harcourt Publishing Company • Image credits: (bg) Jim Merli/Visuals Unlimited/Getty Images; (tl) Bon Appetit/Alamy; (bl) Dorling Kindersley/Getty Images • Image credits: (bg) JG Paterson Grenon/All Canada Photos/Corbis

Science

How are all these plants the same?

Write About the Story

Draw a purple flower. Make it shorter than the orange flower and taller than the yellow flower.

Vocabulary Review

longer	taller
shorter	same

Longer and Shorter

1. Look at the carrot. Draw a shorter carrot on the left.
Draw a longer carrot on the right.

2. Look at the leaf.
Draw a longer leaf
above it.
Draw a shorter leaf
below it.

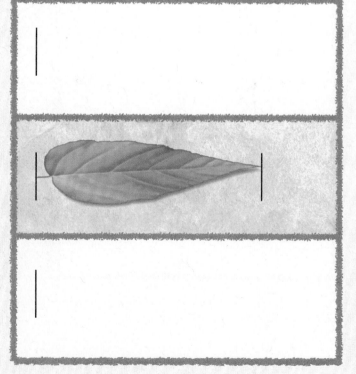

Chapter 11 Measurement

Curious About Math with Curious George

A playground is an area designed for children to play.

- **Which person on the park bench is bigger?**

Name _____

Show What You Know

More and Fewer

_____   _____

_ _ _ _ _ _ _   _ _ _ _ _ _ _

_____   _____

 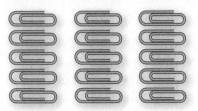 

_____   _____

_ _ _ _ _ _ _   _ _ _ _ _ _ _

_____

Compare Numbers

_____

_ _ _ _ _ _ _

_____

This page checks understanding of important skills needed for success in Chapter 11.

DIRECTIONS 1. Write how many in each set. Circle the set with fewer objects. 2. Write how many in each set. Circle the set with more objects. 3. Write how many cubes in each set. Circle the greater number.

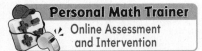

Personal Math Trainer
Online Assessment and Intervention

Name _____

Vocabulary Builder

bigger

smaller

DIRECTIONS Are there more flowers in the bigger pot or the smaller pot? Circle to show the pot with more flowers.

GO DIGITAL
• Interactive Student Edition
• Multimedia eGlossary

© Houghton Mifflin Harcourt Publishing Company

Chapter 11

four hundred sixty-seven **467**

Chapter 11 Game

Connecting Cube Challenge

DIRECTIONS Take turns with a partner tossing the number cube. Move your marker that number of spaces. If a player lands on a cube, he or she takes a cube for making a cube train. At the end of the game, players compare cube trains. Each player identifies the number of cubes in his or her cube train. If one player has a greater number of cubes, partners should identify that as the larger quantity of cubes.

MATERIALS game markers, number cube (1–6), connecting cubes

© Houghton Mifflin Harcourt Publishing Company

468 four hundred sixty-eight

Name _____

Compare Lengths

Essential Question How can you compare the lengths of two objects?

 Measurement and Data—K.MD.2

MATHEMATICAL PRACTICES
MP.3, MP.5, MP.6

Listen and Draw *Real World*

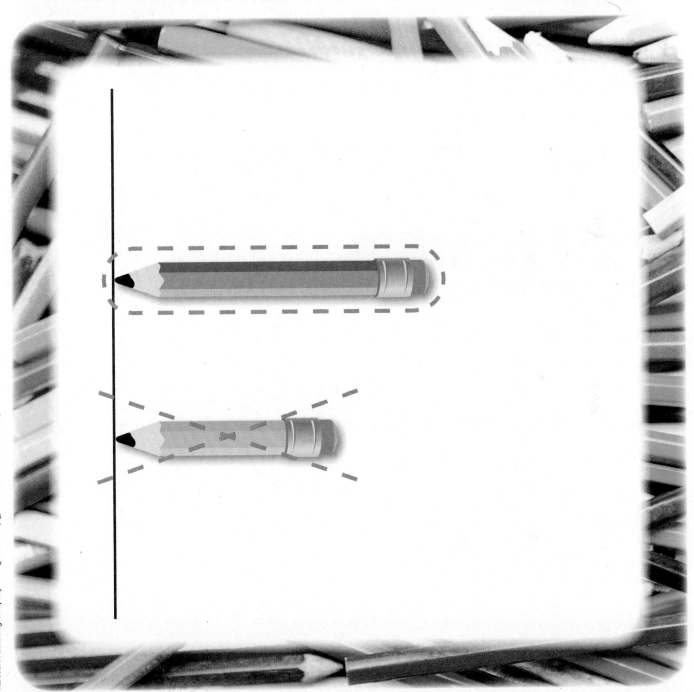

DIRECTIONS Look at the pencils. Compare the lengths of the two pencils. Use the words *longer than*, *shorter than*, or *about the same length* to describe the lengths. Trace the circle around the longer pencil. Trace the X on the shorter pencil.

Chapter 11 • Lesson 1

four hundred sixty-nine **469**

© Houghton Mifflin Harcourt Publishing Company • Image Credits: (bg) ©Corbis Premium RF/Alamy

1

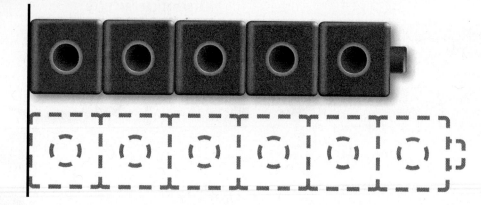

2

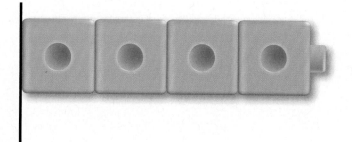

3 ✓

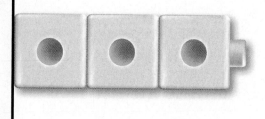

DIRECTIONS 1. Place cubes on the longer cube train. Trace and color the cube train. **2–3.** Make a cube train that is longer than the cube train shown. Draw and color the cube train.

Name _____

4 ✓

5

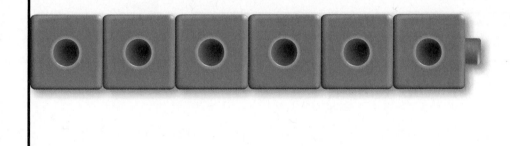

6

DIRECTIONS   4–6. Make a cube train that is shorter than the cube train shown. Draw and color the cube train.

© Houghton Mifflin Harcourt Publishing Company

Problem Solving • Applications

7

8

DIRECTIONS **7.** Two of these pencils are about the same length. Color those pencils. **8.** Draw to show what you know about two objects that are about the same length. Tell a friend about your drawing.

HOME ACTIVITY • Show your child a pencil and ask him or her to find an object that is longer than the pencil. Repeat with an object that is shorter than the pencil.

472 four hundred seventy-two

FOR MORE PRACTICE:
Standards Practice Book

Name _____

Compare Heights

Essential Question How can you compare the heights of two objects?

 Measurement and Data—K.MD.2

MATHEMATICAL PRACTICES
MP.3, MP.5, MP.6

Listen and Draw Real World

DIRECTIONS Look at the chairs. Compare the heights of the two chairs. Use the words *taller than*, *shorter than*, or *about the same height* to describe the heights. Trace the circle on the taller chair. Trace the X on the shorter chair.

Chapter 11 • Lesson 2

four hundred seventy-three **473**

1

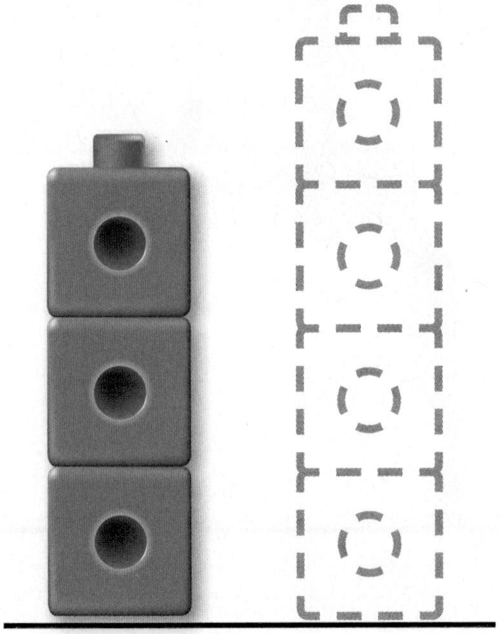

2 ☑

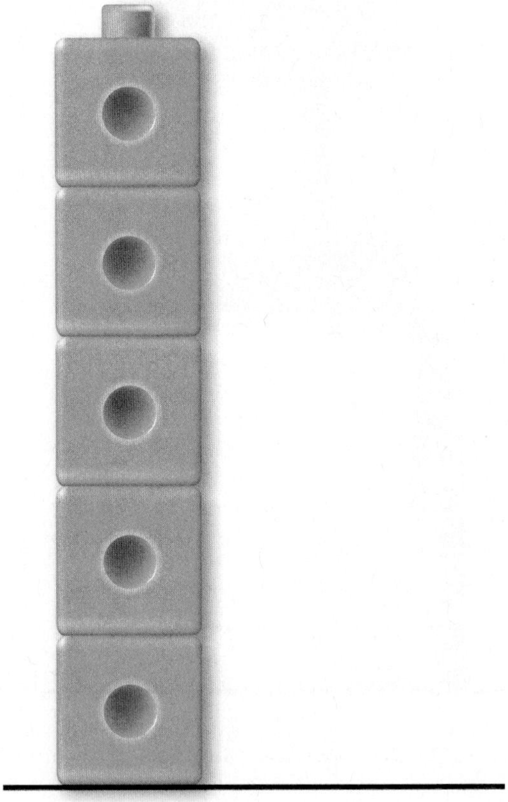

DIRECTIONS **I.** Place cubes on the taller cube tower. Trace and color the cube tower. **2.** Make a cube tower that is taller than the cube tower shown. Draw and color the cube tower.

474 four hundred seventy-four

Name _____

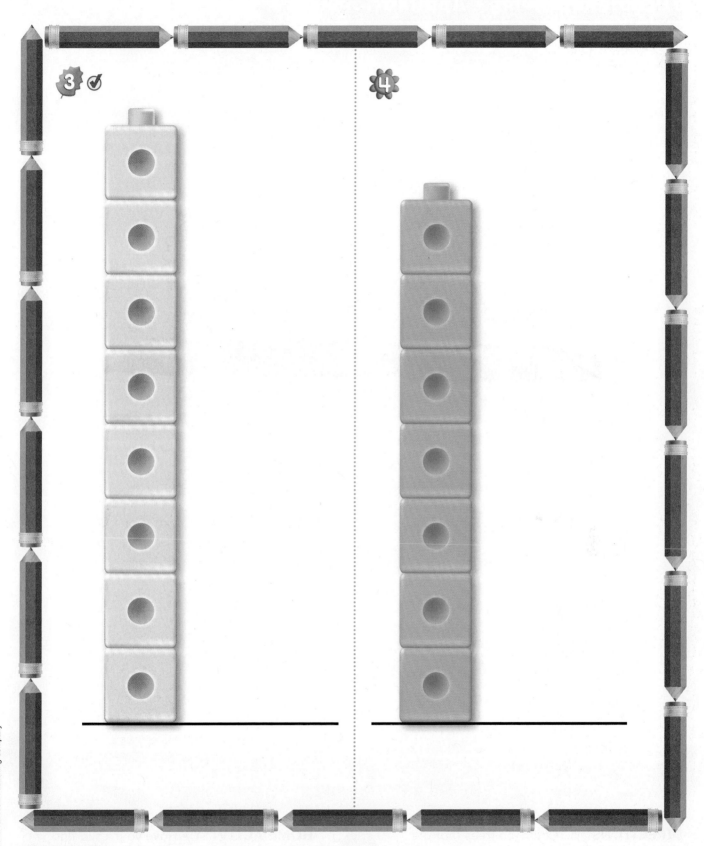

DIRECTIONS 3–4. Make a cube tower that is shorter than the cube tower shown. Draw and color the cube tower.

Problem Solving • Applications

5

6

DIRECTIONS **5.** Color the trees that are about the same height. **6.** Draw to show what you know about two cube towers that are about the same height. Tell a friend about your drawing.

HOME ACTIVITY • Have your child find two objects, such as plastic toys or stuffed animals. Have him or her place the objects side by side to compare the heights. Ask your child which object is taller and which object is shorter.

476 four hundred seventy-six

FOR MORE PRACTICE:
Standards Practice Book

Problem Solving • Direct Comparison

Essential Question How can you solve problems using the strategy *draw a picture?*

Measurement and Data—K.MD.2
MATHEMATICAL PRACTICES
MP.1, MP.3, MP.6

 Unlock the Problem Real World   Hands On

DIRECTIONS Compare the lengths or heights of two classroom objects. Draw the objects. Tell a friend about your drawing.

Chapter II • Lesson 3

four hundred seventy-seven **477**

DIRECTIONS 1. Find two small classroom objects. Place one end of each object on the line. Compare the lengths. Draw the objects. Say *longer than*, *shorter than*, or *about the same length* to describe the lengths. Circle the longer object.

Share and Show

DIRECTIONS   2. Find two small classroom objects. Place one end of each object on the line. Compare the heights. Draw the objects. Say *taller than*, *shorter than*, or *about the same height* to describe the heights. Circle the shorter object.

HOME ACTIVITY • Show your child two objects of different lengths. Have him or her put the ends of the objects on a straight line to compare the lengths and tell which object is shorter and which object is longer.

Chapter 11 • Lesson 3

FOR MORE PRACTICE:
Standards Practice Book

four hundred seventy-nine **479**

Concepts and Skills

❶

② 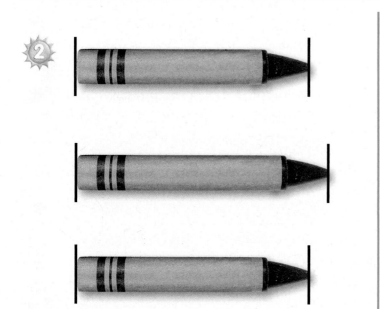   **③**

④ *THINK SMARTER*

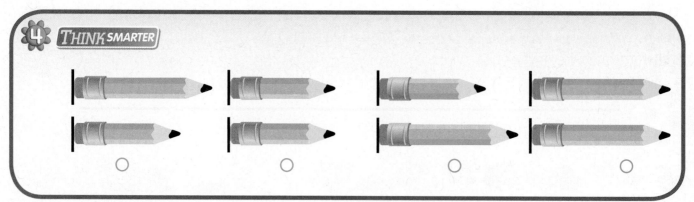

DIRECTIONS **1.** Make a cube train that is shorter than the one shown. Draw the cube train. (K.MD.2)   **2.** Circle the crayons that are about the same length. (K.MD.2)   **3.** Circle the crayon that is shorter. (.K.MD.2)
4. Choose all the sets with two pencils that are about the same length. (K.MD.2)

480 four hundred eighty

Name _____

Compare Weights

Essential Question How can you compare the weights of two objects?

 Measurement and Data—K.MD.2

MATHEMATICAL PRACTICES
MP.3, MP.5, MP.6

Listen and Draw Real World

DIRECTIONS Look at the picture. Compare the weights of the two objects. Use the words *heavier than*, *lighter than*, or *about the same weight* to describe the weights. Trace the circle around the lighter object. Trace the X on the heavier object.

Chapter 11 • Lesson 4

four hundred eighty-one **481**

 left    right

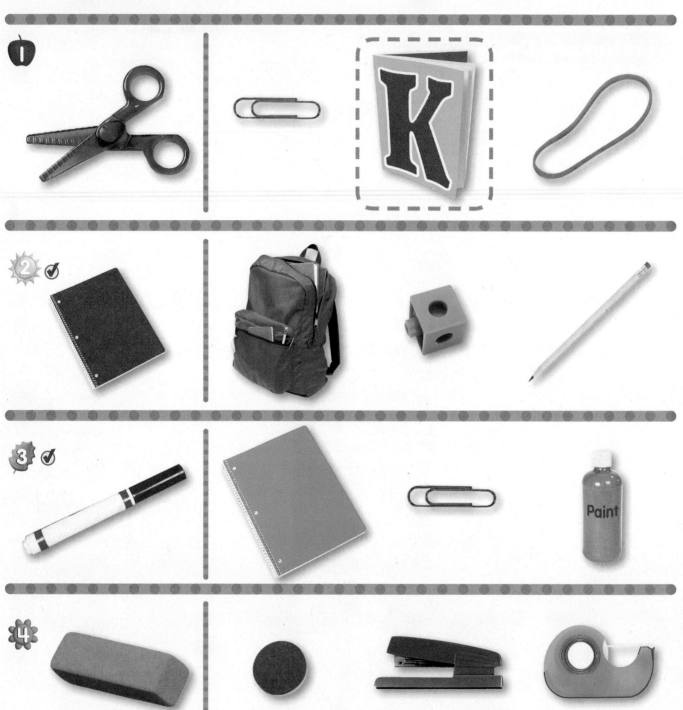

DIRECTIONS Find the first object in the row, and hold it in your left hand. Find the rest of the objects in the row, and take turns holding each of the objects in your right hand. **1.** Trace to show the object that is heavier than the object in your left hand. **2.** Circle the object that is heavier than the object in your left hand. **3–4.** Circle the object that is lighter than the object in your left hand.

482 four hundred eighty-two

Name _____

5

6

DIRECTIONS Find a book in the classroom. **5.** Find a classroom object that is lighter than the book. Draw it in the work space. **6.** Find a classroom object that is heavier than the book. Draw it in the work space.

Problem Solving • Applications

7

WRITE
Math

DIRECTIONS **7.** Draw to show what you know about comparing the weights of two objects. Tell a friend about your drawing.

484 four hundred eighty-four

HOME ACTIVITY • Have your child compare the weights of two objects in a house. Then have him or her use the terms *heavier* and *lighter* to describe the weights.

FOR MORE PRACTICE:
Standards Practice Book

Length, Height, and Weight

Essential Question How can you describe several ways to measure one object?

Measurement and Data—K.MD.1

MATHEMATICAL PRACTICES
MP.1, MP.3, MP.6

Listen and Draw Real World

height

length

© Houghton Mifflin Harcourt Publishing Company • Image Credits: (bg) ©Corbis Premium RF/Alamy

DIRECTIONS Look at the book. Trace your finger over the line that shows how to measure the height of the book. Trace your finger over the line that shows how to measure the length of the book. Talk about another way to measure the book.

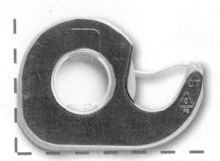

DIRECTIONS 1–2. Use red to trace the line that shows how to measure the length. Use blue to trace the line that shows how to measure the height. Talk about another way to measure the object.

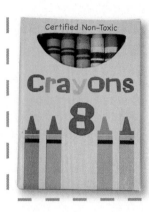

Certified Non-Toxic

Crayons 8

Grape Juice

PREMIUM

100% Pure

6.75 fl oz (200 mL)

DIRECTIONS   3–6. Use red to trace the line that shows how to measure the length. Use blue to trace the line that shows how to measure the height. Talk about another way to measure the object.

Chapter 11 • Lesson 5

Problem Solving • Applications

Real World

WRITE Math

7

DIRECTIONS **7.** Draw to show what you know about measuring an object in more than one way.

HOME ACTIVITY • Show your child an object in a house that can be easily measured by length, height, and weight. Ask him or her to describe the different ways to measure the object.

488 four hundred eighty-eight

FOR MORE PRACTICE:
Standards Practice Book

Name _____

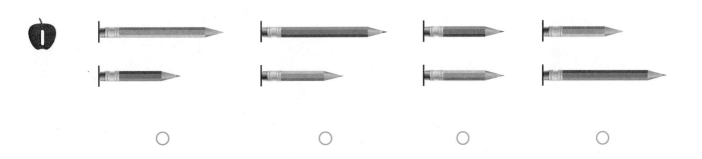 **Chapter 11 Review/Test**

 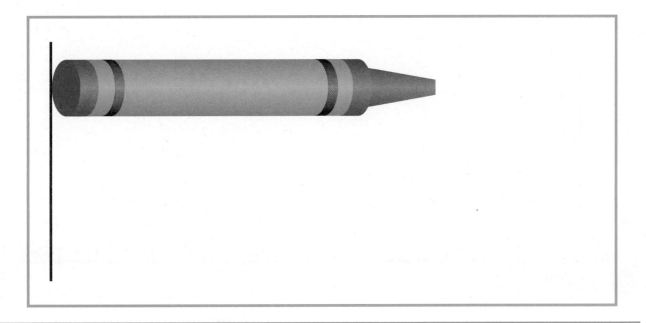

○   ○   ○   ○

DIRECTIONS 1. Choose all the sets that have a green pencil that is longer than the orange pencil. 2. Draw a crayon that is shorter. 3. Circle the tree that is taller.

© Houghton Mifflin Harcourt Publishing Company

Personal Math Trainer

6 THINK SMARTER +

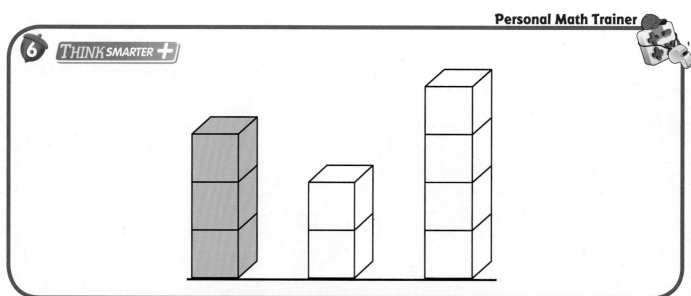

DIRECTIONS **4.** This tree is taller than another tree. Draw to show the other tree.   **5.** Draw two pieces of yarn of different lengths. Draw a circle around the yarn that is longer.   **6.** Which cube tower is shorter than the green cube tower? Color it blue. Which cube tower is taller than the green cube tower? Color it red.

Name _____

 ○ Yes ○ No

  ○ Yes ○ No

 ○ Yes ○ No

Personal Math Trainer

THINK SMARTER +

DIRECTIONS **7.** Circle all the objects that are lighter than the book. **8.** Is the object heavier than the tape dispenser? Choose Yes or No. **9.** Draw a line to show the height of the juice box. Draw a line to show the length of the lunchbox.

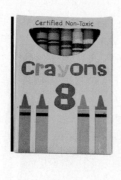

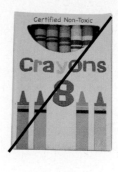

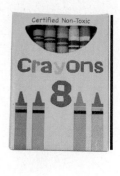

○   ○   ○   ○

DIRECTIONS **10.** Choose all of the pictures that have lines that show how to measure height.   **11.** Look at the objects. Mark an X on the lighter object. Circle the heavier object.   **12.** Draw an object that is heavier than the pencil.

12

Classify and Sort Data

Curious About Math with

Curious George

Primary colors are blue, red, and yellow.

• How many primary colors is the girl sorting?

Show What You Know ✓

Color and Shape

Compare Sets

_____

- - - - - - - - - - - - -

_____

_____

- - - - - - - - - - - - -

_____

_____

- - - - - - - - - - - - -

_____

- - - - - - - - - - - - -

_____

This page checks understanding of important skills needed for success in Chapter 12.

DIRECTIONS 1. Circle the fruits that are red. 2. Circle the triangles. 3. Count and write how many in each set. Circle the set with more objects. 4. Count and write how many in each set. Circle the set with fewer objects.

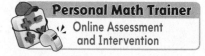

Personal Math Trainer
Online Assessment
and Intervention

Name _____

Vocabulary Builder

different

alike

DIRECTIONS Tell what you know about the ladybugs. Some of the ladybugs are different. Circle those ladybugs and tell why they are different. Tell what you know about the butterflies.

• **Interactive Student Edition**
• **Multimedia *eGlossary***

Game At the Farm

DIRECTIONS Use the picture to play I Spy with a partner. Decide who will go first. Player 1 looks at the picture, selects an object, and tells Player 2 the color of the object. Player 2 must guess what Player 1 sees. Once Player 2 guesses correctly, it is his or her turn to choose an object and have Player 1 guess.

496 four hundred ninety-six

Algebra • Classify and Count by Color

Essential Question How can you classify and count objects by color?

Measurement and Data—
K.MD.3
MATHEMATICAL PRACTICES
MP.2, MP.5, MP.6

Listen and Draw

not

DIRECTIONS Choose a color. Use that color crayon to color the clouds. Sort and classify a handful of shapes into a set of that color and a set of not that color. Draw and color the shapes.

1 ✓

| red | blue |
| yellow | green |

DIRECTIONS 1. Place shapes as shown. Sort and classify the shapes by the category of color. Draw and color the shapes in each category.

②

1

red	blue
yellow	green

_____
- - - - - - - - - - - - -
_____

③

2

red	blue
yellow	green

_____
- - - - - - - - - - - - -
_____

④

3

red	blue
yellow	green

_____
- - - - - - - - - - - - -
_____

DIRECTIONS Look at the categories of color in Exercise 1. Count how many in each category. **2.** Circle the categories of color that have one shape. Write the number. **3.** Circle the category that has two shapes. Write the number. **4.** Circle the category that has 3 shapes. Write the number.

Problem Solving • Applications

5

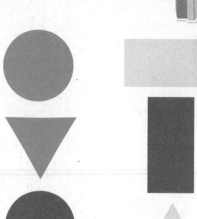

6

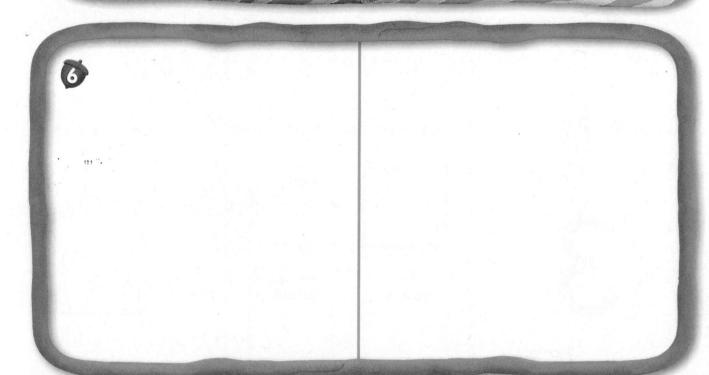

DIRECTIONS **5.** Ava placed her shapes as shown. How did she sort and classify her shapes? Draw one more shape in each category. **6.** Draw to show what you know about sorting and classifying by color.

HOME ACTIVITY • Provide your child with different colors of the same objects, such as straws, socks, or toys. Ask him or her to sort and classify the objects into two sets, a set of all one color and a set of all the other colors.

500 five hundred

FOR MORE PRACTICE: Standards Practice Book

Name _____

Algebra • Classify and Count by Shape

Essential Question How can you classify and count objects by shape?

 Measurement and Data—K.MD.3
MATHEMATICAL PRACTICES
MP.2, MP.5, MP.6

Listen and Draw

	not

DIRECTIONS Choose a shape. Draw the shape at the top of each side. Sort and classify a handful of shapes into a set of the shape you chose and a set that is not that shape. Draw and color the shapes.

Chapter 12 • Lesson 2

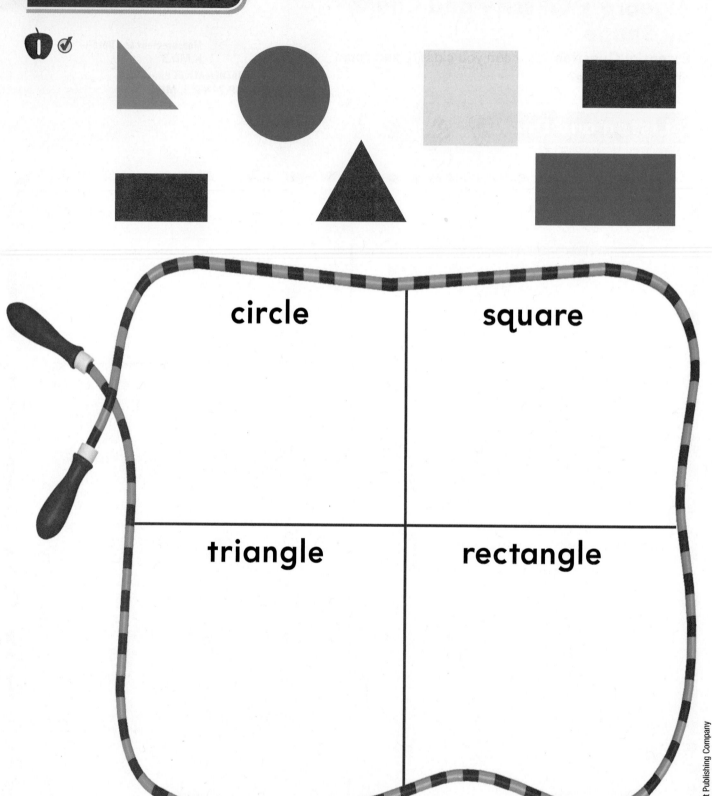

circle

square

triangle

rectangle

DIRECTIONS 1. Place shapes as shown. Sort and classify the shapes by the category of shape. Draw and color the shapes in each category.

2

1

| circle | square |
| triangle | rectangle |

_____
- - - - - - - - -
_____

3

2

| circle | square |
| triangle | rectangle |

_____
- - - - - - - - -
_____

4

3

| circle | square |
| triangle | rectangle |

_____
- - - - - - - - -
_____

DIRECTIONS Look at the categories of shapes in Exercise I. Count how many in each category. **2.** Circle the categories of shapes that have one shape. Write the number. **3.** Circle the category that has two shapes. Write the number. **4.** Circle the category that has three shapes. Write the number.

Problem Solving • Applications

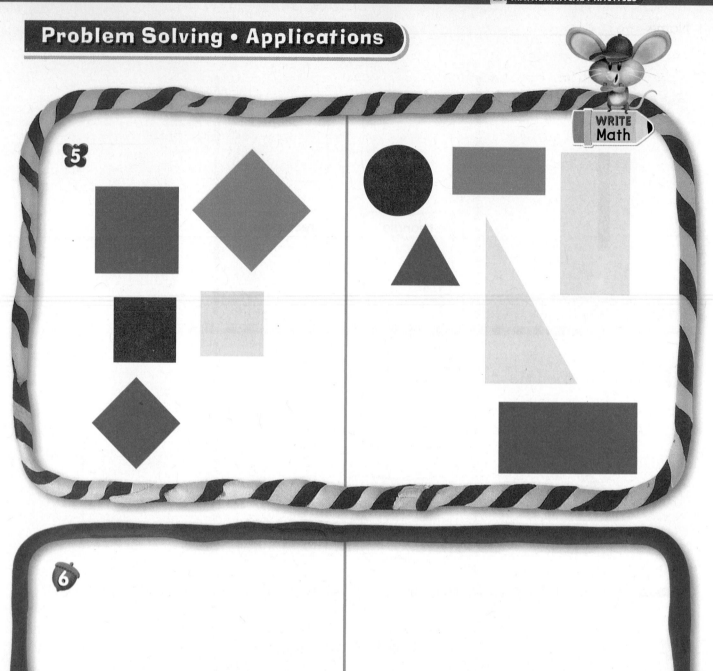

DIRECTIONS 5. Brandon used his shapes. How did he sort and classify his shapes? Draw one more shape in each category. 6. Using the same shapes, draw to show what you know about sorting and classifying by shape in a different way.

HOME ACTIVITY • Have your child sort objects in a house into categories of shape.

FOR MORE PRACTICE:
Standards Practice Book

Name _____

Algebra • Classify and Count by Size

Essential Question How can you classify and count objects by size?

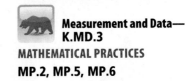

**Measurement and Data—
K.MD.3**

MATHEMATICAL PRACTICES
MP.2, MP.5, MP.6

Listen and Draw

big	small

DIRECTIONS Sort and classify a handful of shapes by size.
Draw and color the shapes.

Chapter 12 • Lesson 3

five hundred five **505**

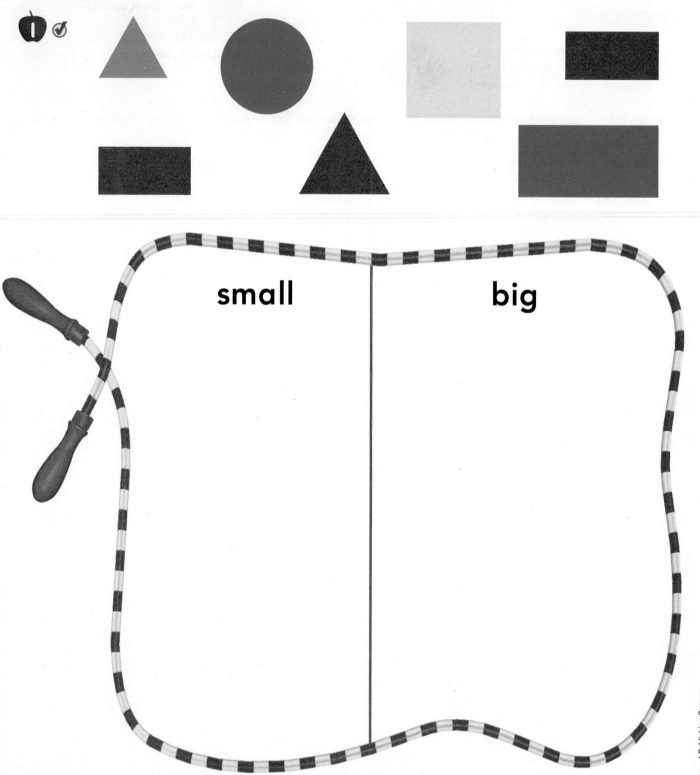

small   **big**

DIRECTIONS   1. Place shapes as shown. Sort and classify the shapes by the category of size. Draw and color the shapes in each category.

Name _____

3

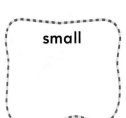

small

big

_____

- - - - - - -

_____

4

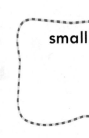

small

big

_____

- - - - - - -

_____

DIRECTIONS Look at the categories of size in Exercise I. Count how many in each category.
2. Circle the category that has three per category. Write the number. **3.** Circle the category that has four per category. Write the number.

HOME ACTIVITY • Have your child sort objects in a house into categories of size.

FOR MORE PRACTICE:
Standards Practice Book

Chapter 12 • Lesson 3

Concepts and Skills

1

2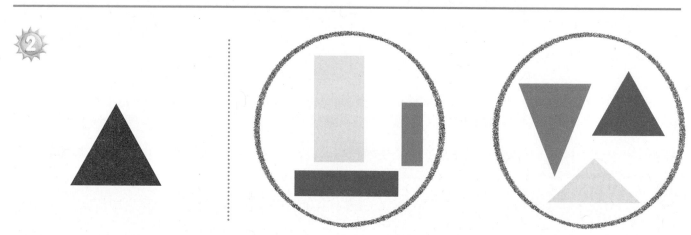

3 THINK SMARTER

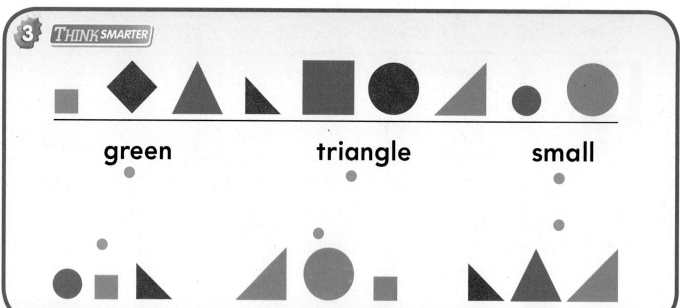

green

triangle

small

DIRECTIONS 1. Look at the set at the beginning of the row. Circle the shape that belongs in that set. (K.MD.3) 2. Look at the shape at the beginning of the row. Mark an X on the set in which the shape belongs. (K.MD.3) 3. Draw lines to match the shapes to the category. (K.MD.3)

Name _____

Make a Concrete Graph

Essential Question How can you make a graph to count objects that have been classified into categories?

Measurement and Data—K.MD.3
Also K.CC.6
MATHEMATICAL PRACTICES
MP.2, MP.6, MP.8

 **Listen and Draw**

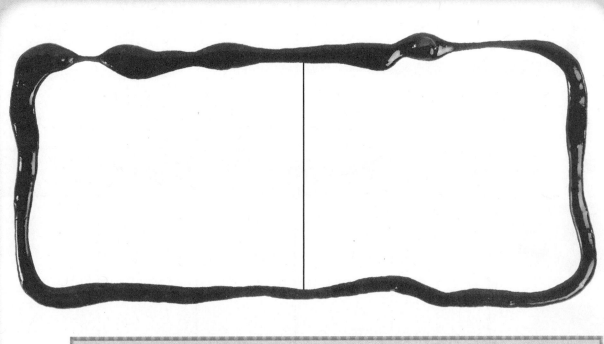

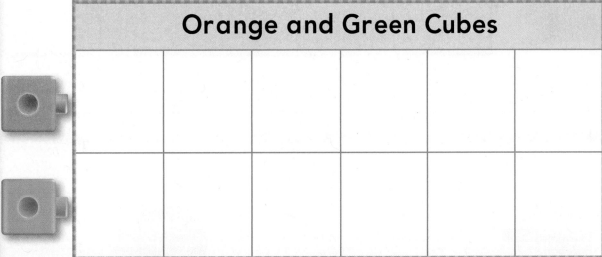

Orange and Green Cubes

DIRECTIONS Place a handful of orange and green cubes on the workspace. Sort and classify the cubes by the category of color. Move the cubes to the graph by category. Draw and color the cubes. Tell a friend how many in each category.

Chapter 12 • Lesson 4

1

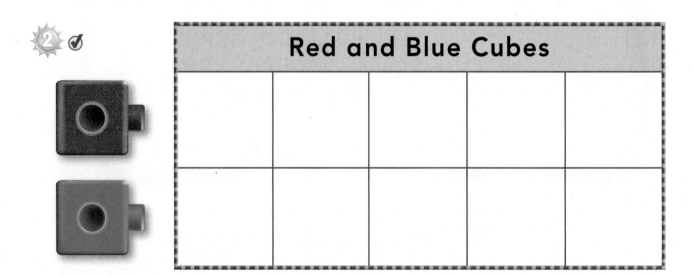

2 ✓

Red and Blue Cubes

3 ✓

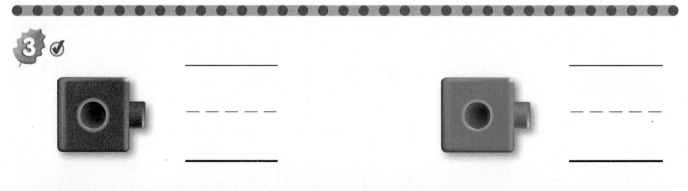

_____

- - - - - - - -

_____

_____

- - - - - - - -

_____

DIRECTIONS 1. Place a handful of red and blue cubes on the workspace. Sort and classify the cubes by category. 2. Move the cubes to the graph. Draw and color the cubes. 3. Write how many of each cube.

510 five hundred ten

4

5

Green Circles and Triangles

6

_____   _____

- - - - -   - - - - -

_____   _____

DIRECTIONS **4.** Place a handful of green circles and triangles on the workspace. Sort and classify the shapes by category. **5.** Move the shapes to the graph. Draw and color the shapes. **6.** Write how many of each shape.

Problem Solving • Applications

7

WRITE Math

My Graph

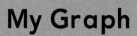

 _____

— — — —

 _____

— — — —

_____

DIRECTIONS 7. Use five cubes of two colors. Color the cubes to show the categories. Draw and color to show what you know about making a graph with those cubes. How many in each category? Write the numbers.

 HOME ACTIVITY • Have your child tell about the graph that he or she made on this page.

512 five hundred twelve

FOR MORE PRACTICE:
Standards Practice Book

Name _____

Problem Solving • Read a Graph

Essential Question How can you read a graph to count objects that have been classified into categories?

Measurement and Data—K.MD.3
Also K.CC.6

MATHEMATICAL PRACTICES
MP.2, MP.6, MP.8

Unlock the Problem

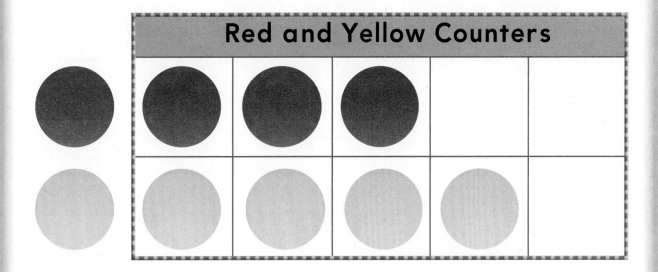

Red and Yellow Counters

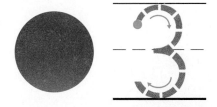

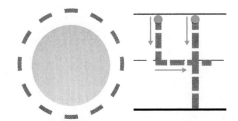

DIRECTIONS Erin made a graph of her counters. How many counters are in each category? Trace the numbers. Trace the circle to show which category has more counters.

Chapter 12 • Lesson 5

© Houghton Mifflin Harcourt Publishing Company

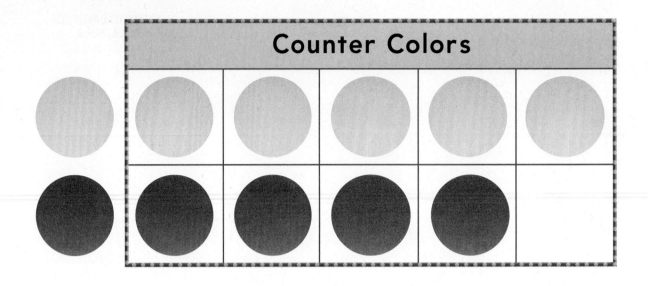

Counter Colors

DIRECTIONS **1.** Billy made a graph showing his counters. Color the counters to show his categories. How many counters are in each category? Write the numbers. **2.** Circle the category that has more counters on the graph.

Share and Show

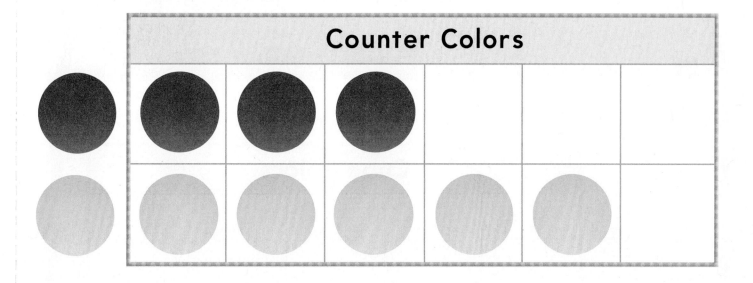

Counter Colors

 3 ✓

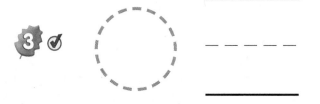

4 ✓

DIRECTIONS **3.** Rong made a graph of her counters. Color the counters to show her categories. How many counters are in each category? Write the numbers.
4. Circle the category that has fewer counters on the graph.

Chapter 12 • Lesson 5

On Your Own · Real World

5

Cube Colors

_____

_____

DIRECTIONS   5. Brian has more blue cubes than red cubes. Draw and color to show his cubes on the graph. Count how many in each category. Write the numbers.

HOME ACTIVITY • Have your child tell about the graph he or she made on this page. Ask him or her which category has more cubes and which category has fewer cubes.

516 five hundred sixteen

FOR MORE PRACTICE:
Standards Practice Book

 **Chapter 12 Review/Test**

1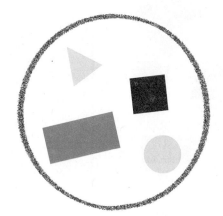

2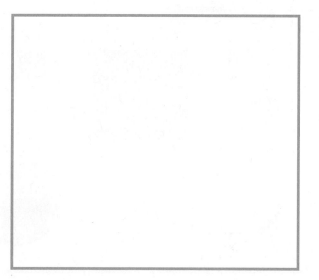

3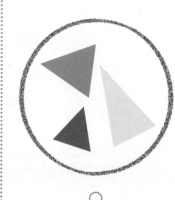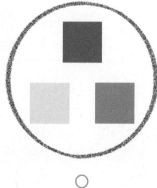

○   ○   ○

DIRECTIONS **1.** Lin sorted some shapes into categories by color. Look at the shape at the beginning of the row. Mark an X on the category that shows where the shape belongs. **2.** Draw and color a shape that belongs in this category. **3.** Look at the shape at the beginning of the row. Mark under all of the categories the shape can belong.

Personal Math Trainer

5 *THINK* SMARTER ➕

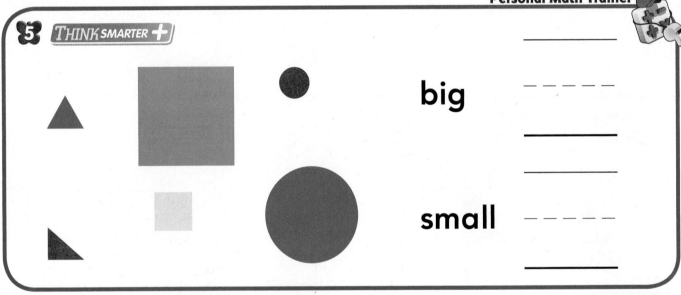

big

_____

— — — — — —

_____

small

— — — — — —

_____

6

red

big

DIRECTIONS **4.** Draw and color a shape that belongs in this category.
5. Mark an X on each big shape. Write how many large objects. Draw a circle
around each of the small objects. Write how many small objects. **6.** Draw
lines to match the shapes to the way they were sorted.

518 five hundred eighteen

7 THINK SMARTER ✚

Triangles and Circles

_____ _____

- - - - - - - - - - - - - -

 _____   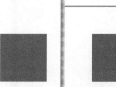 _____

8 🐟

Blue Squares and Circles

DIRECTIONS   7. Sort and classify the shapes by category. Draw each shape on the graph. Write how many of each shape.   **8.** Jake sorted some shapes. Then he made a graph. Count how many shapes there are in each category. Mark an X on the category that has more shapes.

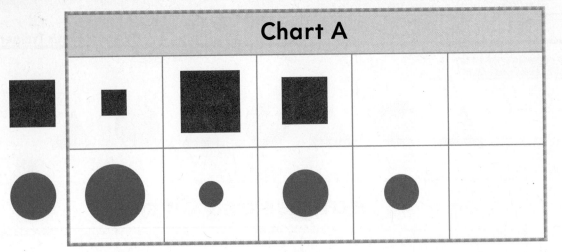

Chart A

color   Yes ○   No ○

size   Yes ○   No ○

shape   Yes ○   No ○

triangle

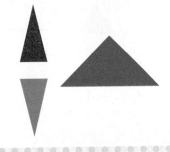

○

rectangle

○

circle

○

square

○

DIRECTIONS **9.** Is this chart sorted by color, size, and shape? Choose
Yes or No. **10.** Choose all of the sets with the same number of objects.

520 five hundred twenty

Picture Glossary

above [arriba, encima]

The kite is **above** the rabbit.

add [sumar]

3 + 2 = 5

alike [igual]

and [y]

 **and**

2 + 2

behind [detrás]

The box is **behind** the girl.

below [debajo]

The rabbit is **below** the kite.

beside [al lado]

The tree is **beside** the bush.

big [grande]

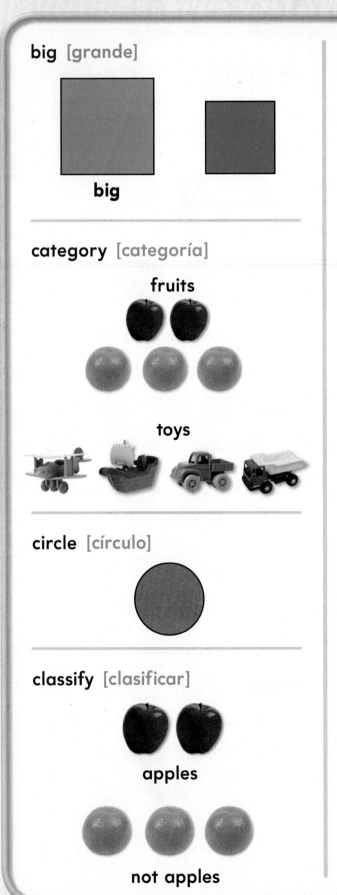

big

category [categoría]

fruits

toys

circle [círculo]

classify [clasificar]

apples

not apples

color [color]

red
[rojo]

blue
[azul]

yellow
[amarillo]

green
[verde]

orange
[anaranjado]

compare [comparar]

cone [cono]

corner [esquina]

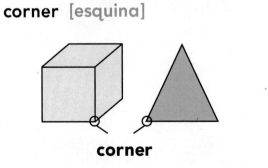

corner

cube [cubo]

curve [curva]

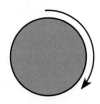

curved surface
[superficie curva]

Some solids have
a **curved surface.**

cylinder [cilindro]

different [diferente]

eight [ocho]

eighteen [dieciocho]

eleven [once]

fewer [menos]

3 **fewer** birds

fifteen [quince]

fifty [cincuenta]

1	2	3	4	5	6	7	8	9	10
11	12	13	14	15	16	17	18	19	20
21	22	23	24	25	26	27	28	29	30
31	32	33	34	35	36	37	38	39	40
41	42	43	44	45	46	47	48	49	50

five [cinco]

flat [plano]

A circle is a **flat** shape.

flat surface [superficie plana]

Some solids have a flat **surface**.

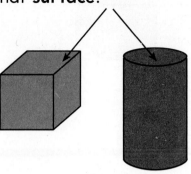

four [cuatro]

fourteen [catorce]

graph [gráfica]

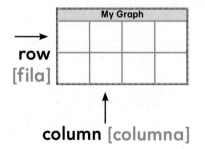

row [fila]

column [columna]

greater [mayor]

9 is greater than 6

6
9

heavier [más pesado]

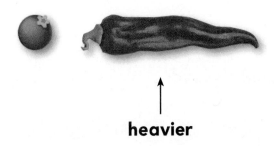

↑
heavier

hexagon [hexágono]

in front of [delante de]

The box is **in front of** the girl.

is equal to [es igual a]

3 + 2 = 5

3 + 2 **is equal to** 5

larger [más grande]

2   3

A quantity of 3 is **larger** than a quantity of 2.

less [menor/menos]

9 is **less** than 11

9
11

lighter [más liviano]

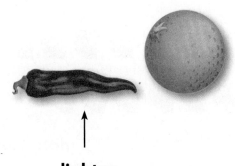

↑
lighter

longer [más largo]

 **longer**

match [emparejar]

minus – [menos]

$$4 - 3 = 1$$

4 **minus** 3 is equal to 1

more [más]

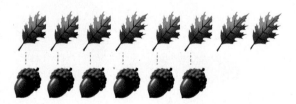

2 **more** leaves

next to [al lado de]

The bush is **next to** the tree.

nine [nueve]

nineteen [diecinueve]

one [uno]

one hundred [cien]

1	2	3	4	5	6	7	8	9	10
11	12	13	14	15	16	17	18	19	20
21	22	23	24	25	26	27	28	29	30
31	32	33	34	35	36	37	38	39	40
41	42	43	44	45	46	47	48	49	50
51	52	53	54	55	56	57	58	59	60
61	62	63	64	65	66	67	68	69	70
71	72	73	74	75	76	77	78	79	80
81	82	83	84	85	86	87	88	89	90
91	92	93	94	95	96	97	98	99	100

ones [unidades]

3 ones

pairs [pares]

3

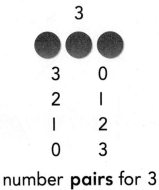

3	0
2	1
1	2
0	3

number **pairs** for 3

plus + [más]

2 **plus** 1 is equal to 3

$2 + 1 = 3$

rectangle [rectángulo]

roll [rodar]

same height
[de la misma altura]

same length [del mismo largo]

same number
[el mismo número]

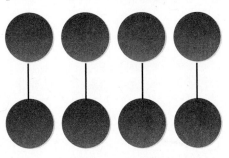

same weight [del mismo peso]

seven [siete]

seventeen [diecisiete]

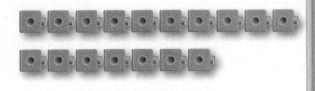

shape [forma]

shorter [más corto]

shorter

side [lado]

side

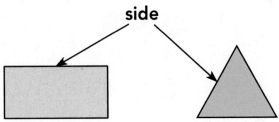

sides of equal length [lados del mismo largo]

six [seis]

sixteen [dieciséis]

size [tamaño]

big　　**small**

slide [deslizar]

small [pequeño]

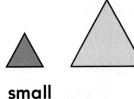

small

solid [sólido]

solid

A cylinder is a **solid** shape.

sphere [esfera]

square [cuadrado]

stack [apilar]

subtract [restar]

Subtract to find out how many are left.

taller [más alto]

taller

ten [diez]

tens [decenas]

1	2	3	4	5	6	7	8	9	10
11	12	13	14	15	16	17	18	19	20
21	22	23	24	25	26	27	28	29	30
31	32	33	34	35	36	37	38	39	40
41	42	43	44	45	46	47	48	49	50
51	52	53	54	55	56	57	58	59	60
61	62	63	64	65	66	67	68	69	70
71	72	73	74	75	76	77	78	79	80
81	82	83	84	85	86	87	88	89	90
91	92	93	94	95	96	97	98	99	100

tens

thirteen [trece]

twelve [doce]

three [tres]

twenty [veinte]

three-dimensional shapes
[figuras tridimensionales]

two [dos]

triangle [triángulo]

two-dimensional shapes
[figuras bidimensionales]

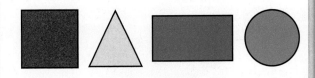

vertex [vértice]

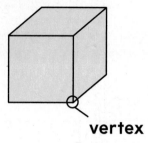

vertex

vertices [vértices]

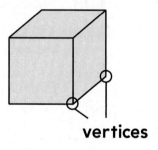

vertices

zero, none [cero, ninguno]

zero fish

Correlations

 CALIFORNIA COMMON CORE STATE STANDARDS

Standards You Will Learn		Student Edition Lessons
Mathematical Practices		
MP.1	Make sense of problems and persevere in solving them.	Lessons 1.3, 1.5, 1.9, 3.9, 5.1, 5.2, 5.3, 5.4, 5.6, 5.7, 6.1, 6.3, 6.4, 6.5, 6.6, 7.6, 11.3, 11.5
MP.2	Reason abstractly and quantitatively.	Lessons 1.1, 1.2, 1.3, 1.4, 1.5, 1.6, 1.8, 1.9, 1.10, 2.2, 2.3, 2.5, 3.2, 3.4, 3.6, 3.8, 4.2, 4.4, 5.1, 5.2, 5.3, 5.4, 5.5, 5.6, 5.7, 5.8, 5.9, 5.10, 5.11, 5.12, 6.1, 6.2, 6.3, 6.4, 6.5, 6.6, 6.7, 7.1, 7.2, 7.3, 7.4, 7.5, 7.6, 7.7, 7.8, 7.9, 7.10, 8.1, 8.2, 8.3, 9.4, 9.6, 9.8, 9.10, 10.3, 10.4, 10.5, 12.1, 12.2, 12.3, 12.4, 12.5
MP.3	Construct viable arguments and critique the reasoning of others.	Lessons 2.1, 2.3, 2.4, 2.5, 3.9, 7.1, 7.3, 7.7, 7.9, 8.4, 10.7, 10.9, 10.10, 11.1, 11.2, 11.3, 11.4, 11.5
MP.4	Model with mathematics.	Lessons 1.7, 1.9, 2.4, 3.1, 3.9, 4.1, 4.3, 4.5, 5.2, 5.4, 6.2, 6.3, 6.4, 7.6, 8.4, 9.9, 10.6, 10.8, 10.9, 10.10
MP.5	Use appropriate tools strategically.	Lessons 1.8, 2.1, 2.2, 2.3, 2.4, 3.1, 3.3, 3.5, 3.7, 4.1, 4.5, 6.2, 6.7, 7.5, 8.1, 8.4, 9.1, 9.2, 9.3, 9.5, 9.7, 9.9, 9.11, 9.12, 10.1, 10.2, 10.3, 10.4, 10.5, 10.6, 11.1, 11.2, 11.4, 12.1, 12.2, 12.3
MP.6	Attend to precision.	Lessons 2.5, 4.6, 4.7, 8.1, 8.7, 9.1, 9.3, 9.5, 9.7, 10.1, 10.2, 10.3, 10.4, 10.5, 10.9, 10.10, 11.1, 11.2, 11.3, 11.4, 11.5, 12.1, 12.2, 12.3, 12.4, 12.5
MP.7	Look for and make use of structure.	Lessons 1.7, 1.8, 3.1, 3.3, 3.5, 3.7, 4.3, 5.5, 5.8, 5.9, 5.10, 5.11, 5.12, 7.1, 7.2, 7.3, 7.4, 7.5, 7.7, 7.8, 7.9, 7.10, 8.5, 8.6, 8.7, 8.8, 9.1, 9.2, 9.3, 9.4, 9.5, 9.6, 9.7, 9.8, 9.9, 9.10, 9.11, 9.12, 10.1, 10.2, 10.6

Standards You Will Learn

Mathematical Practices

MP.8	Look for and express regularity in repeated reasoning.	Lessons 3.3, 3.5, 3.7, 4.5, 4.6, 4.7, 5.5, 6.7, 7.2, 7.4, 7.8, 7.10, 8.5, 8.6, 8.7, 8.8, 9.4, 9.6, 9.8, 9.10, 9.11, 9.12, 10.7, 12.4, 12.5

Domain: Counting and Cardinality

Know number names and the count sequence.

K.CC.1	Count to 100 by ones and by tens.	Lessons 8.5, 8.6, 8.7, 8.8
K.CC.2	Count forward beginning from a given number within the known.	Lessons 4.4, 4.5, 8.3
K.CC.3	Write numbers from 0 to 20. Represent a number of objects with a written numeral 0–20 (with 0 representing a count of no objects).	Lessons 1.2, 1.4, 1.6, 1.9, 1.10, 3.2, 3.4, 3.6, 3.8, 4.2, 8.2
K.CC.4a	Understand the relationship between numbers and quantities; connect counting to cardinality. a. When counting objects, say the number names in the standard order, pairing each object with one and only one number name and each number name with one and only one object.	Lessons 1.1, 1.3, 1.5
K.CC.4b	Understand the relationship between numbers and quantities; connect counting to cardinality. b. Understand that the last number name said tells the number of objects counted. The number of objects is the same regardless of their arrangement or the order in which they were counted.	Lesson 1.7
K.CC.4c	Understand the relationship between numbers and quantities; connect counting to cardinality. c. Understand that each successive number name refers to a quantity that is one larger.	Lesson 1.8

Standards You Will Learn

Domain: Counting and Cardinality		
Know number names and the count sequence.		
K.CC.5	Count to answer "how many?" questions about as many as 20 things arranged in a line, a rectangular array, or a circle, or as many as 10 things in a scattered configuration; given a number from 1–20, count out that many objects.	Lessons 3.1, 3.3, 3.5, 3.7, 4.1, 8.1
Compare numbers.		
K.CC.6	Identify whether the number of objects in one group is greater than, less than, or equal to the number of objects in another group, e.g., by using matching and counting strategies.	Lessons 2.1, 2.2, 2.3, 2.4, 2.5, 3.9, 4.5, 4.6, 7.6, 8.4
K.CC.7	Compare two numbers between 1 and 10 presented as written.	Lesson 4.7
Domain: Operations and Algebraic Thinking		
Understand addition as putting together and adding to, and understand subtraction as taking apart and taking from.		
K.OA.1	Represent addition and subtraction with objects, fingers, mental images, drawings, sounds (e.g., claps), acting out situations, verbal explanations, expressions, or equations.	Lessons 5.1, 5.2, 5.3, 6.1, 6.2, 6.3
K.OA.2	Solve addition and subtraction word problems, and add and subtract within 10, e.g., by using objects or drawings to represent the problem.	Lessons 5.7, 6.6, 6.7
K.OA.3	Decompose numbers less than or equal to 10 into pairs in more than one way, e.g., by using objects or drawings, and record each decomposition by a drawing or equation (e.g., $5 = 2 + 3$ and $5 = 4 + 1$).	Lessons 5.8, 5.9, 5.10, 5.11, 5.12

HI5

Domain: Operations and Algebraic Thinking		
Understand addition as putting together and adding to, and understand subtraction as taking apart and taking from.		
K.OA.4	For any number from 1 to 9, find the number that makes 10 when added to the given number, e.g., by using objects or drawings, and record the answer with a drawing or equation.	Lessons 4.3, 5.5
K.OA.5	Fluently add and subtract within 5.	Lessons 5.4, 5.6, 6.4, 6.5
Domain: Number and Operations in Base Ten		
Work with numbers 11–19 to gain foundations for place value.		
K.NBT.1	Compose and decompose numbers from 11 to 19 into ten ones and some further ones, e.g., by using objects or drawings, and record each composition or decomposition by a drawing or equation (e.g., 18 5 10 1 8); understand that these numbers are composed of ten ones and one, two, three, four, five, six, seven, eight, or nine ones.	Lessons 7.1, 7.2, 7.3, 7.4, 7.5, 7.7, 7.8, 7.9, 7.10
Domain: Measurement and Data		
Describe and compare measurable attributes.		
K.MD.1	Describe measurable attributes of objects, such as length or weight. Describe several measurable attributes of a single object.	Lesson 11.5
K.MD.2	Directly compare two objects with a measurable attribute in common, to see which object has "more of"/ "less of" the attribute, and describe the difference. For example, directly compare the heights of two children and describe one child as taller/ shorter.	Lessons 11.1, 11.2, 11.3, 11.4

Domain: Measurement and Data		
Classify objects and count the number of objects in each category.		
K.MD.3	Classify objects into given categories; count the numbers of objects in each category and sort the categories by count.	Lessons 12.1, 12.2, 12.3, 12.4, 12.5
Domain: Geometry		
Identify and describe shapes (squares, circles, triangles, rectangles, hexagons, cubes, cones, cylinders, and spheres).		
K.G.1	Describe objects in the environment using names of shapes, and describe the relative positions of these objects using terms such as above, below, beside, in front of, behind, and next to.	Lessons 10.8, 10.9, 10.10
K.G.2	Correctly name shapes regardless of their orientations or overall size.	Lessons 9.1, 9.3, 9.5, 9.7, 9.9, 10.2, 10.3, 10.4, 10.5
K.G.3	Identify shapes as two-dimensional (lying in a plane, "flat") or three-dimensional ("solid").	Lesson 10.6
Analyze, compare, create, and compose shapes.		
K.G.4	Analyze and compare two- and three-dimensional shapes, in different sizes and orientations, using informal language to describe their similarities, differences, parts (e.g., number of sides and vertices / "corners") and other attributes (e.g., having sides of equal length).	Lessons 9.2, 9.4, 9.6, 9.8, 9.10, 9.11, 10.1
K.G.5	Model shapes in the world by building shapes from components (e.g., sticks and clay balls) and drawing shapes.	Lesson 10.7
K.G.6	Compose simple shapes to form larger shapes. For example, "Can you join these two triangles with full sides touching to make a rectangle?"	Lesson 9.12

Index

C

California Common Core State Standards, H13-H17

Category, 498–500, 501–504, 505, 507

Chapter Review/Test, 53–56, 81–84, 125–128, 161–164, 217–220, 253–256, 301–304, 341–344, 405–408, 453–456, 489–492, 517–520

Circle
curve, 361–364
describe, 361–364
identify and name, 357–360
sort, 357–360

Classify
and count by color, 497–500
and count by shape, 501–504
and count by size, 505–507

Color
sort by, 497–500

Compare
by counting
sets to 5, 77–80
sets to 10, 153–156
heights, 473–479, 485–488
lengths, 469–472, 485–488
by matching
sets to 5, 73–76
sets to 10, 149–152
numbers/sets
to five, 73–76, 77–80
greater, 65–68
less, 69–71
same, 61–64
to ten, 149–152, 153–156
to twenty, 321–323
two-dimensional shapes, 397–400
two numbers, 157–160
weights, 481–484, 485–488

Cone
curved surface, 429–431
flat surface, 430
identify, name, and describe, 429–431
sort, 429

Corners. *See* **Vertices**

Correlations
California Common Core State Standards, H13-H17

Count
compare by, 77–80, 153–156
forward
to fifty, 325–328
to one hundred, 329–332, 333–336, 337–340
to twenty, 309–312, 313–316, 317–320
model and, 13–16, 21–24, 29–32, 49–52, 89–92, 97–100, 105–108, 113–116, 133–136, 261–264, 269–272, 277–280, 285–288, 293–296, 309–312
and write, 17–20, 25–27, 33–36, 49–52, 93–96, 101–103, 109–112, 117–120, 137–140, 265–267, 273–276, 277–280, 289–292, 297–300, 313–316
numbers. *See* Numbers
by ones, 325–328, 329–332
by tens, 333–336, 337–340

Cube
flat surfaces, 422
identify, name, and describe, 421–424
sort, 421–424

Curious George®, Curious About Math, 9, 57, 85, 129, 165, 221, 257, 305, 353, 409, 485, 493

Curve
of circle, 361–364
sort by, 397–400

Curved surface, 418, 426, 430

Cylinder
curved surface, 426
flat surfaces, 426
identify, name, and describe, 425–428
sort, 425–428

Data
classify and count, 497–500, 501–504, 505–507
graphs, concrete, 509–512, 513–516

Different, 397–400

O

P

R

Z